EX · LIBRIS

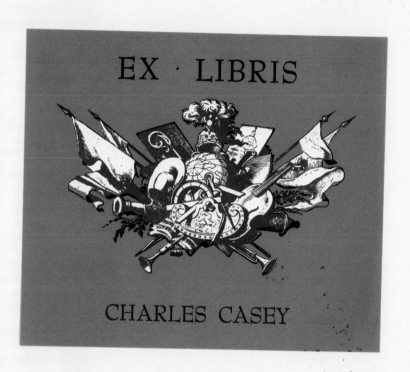

CHARLES CASEY

Books by CARLETON S. COON

THE SEVEN CAVES

(1957)

THE STORY OF MAN

(1954)

THESE ARE BORZOI BOOKS
PUBLISHED BY ALFRED A. KNOPF IN NEW YORK

THE SEVEN CAVES

THE
SEVEN CAVES

*Archæological Explorations
in the Middle East*

by CARLETON S. COON

NEW YORK   ALFRED A. KNOPF   1957

L.C. catalog card number: 56–8918
© *Carleton S. Coon, 1956*

☘ THIS IS A BORZOI BOOK ☘
PUBLISHED BY ALFRED A. KNOPF, INC.

FIRST EDITION

To

Lisa Dougherty Coon

PREFACE

THIS BOOK is an experiment in archæological writing. Now-adays the discovery of Paleolithic flints and bones in a Middle Eastern cave is front-page news. The public wants to know, within a reasonable length of time, what the flints and bones mean. Yet the procedure of Paleolithic archæ-ologists is still geared to public apathy, and archæologists write principally for one another. Because they keep in touch with one another's work informally, it does not greatly matter to them if publication is delayed. Indeed, ten or even twenty years may pass between the digging and the formal publication of a site, because many sepa-rate studies have to be made by specialists in as many dis-ciplines, and their reports have to be brought together and co-ordinated. Although these reports are usually couched in technical terms, the specialists understand them, and no one else used to be interested.

Unlike such ponderous publications, this book is writ-ten in plain English and is being published within an av-erage of five years after the digging of the sites described in it. It also differs from the popular books on archæology written by journalists and professional science writers in that the author is the man who did the digging. These differences make the writer vulnerable to attacks from many quarters. Professionals may accuse him of haste. However, a large number of them have been consulted, and every word has been read in manuscript or proof by top men in the field. Functionaries in the countries in which I dug may find the plain language of this book too frank for comfort, but most of the officials with whom I have dealt are my firm friends, and I am certain that a breath of fresh air will not impair our relationships.

Part of the experiment, the plain English part, is to do away with the technical terms that have tied Stone Age archæology down flat on its back like the cords that bound Gulliver in Liliput. Words like Mousterian and Aurignacian which we see everyday in archæological writing are tyrants with long mustaches. When the Russians announce that they have found Aurignacian flints in Siberia, the chances are that their finds bear no more relationship to those of Aurignac in France that Koniak does to Cognac. Yet the readers of the announcement, including some professionals, find themselves steered by this verbal tyranny into stereotyped channels of thought. With the encouragement of specialist friends I have eliminated as many as possible of these words to promote easy reading and clear thinking.

Paleolithic archæology is far less complicated and abstruse than either nuclear physics or the structure of the human brain, yet both these difficult subjects have been explained in words that anyone who owns a dictionary can understand. There is no reason why Paleolithic archæology should not be similarly opened to public consumption. Now that the interest is abundantly at hand, books on archæology are multiplying like rabbits. This one, I hope, may turn out to be a rabbit of odd color and habits. Perhaps it will be devoured by hawks on account of its unexpectedly simple coat pattern. Perhaps it will survive to start a new breed.

Between accounts of the discovery and interpretation of caves, flints, soils, and bones I have taken the liberty of telling a few simple stories about what happened to me and my companions on our expeditions. While I hope the reader will find these incidents of travel and work amusing, dramatic, and anthropologically interesting, he can skip them without loss of archæological content. I am sure that Persians, Afghans, and Arabs who see this book will not ignore them. In the anecdotes I hope that they will see no more than I intended: an attempt to capture the character of their common people, whom I regard with admiration and affection.

In every country I have worked in except the International Zone of Morocco, my activities have come under the jurisdiction of a Department of Antiquities, which is a branch of the Ministry of Education, itself subject to the Council of Ministers. In Syria, Iraq, Iran, and Afghanistan I have always worked with permits from the Directors of Antiquities: Dr. Selim Abd el-Haqq of Syria, Dr. Naji al-Asil of Iraq, Mr. Mohammed Mostafavi of Iran, and Dr. Ahmad Ali Kohzad of Afghanistan. My first acknowledgments in this book go to them and to the governments they represent.

I owe an equal debt to Dr. Froelich Rainey, Director of the University Museum of the University of Pennsylvania, under whose direction and guidance I have dug all the caves mentioned in this book except those at Tangier. Both Dr. Rainey and his field men, including myself, are very lucky that we have the enthusiastic support of an outstanding board of trustees, headed by Mr. Percy C. Madeira, Jr., who have provided for us generously in our work. Funds from outside the Museum were received also from the American Philosophical Society, the Social Science Research Council, and the Wenner Gren Foundation. My work at Tangier in 1939 was supported by Dr. Donald Scott, then Director of the Peabody Museum at Harvard, who contributed toward the expenses of the excavation. In 1947 I worked there again on the staff of Dr. Hugh Hencken, Director of the American School of Prehistoric Research, who was in charge of financial arrangements, including my wife's and my expenses.

In the field we were helped everywhere by members of

our splendid diplomatic and consular staff, including one of my sons, and in Iran we became greatly indebted to the American Presbyterian Mission for quarters, advice, and personnel. On every expedition I have been accompanied by my wife, and on most of them by one or both of my sons. In 1947, while working for Hugh Hencken, I also had the pleasure of the company of Bruce Howe and Charles Stearns. In 1949 I was accompanied by David Elder and Paul Schumacher, in 1951 by Louis and Anne Dupree, and in 1954 by Henry Coulter. We are all still good friends.

My debts on the home front are even greater than those incurred in the field, for I can easily create a list of over forty persons who helped me in one or more essential ways, often by doing something of which I was personally incapable, like making Carbon-14 tests on our charcoal samples or identifying the species of bird bones. This list is appended. In it three names are archæologically outstanding. Hallam Movius, whom I taught as an undergraduate, has taught me much more as a friend and colleague. Ever since I began digging caves I have taken my flints to him for study, and we have hashed over many a problem for nearly two decades. So encyclopedic is his knowledge of the Paleolithic that, like many others, I have become dependent on him and do not know where his ideas leave off and my own begin. Bruce Howe has also been a constant and indispensable consultant since our days of digging together in Tangier; he has read the manuscript of this book several times, and has helped me with all of it, particularly Chapter Two. John d'Arcy Waechter, a newer friend, has sorted every flint from every cave except Tangier, and gone over every chapter in fine detail. Without Movius, Howe, and Waechter I would not dare to present this book to the publishers.

My deepest gratitude is expressed to these three men and to their companions on the following list.

NAME   INSTITUTION AND SUBJECT

GLOVER M. ALLEN (DECEASED)
   Harvard: Animal Bones

J. LAWRENCE ANGEL
   Jefferson Medical: Human Bones

LINDA BRAIDWOOD
   Oriental Inst. Chicago: Flint

ROBERT BRAIDWOOD
   Oriental Inst. Chicago: Flint & Pottery

WENDELL H. CAMP
   Acad. Nat. Sci. Phila. & U. of Pa.:   Botany

THERESA H. CARTER
   University Mus., U. of Pa.:   Animal Bones

ROGER CONANT
   Phila. Zoo: Snakes

HENRY W. COULTER, JR.
   U.S. Geol. Survey: Geology & Soils

MARGARET CURRIER
   Peabody Museum, Harvard: Library

BURTON DYSON, M.D.
   Presbyterian Mission: Iranian Chapters

ROBERT DYSON, JR.
   University Museum: Pottery & General

G. J. FERGUSSON
   New Zealand Dom. Phys. Lab.:   Carbon-14

HENRY FOWLER
   Acad. Nat. Sci. Phila.:   Fish Bones

F. C. FRASER
   Brit. Mus. Nat. Hist.:   Animal Bones

NAME   INSTITUTION AND SUBJECT

JANE C. GOODALE
    University Mus.: General

CYNTHIA GRIFFIN
    University Museum: Library

BRUCE HOWE
    Harvard & Am. Sch. Pre. Res.: Flints & General

C. D. JEFFRIES
    Penn. State: Soils

ALFRED KIDDER II
    University Museum: Flints & General

JUDITH E. KING
    Brit. Mus. Nat. Hist.: Animal Bones

J. LAURENCE KULP
    Columbia: Carbon-14

W. F. LIBBY
    U. of Chicago: Carbon-14

W. J. VAN LIERE
    F.A.O., United Nations: Soils

PAUL MANGELSDORF
    Harvard: Botany

FRED R. MATSON
    Penn. State: Pottery

DONALD MCCOWN
    Oriental Institute, Chicago: Pottery

JOHN MILLER
    Penn. State & Harvard: Soils

HALLAM L. MOVIUS, JR.
    Harvard: Flints, General

KENNETH P. OAKLEY
    Brit. Mus. Nat. Hist.: Flints, Fluorine, General

RUSSELL OLSEN
    Harvard: Fluorine

NAME   INSTITUTION AND SUBJECT

DEXTER PERKINS, JR.
Univ. Mus. & Harvard: Animal Bones

ELIZABETH K. RALPH
U. of Pa.:   Carbon-14

CHARLES REID
Illinois Col. of Pharm.:   Animal Bones

HORACE RICHARDS, JR.
Acad. Nat. Sci. Phila. & U. of Pa.:   Mollusks & Minerals

BARBARA LAWRENCE SCHEVILL
Mus. of Comp. Zool., Harvard: Animal Bones

HENRY SETZER
U.S. Natl. Mus.:   Animal Bones

G. G. SIMPSON
Am. Mus. Nat. Hist.:   Horse Teeth

RALPH SOLECKI
Columbia U.:   Flints

CHARLES STEARNS
Tufts University: Geology

HANS SUESS
U.S. Geol. Survey: Carbon-14

FRED ULLMER
Philadelphia Zoo: Animal Bones

JOHN D'A. WAECHTER
Arch. Inst., U. of London: Flints

LAURISTON WARD
Harvard: Pottery

ALEXANDER WETMORE
Smithsonian Inst.:   Bird Bones

CARLETON S. COON

Devon, Pennsylvania
August 7, 1956

CONTENTS

LINE DRAWINGS IN THE TEXT

Flints drawn by MARGARET DAY DILKS.
Plans, sections, bones, and lettering by JOHN R. RILE.

NOTE: *All flints are scaled to one-half actual size, unless otherwise noted.*

MAPS
Prepared by C. S. COON and GUY FLEMING

LIST OF PLATES

THE SEVEN CAVES

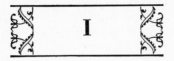

I

WHY SOME PEOPLE DIG CAVES

Dᴜʀɪɴɢ ᴛʜᴇ ᴇᴀʀʟʏ sᴘʀɪɴɢ of 1939, while bored with doing very little on a half-sabbatical leave in the Azores, I wrote the first few scenes of a play, the manuscript of which was lost during the war. Although I had never really dug at the time, I named this dramatic effort *The Cave*. Its scene is a grotto in the south of France, where the major part of the world's cave-digging has been done. The audience sits inside the cave, watching events that take place in its mouth. Outside is a hilly landscape, represented by a series of consecutive scenes built on a turntable. The first is a glacial vista, full of snow and ice. Later comes a temperate forest, with a few straw huts emitting curls of smoke in the distance; next we have a hilltop fort of the Gallic period, a factory town of the late nineteenth century, then a devasted landscape, and finally snow and ice again. Changing scenes is a simple matter, rotating the turntable from one ice age to another.

In the first scene the actors are bears. One of them is complaining to the others that a new animal has entered the valley, a two-legged animal armed with an unfair secret weapon that makes him invincible. That weapon is fire. With it he is chasing the other animals out of their comfortable caves, and before long this very grotto will be the scene of a disastrous conflict. While the bears have little chance of winning, they resolve to stand their ground and die heroically rather than allow themselves to be driven ignominiously from cave after cave and valley after valley. As one might suspect, the last scene is the same as the first, and the bears, who ran away after all, are back again, expressing relief that man—that troublesome if ephemeral creature —is only a bitter memory.

The scenes between are easily filled in by anyone's imagination. Cro-Magnon man is painting his animal pictures on the walls; a procession of Neolithic farmers is carrying in a corpse for burial in the floor; Vercingetorix—who, being a Celt, resembles my friend the Honorable James Michael Curley, formerly a frequent mayor of Boston—is nobly and tragically surrendering to Julius Cæsar, who resembles the late Benito Mussolini. This scene was my favorite because it was all in limericks. After that I planned to show Attila's death and several other events of historical importance up to the beginning of World War II, when a covey of archæologists, digging in the floor, hears the news of the outbreak of that particular conflict over a portable radio.

Although my manuscript has been lost and I will probably never attempt to rewrite it, the point can still be made that caves are fine vantage points from which to look out on the world. That same year, 1939, marked my first serious venture into the digging of caves, an occupation I have followed, between other jobs, when ever possible from that day to this. I consider it the prince of sports and a solace to the nervous system in these days of a dizzily whirling world.

It must be stated clearly before going any further that I am not an archæologist by profession, but a physical anthropologist seeking human bones in flint-strewn caves. While I process the flints, I also show them to specialists in that field when I get home. These specialists are men who do little else but study the tools of prehistoric men, and who sit in the final court of judgment on the meaning of what people like myself bring in. Just as the science of botany has plant-explorers, so I am a cave-explorer looking for bones of early people and of the creatures they ate, rather than a specialist in the entire contents of caves. While knowing something about flint in an amateurish way, I profess almost complete ignorance about pottery and metal, which I turn over to others *in toto* with the same feeling of relief with which I relinquish charcoal samples to atomic physicists whose techniques of determining the ages of different levels in our caves are beyond my comprehension.

Much that I will say in these pages will be controversial and provisional. Please do not take me too literally, and when I urge caution it is because it is needed and not because of modesty. A teacher always has to summarize the existing material on his subject. He can neither refuse to address his class because his material is in a state of change, nor wait for matters to clear up or settle down. An author reporting on any branch of science is in the same position. He must have something to say which makes sense internally and rounds out a picture, even if he finds it necessary to present several alternative pictures, of which only one, or none, may turn out to be true.

Little will be learned if the narrative is riddled with gaps in anticipation of the final publication of technical reports, which, in archæology, are often ten years late because some expert has not found time to identify some category of rocks, soils, bones, or tools. Even if we wait ten years, other problems will have arisen which will present fresh gaps and we will be caught in a vicious circle. So here we go, jumping without a parachute and praying for a haystack below.

I am well aware of the interpretation placed on a fondness for caves by Freudian psychoanalysts. It has been suggested to me several times that I am crawling back into my mother's womb, trying to escape the buffeting of everyday life, acting immaturely or even schizophrenically. Perhaps this may be so, but if so, what of it? Out of a cave in Delphi came many words of ancient wisdom, however obscurely phrased, and it was in a cave containing a manger, as everyone who has been to Bethlehem knows, that the Christ Child was born. The Dome of the Rock surmounts a cave, and in another cave Muhammad received his first divine messages.

I refer to these holy uses of caves merely to indicate the part that they play in the ritual imagination of peoples in the Middle East, and how firmly rooted they are in tradition, for indeed we have found that people lived in caves before they left the Garden of Eden, the food-gatherer's simple paradise, to take up the onerous life of agriculture. If one is returning to a former state symbolically in digging caves, it is to that of the hunter, the happy state in which our ancestors spent the vast majority of the life of our species.

Cave-digging is a very busy and active occupation. First of all, much time and energy must be spent in deciding where in general to seek for caves; then it is necessary to raise the money to dig with, and to get permission from the government in whose territory the cave is located. Then come the collection of suitable vehicles, camping equipment, and technical devices and the search for suitable field companions before one even starts to look for a cave. Once overseas and squared away with the authorities, the cave-digger begins his frantic search, and this is the most exciting and dramatic aspect of the job. After several caves have been located, the fateful decision must be made as to which shall be dug; if it turns out to be a dud, as sometimes happens, a quick shift must be made. The cave-digger is fighting against time, for there are seasons when it is too hot or too cold to work, and also religious holidays and months of fasting to interfere with the work and to impose deadlines. Often he has to argue with farmers who keep their lambs or kids in the cave during the winter and do not want the floor disturbed. Finally, labor problems arise, magnified by the temporary nature of the employment.

The work itself is the functioning of a little kingdom. A tightly organized group of from ten to forty men work closely together for a period varying from a week to three months, sharing exercise and a certain amount of physical danger. They are forced to co-ordinate their individual efforts in a pattern of teamwork, as pick man feeds earth and its contents to shovel man, to bucket man, to sieve man, to washer of specimens, to the head of the expedition, who sorts specimens from scrap and hands the objects worthy of being kept to the labelers and baggers. This processing-line is almost as rigid in its requirements for co-ordination as that of a shoe factory, and a bottleneck in any department can clog the total machine and stop the work. If the earth is nearly sterile—that is, empty of man-made objects—it is quickly excavated and the foreman puts extra men on the bucket line and at the shovels. If it is rich, the extras are assigned to the washbasins and sieves.

Before the digging season many of the men have never seen one another and after it they will part forever. People of different nations, languages, religions, income brackets, ages, and degrees of education will be thrown together intimately for a few weeks. The personality ad-

justments that must be made are profound if temporary.
The wise archæologist gets to know each workman's name
the first day and studies his character. Among them he
will find bright men who, had they had a chance, could
have been presidents of corporations, and stupid men
who could never have risen far above their current stations. He will find leaders and followers, boasters and
meek men who become dangerous if overly teased, jokers,
poets, and men gifted in the use of their hands. He will
discover the deep antagonisms between village men and
townees, and between country people and the sophisticated products of cities. Men will be hurt, some rarely
and others repeatedly; some will become too ill to work,
while others will be found frequently scuttling around
the corner of a cliff because of dysentery.

It does not take long to dig a cave, but digging a
cave is a lifetime of experience in human relations all in
a capsule. To be the leader of a cave-digging expedition
gives an ordinary man enough feeling of power to make
up for the knowledge that he will never be President of
the United States or Pope of Rome, enough responsibility
and opportunity for decision to satisfy the Odysseus and
Solomon lurking in all of us.

The peak of the sequence, the climax of the orchestra-
tion with all strings and wind instruments welling out
of the pit and the cymbals ready to be clashed, is the
discovery, in which everyone participates. When a skull
is found, sieves and buckets are abandoned. I have seen
a strong man, an illiterate farmer who had never
before known that a piece of flint was anything more
than a kind of rock to be thrown at a dog, weep as he
wiped the sticky clay off the edge of a particularly large
and lovely blade. I have also seen an elderly man, a
barber, get the thrill of his life in the gradual cleaning,

with penknife and brushes, of the curved surfaces of an ancient skull.

Sometimes we fail. The cave is empty, save for the fossilized droppings of man's scavenging enemy, the hyena, and our faces are long as we take down the sieves and roll up our tents. Then comes the test of true companionship as we move on to another site. Crawling back into a womb, bah! Crawling into a hornet's nest is a more accurate metaphor. This I have been doing on and off for seventeen years, in a dozen caves, of which only seven merit the amount of description they will receive in this volume. As far as I know, no man has dug more caves than I, but I may be wrong. This piece of information is produced not by way of boasting—it is nothing to be particularly proud of, any more than winning a pie-eating championship or some other endurance contest—but simply to assure the reader that the pages which follow are based on a sufficient amount of experience.

Cave-digging is of importance, not just to professionals like me, but to everyone interested in following the grand sweep of human history, because caves were principally occupied during that critical period when modern European men first appeared on the scene. During cave-dwelling times our ancestors passed from the hand-to-mouth existence of simple hunters and gatherers, their stomachs empty one day and crammed with meat the next, to a planned economy in which, by the systematic slaughtering of herd animals, they could acquire masses of food at once, let it freeze, and parcel it out day by day as needed.

In Europe and the Middle East people dwelt in caves, off and on, for about one hundred thousand years. This estimate is tentative because geologists lack accurate techniques of dating deposits more than forty thousand years old, and because very few of the world's caves have been dug. In China, at Chou Kou Tien near Peking, a limestone fissure was found to contain human remains several hundreds of thousands of years old.

Why the caves that have been excavated in other parts of the world were not inhabited as early as Chou Kou Tien is not fully known. It could hardly have been for lack of fire, which burns the damp chill out of the air in caves and frightens off bears and hyenas competing for their shelter. The cave men of China had fire hundreds of thousands of years earlier than the earliest known occupation of European caves, and it is extremely unlikely that the knowledge of fire remained limited to China for very long.

One possible reason is that all the world's caves are not equally ancient. The limestone deposits out of which caves are formed were laid down at different geological ages; they vary in degree of solubility; and the amount of water available to dissolve the limestone and so to form caves also varies greatly in different places. Many European and Middle Eastern caves that have been dug to bedrock are little older than the deposits found in them, while others that have been incompletely dug may yield deposits as old as Chou Kou Tien when archæologists reach their bottoms. Who knows?

In Europe and the Middle East, caves were inhabited, regularly or intermittently, by families and bands hunting in their neighborhoods down to the time when agriculture was invented, about seven or eight thousand years ago. The introduction of the agricultural life made human communities too populous for cave-dwelling. Since then, people living near caves have used them as workshops, picnic grounds, amatory nooks, and burial places, and sometimes as the depositories of precious objects, such as the Dead Sea scrolls.

The floor of a cave is built up of a number of layers of earth, each deposited at a different period and each containing bones, flints, potsherds, metal objects, and whatever other kinds of imperishable objects may have been left there by people. The soil in a cave is stratified in layers that differ in consistency and appearance because the climatic conditions under which it was deposited varied from period to period, and because of human and animal occupation. Soils laid down by water action in a damp era will be different from those carried in by the wind during a period of drought. Even if all the soils are wind-borne, the soil blown in from one end of a valley may differ from that coming from the other end. Human beings have a habit of carrying bundles of leaves and grass into caves to make beds, and these organic materials produce humus as they decay, just as in compost heaps. If one excavates carefully, it is not difficult to recognize the individual layers and keep the objects found in each level separate from the others. Now and then early men dug holes in the floors of their caves, but the disturbance of the layers is easy to recognize and we know that the materials found in disturbed soil go with the layer above the highest one through which the hole was cut.

In several ways cave-digging is easier and more satisfactory than the excavation of the commoner and better-known type of archæological site, that found in open air. The number of objects in a cubic meter of earth is many times greater in caves than in open sites like Schliemann's Troy or Sir Leonard Woolley's Ur of the Chaldees. Caves are also less subject to the vagaries of the weather than open digging-grounds; if outdoor sifting can be dispensed with, caves can be excavated when it is raining or even snowing outside.

The oldest open-air sites, seven hundred thousand to a million years old, are nothing but gravel banks plowed up and dumped by the lips of ancient ice sheets, or laid down by the flooding of ice-nurtured streams. In them we find stone tools torn from the original camp-sites where early men had left them, their edges blunted and smoothed by the rolling and buffeting of their chilly journey. Only rarely does a scrap of human bone turn up in a gravel bank, and when it does its discovery is front-page news.

As gravel sites are secondary deposits, they do not contain the orderly association of tools, animal bones, and hearths which we uncover in the sheltered and un-disturbed earth layers of caves. A few undisturbed early campsites have been found, including one in Spain, of Lower Paleolithic date.[1] It was occupied during a single period only.

Upper Paleolithic sites in the open air, as old as cave deposits elsewhere, have been excavated in the plain of central Europe, from Czechoslovakia to Russia. They were the camping-grounds of hunters whose cousins dwelt in caves in France and Spain. When undisturbed, these sites contain the outlines of house pits, fireplaces, tools, and neatly arranged stacks of mammoth bones. But because they are single occupations, these too lack the time depth found in the superimposed layers of caves.

Still younger open-air sites are man-made mounds, decayed villages, crumbled cities, and royal tombs, built during the last seven thousand years. Mound-ex-cavating is a specialized occupation requiring much patience and endurance, for a single dig may involve

[1] The Paleolithic period, or Old Stone Age, which is the age of man as a hunter within the bounds of the Pleistocene, is commonly divided into Lower (early), Middle, and Upper (late) eras.

hundreds of workmen and may take many years. Mound-digging archæologists are divided into excavators, architects, experts at ancient writing, pottery experts, photographers, and the like. Their most difficult problem in the field is keeping out of one another's hair.

Many archæologists have long believed that the focal point for the history of man during the cave-dwelling epoch was the south of France, because that is where most of the caves that have been excavated to date are located. Also, nowhere else in the world except in the north of Spain have such magnificent works of early art been discovered as the well-known animal paintings that these caverns contain. These works of art are of Upper Paleolithic date, made during the second half of the hundred-thousand-year period during which European caves are known to have been occupied.

In a few recently excavated French caves certain very late Lower Paleolithic remains, probably no more than one hundred thousand years old, have been found. The bottom layers of most French caves, however, contain the Middle Paleolithic flints, broken animal bones, and sometimes the skulls and long bones of Neanderthal men. At the end of their Middle Paleolithic occupancy most caves north of the Pyrenees were left vacant over the peak of an entire cold period, and after that, new tenants moved in.

These new settlers were the Upper Paleolithic hunters; they were men of modern European race, and may be counted among our ancestors. The varied and cleverly made tools found in their caves indicate that these hunters knew how to survive every change of the weather. Similar remains of equal age, accompanied by the skeletons of similar people, have also been recovered both from caves and from open-air sites in central Europe and southern Russia. Across the whole expanse of northern Europe, from the Bay of Biscay to the Caspian Sea, the situation was the same. It was generally believed that a new people, fully evolved physically and bearing a fully evolved and complex tool-kit, had arrived from somewhere. But where? When I began digging caves, this was one of the most puzzling problems of archæology—a first-class mystery.

The best way to solve a mystery is to follow the deductive method, working backward from the known to the unknown, step by step. In archæology the known was history, the time of written records; the unknown was prehistory. Writing, and therefore history itself, began in a certain geographical focus, in Mesopotamia, Egypt, and Syria, and across Iran and Afghanistan to the Indus valley. This is the stretch of country known as the Middle East. Before the invention of writing, the people of the Middle East had made an even greater invention—agriculture.

Agriculture began about 6000 B.C., along with animal husbandry, pottery-making, and the manufacture of polished-stone axes—traits that, taken together, constitute a way of life known as the Neolithic (New Stone Age) culture. Following the Neolithic, about 3000 B.C., the Middle East provided the setting for the world's earliest manufacture of copper and bronze tools and weapons, its first use of the wheel, and its earliest forms of writing. This combination of traits is called the Bronze Age. Two thousand years later the Iron Age began in the northwestern part of this area, and it was not until about 500 B.C. that the focal point of highest culture moved westward to Greece.

Twenty years ago it seemed obvious that these three great cultural stages—the Neolithic, Bronze, and Iron ages—which had carried modern men from the life of a

hunter to the golden age of Greece, could not have arisen
in a single region without some cogent reason. Why did
these cultures pick the Middle East as their birthplace?
As no one can have planned the choice, the reason must
be geographical. What, in other words, did the Middle
East have at that time which other parts of the world
lacked?

Whatever the secret ingredient, could it not have
been present in pre-Neolithic times as well? Could not
the ancestors of the Upper Paleolithic Europeans have
evolved their culture, and developed it by gradual stages,
in the same stretch of country in which the high cultures
of later times were born? Twenty years ago it seemed
attractive to locate the origin of the European Upper
Paleolithic in the little-known mountains and deserts
of Syria and Palestine, in Iraq, or on the Persian plateau.
The alternative was to suppose that Upper Paleolithic
Europeans had evolved both physically and culturally in
some part of Europe still archæologically unknown. As
much more work had been done in Europe than in the
Middle East, without unequivocal success, the second
area seemed to hold out much promise.

As the geography of the Middle East, and particularly
its relationship to Europe, has meaning only as part of
global geography, our search for its special significance
—its secret ingredient—must begin on a world-wide scale.
Europe, which can be taken as a point of departure, is
only a peninsula of Asia, like Arabia, India, and Southeast Asia. But it differs from all other natural regions of
the world in containing a land mass of over two million
square miles—from Ireland to Russia and from the Alps
almost to the Arctic Circle—which lies above the 45th degree of latitude and, lacking a considerable mountain
barrier, still has a well-watered, temperate, and cloudy
climate. Cloudiness, an essential part of this climatic com-

plex, reduces the amount of sunlight which reaches the earth's surface during the long days of the northern summer, producing cool temperatures. It also reduces the

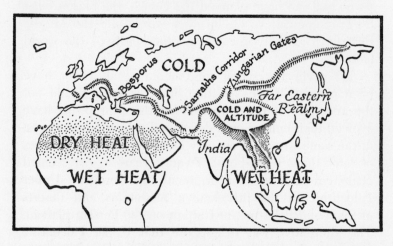

Environmental Stress Zones of the Old World. Mountains and deserts divide the Old World into four principal climatic realms. North of the mountain spine, animals and men face winter cold. South of it, summer brings dry heat. The Far East is both hot and cold, while below the deserts and in Southeast Asia, rainy summer heat is critical. While each realm molds and tests its occupants in its own fashion, none is wholly sealed off. Several world-shattering invasions have passed east-west through the Zungarian Gates, while over the southern beachhead of France, the Bosporus, and the Sarrakhs Corridor, genes and ideas have flowed between the North and the Middle East.

amount of ultra-violet radiation which gets through, permitting the evolution of a blond, white-skinned race.

In the southern hemisphere the only inhabited lands equally far from the equator are the bleak mountains, fiords, and islands of Tierra del Fuego. Eastern Siberia and Labrador also lie at this latitude, but their climates are inclement. Only in the Pacific northwest coast of the United States and Canada is there another area of cool, wet, and cloudy high-latitude climate, but its surface is small because the coastal ranges sweep almost to the sea.

The northwest coasts of America and of Europe both derive their climatic peculiarities from a combination of ocean currents and westerly winds blowing off the sea. In America these winds buffet the crests of the Rockies, dropping their thick blankets of snow on the top and the western side. In Europe they blow unimpeded across the lowland countries, Germany, Poland, and Russia, because the wind-blocking mountains that run north and south in the Americas and in eastern Asia have no counterparts in Europe. Instead, the whole mountain spine of the continent runs east and west, through the Pyrenees, the Alps, and the highlands of southeastern Europe, over to the Caucasus, splitting the westerlies into a northern and a southern stream. The latter flows over the Mediterranean to the mountains of the Middle East.

This east-west axis runs on through western and central Asia, through the mountains of Turkey, Iraq, Iran, and Afghanistan, rising gradually into the colossal barrier of the Himalayas. Beyond Afghanistan the spine of Asia forks northward and eastward to the icy waters of the Bering Sea. At their eastern end the Himalayas turn abruptly, to run in narrow ridges southward in Assam and Burma into the steep range that carries the Malay Peninsula into the sea. By these forking ranges of mountains the continent is divided into three portions; a northwestern, which includes most of Europe, Siberia, and Turkestan; a southwestern, which includes the Arabian and Indian peninsulas and lands between; and a far eastern, which is pinched into small quarters between the cold plateau of Tibet and the Pacific Ocean. Only in northern China is a large, flat land mass to be found at low altitude, and its climate is much colder and more extreme in seasonal variation than that of Europe at the same latitude.

Although the far eastern portion of Eurasia is quite isolated geographically, the northwestern and south-western ones are less so. The mountain barrier between them is breached in several places by easily negotiated gaps. These include the whole southern shore of France, the Bosporus, and the trough between the Indian Ocean and the plains of Russian Turkestan which is known as the Sarrakhs Corridor. Many mountain passes are also free of snow in the summer. While we were working in the Middle East I considered these gaps important places to investigate because in historic times countless migrations have taken place between the two regions over these corridors. On the other hand, movements into and out of the Far East, through the pass known as the Zungarian Gates in central Asia, have been rare, though spectacular.

North of the Alpo-Himalayan mountain barrier it rains throughout the year. South of the mountains the rainfall is scarcer, but as it falls mainly during winter in the whole stretch from Spain to West Pakistan, the water soaks into the ground with relatively little loss through evaporation. Throughout this zone the summers are hot, dry, and trying. The southern belt fades into a desert all the way from North Africa to India, and in Africa, southern Arabia, and India the desert gives way in turn to a tropical region of greater moisture, where the rain falls during the hot season.

Each of these climate zones imposes a different kind of stress on plant and animal life, and each has its characteristic flora and fauna, tailored to its special rigors by a long process of selection. In the northwestern zone of the Old World, all forms need to be able to live through winters of moderate coldness and cool summers. At nearly all times the air is damp and the sky cloudy. As one moves eastward and the influences of the sea are lost, along with the full impact of the westerlies, the climate becomes drier at all times, and colder in winter. The winter cold provides a challenge to all forms of life present, including man. South of the mountains, the winter is a time of growth and comfort, culminating in the beauty and exhilaration of spring. The time of stress is summer, with its heat and drought. In the deserts fringing this zone, dry heat becomes critical. Farther south it is the enervating steamy heat such as one finds in India which screens the fit from the unfit, and creatures that can live in comfort in Scotland will die in Calcutta, and vice versa. In A.D. 1223 Genghiz Khan left India, to retreat over the Hindu Kush to the northern climatic zone in which he had been born and reared; the weather defeated the Mongol emperor as no human army could.

We were searching for the place of origin of a kind of man fully evolved in body and brain and capable of living in a cold, moist, and cloudy climate, a man who, when he first appeared in Ice Age Europe, was equipped with a complete Upper Paleolithic toolkit. According to our hypothesis, his ancestors may have developed their culture in the warm belt of climate south of the mountain barrier—the Middle East. They may then have moved north through one or more of the barrier's breaches shortly before the time of their earliest known European cave deposits. All that was lacking to prove this theory was a series of sites, properly dated, located in between, and early dates for the sites already found in the Middle East. These proofs had not been found when I began cave-digging in 1939.

An argument against this migration theory arises from zoology. When the Upper Paleolithic people migrated anywhere it was in search of food. They moved because their food was mobile. Parasites on flocks and herds of game, they followed their walking meat stores wherever the herds went. As the bone heaps left by Upper Paleolithic men show, they specialized in certain species of animals, such as reindeer, horse, or mammoth, and killed them selectively, choosing individuals of a special age and even sex, just as in a slaughterhouse. This specialization required much training, and yielded the rich reward of a dependable food supply. Hunters so specialized would not be likely to change their source of food unless forced to.

The movements of hunters, therefore, can best be traced by following those of game. But the animals also specialized in their own choice of food—grass of a certain kind, or spruce twigs, or whatever—and their movements were dictated by changes in vegetation. Changes in vegetation, in turn, were brought about by changes in climate. The primary cause of human migration during the period we were investigating was therefore climate, and it was in fact a period of marked climatic change.[2]

The one hundred thousand years of man's cave-dwelling history fall within that great division of geologic time known as the Pleistocene or Ice Age, stretching from nearly a million years ago down to about 8000 B.C. In terms of climate, the Pleistocene's variability stood in great contrast to the preceding Pliocene period, a stretch of ten million years of warm and uneventful weather. In most parts of the world the Pleistocene came in abruptly. Mountains rose, and the earth's surface cooled, probably as a result of an epidemic of sunspots.

[2] This subject is specifically covered in *Climatic Change*, edited by Harlow Shapley (Cambridge, Mass.: Harvard University Press; 1953).

The temperature of our atmosphere was lowered to about 14.4° F. below its present level, which itself is colder than the Pliocene. To a radar-eyed observer posted in outer space and capable of looking through the cowl of clouds which tempered the blow of the sun's rays over many parts of the earth's skin, white spots were beginning to appear on certain portions of the land surface of the planet. The Antarctic continent, thrust above the surface of the surrounding waters to a height of some nine thousand feet at the South Pole, was the first to collect permanent snow and ice. Owing to its sea-locked form, however, it could not fan this glacial icecap equatorward, but dropped into the sea great bergs and floes of gleaming crystal which floated toward the tips of Africa and South America, driving ahead of them, in the atmosphere, great circular areas of high pressure, the breeders of storms.

In the northern hemisphere it was not the watery pole that first accumulated ice, but probably the great plateau of the world's largest island, Greenland. Seeds of glaciation then spread out to northeastern Canada and the United States. Meanwhile, similar white patches had formed on the Alps and on the mountains of Scandinavia. As the American and Scandinavian centers bordered on land to the south, the ice crawled unimpeded for hundreds of miles, pushing the paths of winds before its edges, and moving the zones of vegetation ahead of it like fleeing legions chased by an invincible host. In western Siberia the ice marched inward from a rim of converging mountains, its fingers meeting in the center as in a cup, and the sheet so formed spread westward in the direction of the source of moisture until it crossed the Urals and merged with the Scandinavian mass. In Africa and South America, mountain glaciers formed in high places, as they did in such unlikely spots as the spine of New Guinea; but, owing to the tempering influence of the oceans, nowhere in the southern hemisphere did the ice advance in vast sheets as it did in Europe and North America.

Such mountain glaciers were sluggish streams of ice massively oozing down the courses of valleys, scouring out their bottoms and sides, pushing dikes of gravel before them, and feeding mountain streams at their feet. If the flatland at the foot of the mountains was cold enough and cloudy enough, it too grew a coat of ice. This process of ice-sheet formation took place, in various parts of the world, several times during the Pleistocene period, with intervening periods of warmer climate.

In 1909 Albrecht Penck and Eduard Bruckner published a three-volume work on the Ice Age in the Alps,[3] a magnum opus of such overwhelming authority that it has served as a model of glacial research ever since. They recognized four successive periods of ice-sheet formation in the Alpine region, during each of which the amount of heat which reached the earth from the sun was reduced to about 14.4° F. less than at present, and three intervening periods of warmth when the ice melted and the earth's temperature level rose to 5.4° F. above our present condition. Geologists working in Scandinavia, the Himalayas, the Pamirs, and elsewhere have tried to fit their findings into the Alpine sequence, with varying success.[4] It has been found, for example, that the first recognizable ice sheet in northern Europe corresponds to the second one in the Alps. In the Caucasus only two, presumed to be the last two, have been reported, and in

[3] Albrecht Penck and Eduard Bruckner: *Die Alpen in Eiszeitalter* (Leipzig, 1909).

[4] Penck and Bruckner named the four glacial periods Gunz, Mindel, Riss, and Würm, after sites in the Alps. Although the Scandinavian and other non-Alpine ice sheets have been given separate names, the Alpine terminology is in general use for the whole northern region of the Old World.

Iran no one knows how many there were in the mountains. The New World, like the Alps, had four, but the exact duration of each may not have been the same in the two continents. The ice may have lasted longer in New than in Old England.

During the height of each great glacial advance, so much of the world's supply of water was immobilized in its icecaps that the level of the continent-encircling oceans of the earth was greatly lowered. In the course of one as yet unidentified glacial period the world's shorelines sank nearly three hundred feet below present sea level. During the interglacial periods when the ice melted,[5] high sea levels ranged from about a hundred feet to only fifteen or twenty feet above the world's present beaches. During the fourth glacial period, minor increases in solar radiation melted some of the ice and produced ancient beach levels less than fifteen feet above present height. Owing to subsequent earth movements, these figures are not the same everywhere. In each country where caves are to be dug near the sea, the local sequence of beach levels must be worked out independently.

Warm intervals occurred within each of the four great glaciations, but we do not know how many there were in the first three because subsequent ice and stream action has erased most of their traces. We are not even sure how many occurred during the fourth and last ice period, partly for the same reason, and partly because much of the earth's surface remains geologically unexplored. In the Alps the fourth glacial period consisted of at least three subperiods of greatest cold, with two minor intervals of comparative warmth, probably not quite so warm as today. For the sake of simplicity these will be

[5] Recent work in Greenland and current work in Antarctica indicate that some ice may have remained through one or more interglacials in these regions.

called the first, second, and third advances of the fourth
ice sheet, separated by the first and second warm intervals; [6] these warm intervals are quite distinct, of course,
from the earlier and much warmer interglacials.

In many places outside of western Europe it is impossible to refine the fourth glacial period into three dis-
crete subperiods; not only is much work left to be done,

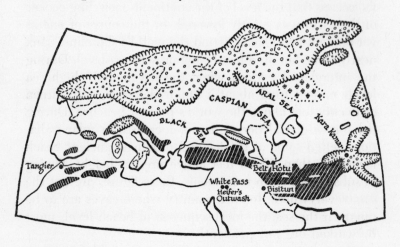

*Europe and the Middle East during the Last Ice Age. At
the height of the last ice age, most of Europe and the ad-
joining portion of central Asia were boxed off from the
rest of the world by a double barrier. Ice sheets covered
the Far North, the Pyrenees, Alps, Caucasus, and mountains of central Asia. Fed by the melting edges of ice, the
inland waters of the Caspian and Aral seas swelled, and
the Caspian water spilled over, through a narrow channel, into the Black Sea, whence it flowed through the
Bosporus into the Mediterranean. The narrow band of
ice-free land from the Atlantic to the Altai became the
home of cold-loving animals and their human parasite,
northern man.*

[6] The advances are technically known as Würm I, II, and III, and the
warm intervals as the Würm I/II and II/III interstadials.

but also it is not certain that regions away from the centers of ice-formation, such as the Arabian desert, were so sensitive to climatic change as those near them, such as southern Germany or northern France. This makes our job of dating the remains found in caves in the Middle East harder than it is in Europe.

Each time a major ice sheet formed, three zones of climate could be seen beyond its edges. Nearest the ice, and averaging about fifty miles wide, was a belt of soggy ground overlying permanently frozen earth; the same kind of terrain still exists in Alaska, where it is called *muskeag*. Its vegetation consisted largely of mosses and dwarf willow. Beyond it lay a stretch of plain formed of a fine, wind-blown, clayey soil called *loess*, which bore a rich annual crop of grass. On this cold steppe or prairie, vast herds of horses and other grazing animals could be hunted by anyone who could live through the winter. Although narrow in western Europe, this grassland reached a width of over a hundred miles in southern Russia, which was a fine hunting-ground indeed. The third zone was one of boreal forest, similar to the Siberian taiga and the woods of Maine, Minnesota, and Canada.

Each time the ice sheet formed, however, the prime hunting-ground of southern Russia lost some of its territory by flooding. The ice sheet that covered Scandinavia and northwestern Russia melted a little around the edges each summer, and the water that ran off flooded the inland basins into which it drained. The Black Sea, which was landlocked before, in pre-glacial times, the Ægean water broke through the Bosporus, was fed by the four D's—Danube, Dniester, Dnieper, and Don —and the Caspian was fed by the mighty Volga. Runoff from the northern slope of the Hindu Kush and the western flank of the Tian Shan reached the Aral Sea. At the height of the flooding the Caspian waters spilled over into the Black Sea, and vast areas that are now dry land were flooded. At its peak the flood caused by the third glacial advance raised the Caspian 300 feet (90 meters) above its present level, which is 85 feet (26 meters) below the present level of the oceans. During the fourth glacial period it reached 250 feet (75 meters) above its present level on one occasion, and then finally it flooded again, just before the end of the Ice Age, to a height of 85 feet (26 meters), or present ocean level. The presence of this vast lake not far from the center of a continental land mass during these glacial times may have had a tempering effect on the local climate.

As the ice disappeared after each advance, the zones of climate followed its edge; the soggy swamps and the cold steppe vanished with the ice itself, while the boreal forest moved north to its present position in Scandinavia, the Baltic states, and northern Russia. Behind it came the hardwood forest of western Europe, in which antlered deer browsed on twigs and leaves and wild boar munched fallen beechnuts and acorns. In the drier east, the borders of the shrinking lakes became grasslands again, but of the kind seen today.

In the Middle East neither the climate nor the vegetation changed nearly so much as in the north. Although local mountain glaciers covered the peaks and high valleys with a snowy mantle, no ice sheet formed. The place of glacial advances was taken by periods of increased rainfall, known as *pluvials*. The warm intervals of the north were correspondingly replaced by periods of relative drought, comparable to the present climate in that area. Geologists working in the Middle East have by no means completed their surveys. In some places they have found two periods of heavy rainfall, in others three, of which the third is minor. It is obvious that the number of climatic fluctuations in the north cannot be matched in a simple fashion against those in the south. The reason may be that only ice movements of major proportions in the north were powerful enough to displace the westerly storm belts.

During times of major climatic change, as from a glacial to an interglacial period in the north, the shifts in temperature and rainfall levels which accompanied the retreat of the ice sheets caused whole zones of vegetation to move, and entire faunas to follow them. Reindeer and mammoth were succeeded by hippopotamus as the tropical forests moved exotically far from the equator. Successions of this nature have been found in western Europe, and even in England. As a matter of course, human populations followed their favorite animals, just as any parasite rides its host.

During times of minor climatic change, like the cold advances and warm fluctuations of the last glacial period, animal species also moved about with their special zones of vegetation in Europe, so that arctic and temperate-forest animals alternately replaced one another. Tropical animals, however, never went north after the last interglacial. Excavations in Palestine in the 1930's were then interpreted as showing that during the last glacial period gazelles and fallow deer took turns predominating along the coast, and this suggested that similar changes might be expected in the desert. There was no evidence, however, that during the last ice age game marched in great herds through the gaps in the east-west mountain barrier or over the mountain passes, nor that any great human movements dependent on the pursuit of wild herds took place.

Nevertheless, people had to migrate between these two great geographical regions at one time or another, either before or after the last ice age if not during it, because Middle Easterners and Europeans are both basically of one race, the white or Caucasian, and because there must have been a time when the people living north of the barrier first learned to hunt arctic animals, after finding means to protect themselves from the winter cold.

Keeping alive in the cold required fire, which we know that both Neanderthal and Upper Paleolithic men had. It also required tools with which warm clothing could be made. We do not know what kind of clothing either Neanderthal or Upper Paleolithic men wore, but we know what kind of garments they could have made. Upper Paleolithic men could have made tailored suits like those of Siberian natives, Eskimos, and American Indians who live in the Arctic. Neanderthal men could have made robes, possibly as warm as those of the guanaco-hunting Indians of Tierra del Fuego. We know what they could have made through a study of their flint and bone tools.

The same is true of housing. Caves are scarce in most parts of the world, and certainly Paleolithic people lived outside caves more than in them. Lower, Middle, and Upper Paleolithic tools were all good enough for felling and trimming poles, peeling off strips of birchbark, skinning animals, dressing their skins, and lacing them together into tent covers. In eastern Siberia modern tribesmen live safely through the Arctic winter, at temperatures as low as −75° F., in conical tents made of poles, bark, and skins. In western Siberia some of the fishermen along the Obi River inhabit semi-subterranean houses similar in plan to the house pits excavated in Upper Paleolithic sites in Czechoslovakia. We have every reason to believe that Upper Paleolithic Europeans found ways to keep warm through the glacial cold, both in caves and in open country. Earlier men might have done the same, as far as the possibilities of working wood, skin, and bark are shown by the tools they left behind them. In other words, we cannot tell by the types of tools *alone* exactly when people first could have lived through the glacial cold of Europe; we can only tell when they could first have done so in some degree of comfort.

Archæologists who study flint tools spend little of their time trying to figure out the exact functions of each class of implement. Their principal task is to sort the tools, count them, and compare the assemblages from different levels of a single site and those from different sites. Some archæologists also study the unused flakes and cores, which toolmakers threw away during their work just as carpenters discard shavings and tag ends of wood. Being equally imperishable, the scrap lasts as long as the finished tools, and cave deposits are full of it. The scrap tells us how the tools were made, even if all the tools were carried away.

When an archæologist finds similar tools in two levels of a single site, he can assume a continuity of occupation. When he finds them in two sites, he has to decide whether the similarity is due to migration, or to the exchange of ideas between neighboring peoples, or to parallel evolution—that is, two different peoples faced with the same needs working out the same methods of tool-making independently. Which choice he accepts depends on how close the sites are to each other in time and space, on what physical barriers lay between them to prevent movement, and on his own good judgment.

Although man does not live by tools alone, and never did, flint implements are nearly all we have to study Paleolithic cultures with. This research is largely a matter of sorting, counting, and comparing the flint tools we dig up by the thousands in caves. Because flint tools are works of art as well as implements (some archæologists deny this), the experts who study them full-time arrive at their

judgments as intuitively as wine-tasters. Only about ten
men in the world are top flint experts. The rest of us, who
merely dig caves, show our flints to as many of these
specialists as we can, partly because of this æsthetic fac-
tor, and partly because no definitive Comparative Anatomy of Flint Tools has yet been written.[7] No one has yet

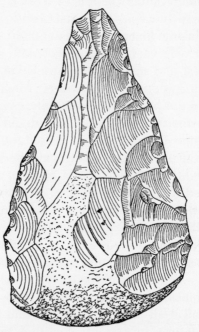

A hand ax: the tool par excellence *of the Lower Paleolithic, all the way from London to Capetown to Bombay.
A pointed tool flaked on both sides and retouched on
both edges, it is a splendid all-purpose cutter, as good as
a steel knife for skinning and butchering an animal, and
adequate for felling saplings and fashioning poles and
hafts. (One-half actual size.)*

[7] Several useful short handbooks are available, particularly Kenneth
P. Oakley's *Man the Tool Maker* (Third edition. London: British Museum
[Natural History]; 1955). See also Lewis Leakey's *Adam's Ancestors*
(Second edition. London: Methuen & Co.; 1955).

completely analyzed the entire technical field, though some are working on it.

For purposes of rapid field analysis, we diggers need to know a few basic facts about the properties of flint and how it was worked. Flint is the best tool-making material that men can pick up off the ground and shape with no other aids than a natural pebble or a stick. With such a hammer he can break it, for flint is brittle and shatters like glass. Making flint tools is essentially a process of breaking flint with varying degrees of skill.

The earliest and simplest stone tools known are pebbles broken to produce a sharp edge. Among the latest and finest are the beautiful, supposedly ceremonial, flint knives of the ancient Egyptians, as hard and sharp as the finest steel, smooth and even of edge, and graceful as Florentine daggers. The first could have been made by a wild creature little brighter than a brilliant ape; the last was fashioned by sophisticated urban human beings highly specialized in their craft. In between lies the world of flint.

Flint in the strict sense is a glassy mineral that comes in more or less globular lumps in beds of chalk; if it is found in other soil, in stream beds, or embedded in limestone, its technical name is *chert*. For purposes of simplification we call it all flint. All of it is found in limestone country, for it was formed as a natural by-product of limestone. As habitable caves are found in limestone cliffs, primitive and ancient cave-dwellers found their tool materials near by.

Some lumps of flint are as small as apples; the tools made of them must be even smaller. Other lumps are as big as watermelons. So flint tools may vary from an inch or so in length to more than a foot. Some flint has a fine grain, and breaks as smoothly as glass. Some of the coarser cherts are rough and granular. Often we find coarse tool

material lying unused near our caves while the implements in the deposit are of fine flint brought from afar.
Stone Age man was choosy about his flint because finer
flint is easier to work and produces a more nearly perfect
tool.

Holding a lump or piece of flint in his hand, the toolmaker has a choice at the start. Shall he make a single
tool out of this lump by knocking pieces off its surface and
trimming it into some shape that will give him one or
more cutting edges? Or shall he break it up and use the
pieces as tools? The simpler and more obvious of these
alternatives is to treat it as a unit. The tool he makes is a
core tool, for the core of the lump is his object of con-
centration. If he breaks it up, he is faced with another
choice. Shall he just knock flake after flake off it more or
less at random until he finds a piece that is of the proper
general shape for a knife or scraper? Or shall he try to
shape the core in advance in some way, in order to strike
off the kind of piece he wants?

Aborigines of one of the living Australian tribes still
use the simplest method of all. They smash their cores
and use whatever flakes they find on the ground. Living
in a bleak desert, they have to travel long distances to get
food and water. As the surface of the ground is strewn
with flint, they make their tools as they need them instead of carrying them around. The crude flakes they
make and abandon after use are good enough for shaping
simple wooden spears and digging-sticks and fashioning
bark baskets to carry water in. They have failed to invent
better tools because they do not need them, and they
prefer not to burden themselves on their desperately long
journeys.

As far back as the second interglacial period, however, people in various parts of the world, including the
Middle East and Europe, began shaping their cores in

advance, perhaps through economy of flint, perhaps to
save time and effort. Intellectually speaking, pre-shaping
a core requires an image of what is wanted in advance
of production, and planning through several steps. The

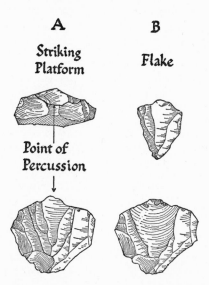

A

Striking
Platform

B

Flake

Point of
Percussion

*Making a flake on a prepared core. (A) The upper draw-
ing represents the butt or top end of a prepared core; its
entire surface is a striking-platform. Lower view shows
the front of the prepared core. In both views, the outline
of the flake to be detached is marked by a heavy line.
(B) The core has been struck by a hammer blow at the
point of percussion and the flake, shown above, removed.
The front of the remaining core is shown below. (After
H. Kelly.) (One-fourth actual size.)*

usual method is to visualize the flake as part of the surface of a lump of flint, and then, by striking off trimming
flakes—intentional waste products—to make a domed surface. That will be the back of the flake. Then the flint-

worker selects one end of the core to be the butt of his
flake. Here he will strike a single, carefully directed blow
that, if successful, will detach the flake in one operation.
As this is the critical act in the whole sequence, he takes
every precaution to insure success. Probably through trial

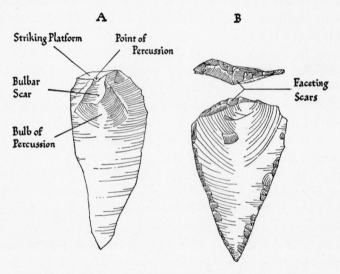

*Anatomy of a flake and faceting. (A) Rear view of a typ-
ical flake removed from a prepared core. The butt end is
the remains of the striking-platform. (B) Two views of a
flake removed from a core. In this case the striking-platform was faceted before the flake was struck off. (One-
half actual size.)*

and error, he or his teachers found out that the very flake
wanted will fly off the core if the force of the blow follows
the direction of the long axis of the flake. This flake will
be long and flat. The bulb of percussion, which is a smooth,
breast-like mound at the base of the detached surface,
will be small. If he strikes the core at a wider angle, the

bulb will be large and awkward, the flake shorter and thicker.

A blow that follows the long axis of the desired flake can be struck only if the surface where the flint is hit stands at an angle of forty-five degrees to the long axis of the flake. The worker may knock off several trimming flakes until one of them has left a striking-platform set at this angle. If he cannot create such a platform by a single blow, he has another trick: he can lean over his flake and nibble at it with his hammer, pecking off a row of small chips, which leave telltale scars or facets. These undulations on his striking-platform are carried over onto the butt of his flake.

A third way of getting flakes was first introduced to Europe and the Middle East in late third-interglacial times; that was the use of the disk core. Instead of tailoring his core for a single flake, our toolmaker trims it into the form of a fat disk, like two saucers glued rim to rim. Now he has a striking platform on each side, and its angle is forty-five degrees or less. He can strike a blow on one side and take off a flake shaped like a cut of pie, then knock off another on the other side, and so around the circle on both sides. This does not produce a better flake than the single prepared core, but is less expensive of time and effort, if not also of flint. Like the single prepared core, its striking-platforms can be faceted if necessary.

Now and then a man making flakes by either of these methods knocks off a long, narrow, flat piece with a small bulb and parallel sides. This is, as far as appearance goes, a blade. A blade is a fine tool for use as a knife, and to use as a blank for reshaping into a number of special implement types. Making blades deliberately and as a standard procedure is a highly skilled technique that not all of the flint-chipping peoples of the world achieved. The Aus-

tralian aborigines and the Bushmen of South Africa were
still using flakes in the present century.

To make blades, the worker selects a lump of fine-

*Two views of a disk-shaped core, showing the scars from
which flakes have been struck from both sides, around
the rim. The original core and the flakes first struck from
it were much larger. (One-half actual size.)*

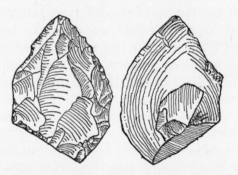

*An implement made on a flake which could have been
struck from a disk-shaped core (shown in two views).
The striking-platform is visible at the lower right edge.
From the Neanderthal type-site of Le Moustier, France.
(After K. P. Oakley.) (One-half actual size.)*

grained flint as long and straight as possible. He trims
this carefully, aiming for a cylindrical shape, or a split
cylinder, which will do as well. Selecting one end for the
striking-platform, he then very carefully strikes off long,

thin, flat, small-bulbed, parallel-sided blades. Instead of striking the platform directly with a hammer, he uses a punch of bone, antler, or some other elastic material. By channeling the force of the blow through the punch he

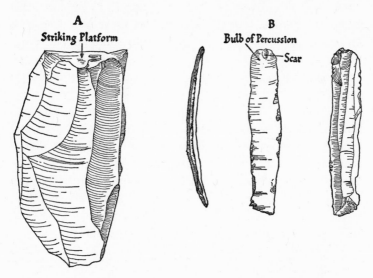

(A) *Blade core of Upper Paleolithic workmanship, from Europe.* (B) *Blade from Kara Kamar, Afghanistan. The three views, side, back, and front, show the small butt, tiny bulb and scar, and the long, thin, and nearly flat shape of the blade itself. It is a fine, economical, all-purpose blank from which many kinds of special tools can be made. (One-half actual size.)*

can make sure of its point of impact and direction, and the butt of the blade will be small. The blade is the acme of the flint-chipper's technique. No better way of producing implement blanks has ever been discovered. The gunflint-makers of Brandon in England, who handle flint as easily and skillfully as sculptors do clay, turn their cores into blades.

Some flakes are ready for use as they come off the core, but most of them are a little uneven here and there and need retouching to produce a straight, even edge. After they have been nicked a few times the whole edge may have to be retouched, just as an old knife can need grinding. Blades, too, get nicked and must be retouched, and often the blade is retouched into some special form to serve, for example, as a chisel. Core tools that have been fashioned by primary flaking also often need retouching.

Retouching itself is as skilled a procedure as the primary removal of flakes and blades from cores, and the techniques employed parallel those of flake- and blade-making, for the two are parts of a single process. The earliest and crudest method of retouching is to strike the edge of the flake or blade a series of short, sharp blows with the tool used as a hammer. This produces nothing but a series of nicks, somewhat like butt facets.

By third-interglacial times flint-workers in Europe and the Middle East had learned to remove small, flattish chips that are described as *squamous* because of their resemblance to the scales of reptiles and fish. Probably these were taken off with a punch, a tool to be used later in blade-making. Not only could a skilled man produce an even edge in this way, but he could also trim the whole surface of an implement into a special shape, even making both sides of it alike.

During the middle of the Upper Paleolithic in Europe flint-workers learned to take off very long, fine, and delicate slivers of flint from the surface of a blade, creating a pattern of shallow channels which reached all the way across the piece. They did this by applying pressure, rather than a blow, with a flaking-tool or punch. This pressure-flaking technique was also used in North America, and in the Old World it was revived in Neolithic times and used on the ceremonial knives of the ancient Egyptians down into the Bronze Age.

Both specialists and professional diggers know that little can be learned by studying individual flints, because most early hunters, unlike the Australian aborigines mentioned, needed several kinds of tools for different purposes. In order to find out as much as possible about the life of the people who made the tools, we need every scrap of evidence we can get. All the tools must be studied to find out both the ratios of tool types to one another, and the variability within each type. The statistical method is just as necessary in archæology as in biology.

The total set of flints from a single site and time span —usually a soil stratum in a site—is known as an assemblage. This assemblage may have a certain proportion of tools made on cores, flakes, and blades. A certain percentage of the flakes will have faceted butts, showing special preparation of the striking-platform before removal from the core. If there are blades, the number of different kinds of special tools made from them will vary from assemblage to assemblage. Or a set of tools may show a characteristic kind of retouch. When he has surveyed all these factors both statistically and intuitively, the flint expert has obtained an idea of the over-all characteristics of his assemblage, and he is ready to compare it with other assemblages previously found and described.

A number of assemblages that are essentially alike, so much so that they were probably made by a single population, is called a *culture*, using that word in a special technical sense. When an archæologist has discovered a new culture he usually gives it a name, using some modification of the name of the site or nearest settlement. For example, the hand axes of the Lower Paleolithic of first-interglacial date are called Abbevillian, after Abbeville in France, where they were first discovered and described.

The single prepared flakes and the finer hand axes of the second and third interglacials are called Acheulian after St.-Acheul. The prepared flakes which sometimes have faceted butts and which appeared during the second interglacial are called Levallois flakes, after a suburb of Paris. Neanderthal man's special flake culture, including disk cores, is known as Mousterian, after Le Moustier, a cave site where this culture was first recognized as such.

Some cultures are small and local. Others are widespread, having been traced across continents. Naming a culture was a thrilling business during the early days of Paleolithic archæology. Once the French list had been filled, from Lower through Middle and Upper Paleolithic cultures, the fashion changed, and archæologists liked to tie newly discovered cultures into old ones; thus the Acheulian came to be discovered as far from France as India and South Africa, and the Mousterian thousands of miles from the known haunts of Neanderthal men. Upon re-examination many of the cultures identified with the original French sequence have been found to be local. Some of them are probably related to one another only in the evolutionary stage each had independently reached. That is why most modern archæologists dislike these old labels, which, by obscuring regional evolutionary sequences, do more harm than good. In this book we will describe the assemblages we found and try to relate them to others when possible without these cultural tags.

In a general way, the evolution of tools during the parts of the Pleistocene which preceded our cave-dwelling period followed an orderly scheme, like the evolution of man himself. In the very beginning people took pebbles out of streams, broke them, and cut things with the broken edges. Later they found how to crack the pebbles on the bias, to get longer and sharper edges than before. This Lower Paleolithic pebble-tool technique was followed by a process of chipping lumps of stone, and then of flint, into single, large, pointed core tools, flaked on both sides and shaped like almonds. These tools are the famous *hand axes*. They are impressive, heavy, and expensive to make, in terms of time and materials.

Proper hand axes began to appear during the first interglacial, and by the second they had acquired an elegant and formal shape. At the same time various cheaper implements in the form of flakes were also being manufactured, and even a few blades. By the dawn of the third interglacial period, hand axes were still fashionable, like Rolls-Royces in the 1930's, but, being very individual and time-consuming things to make, they were growing rare. At the time our story opens, one hundred thousand years ago, in the middle of the third interglacial period, hand axes, random flakes, flakes produced on prepared cores, flakes made from disks, and blades were all being made, and by more than one kind of human being. Nothing of any style that had flourished in the past had been completely forgotten, and nothing notable to be produced in the immediate future had failed to be anticipated. It was a rare period in history. Like the atomic age, it was also a fine time to begin thinking about living in caves.

Sooner or later, in one place or another, caves are bound to give us the answer to our question: what was the origin of our own race? However, it does not pay us to be too optimistic about settling this matter here and now, for we can dig one cave after another for years on end without finding what we hope to see in them. Like lovely ladies, no two caves are alike, and not one of them ever reveals all her secrets at the first intimacy. A digger of caves can never, unless he is foolish, lose his capacity for surprise.

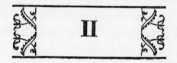

II

TANGIER—THE HIGH CAVE

My INTERMITTENT CAVE-DIGGING CAREER began early in May 1939, following a visit to the American Legation in Tangier. My two young sons, Carl, Jr., and Charles (aged twelve and eight), their mother, and I were on our way from the Azores to French Morocco, having crossed the strait from Gibraltar the previous day. We had no intention to tarry in Tangier, despite its well-known charm, but planned to move southward to Fez, Marrakesh, and the Sous valley in the cool spring weather, during the few perfect weeks of the year when the coastal plain of Morocco is a sweet-smelling garden of daisies and wild iris, and the storks circle overhead, steering their white bodies with their bright orange legs stretched out behind. The boys had never seen Morocco, and we were eager to show it to them.

The Honorable Hooker A. Doolittle, our chargé d'affaires, sat behind his desk in a beautiful old Moorish room in the Legation, a chamber embellished with delicate tile and plasterwork and soft-toned Berber carpets. A Riffian guard, blond-whiskered and yellow-turbaned, served us coffee in small cups. One of these he set noiselessly on Mr. Doolittle's desk. As I watched the movements of the Riffian's hands with professional interest—observing their freckles and blond hair—my glance moved to a shiny black object resting on the edge of a large green blotter. The black object was a Neolithic polished-stone ax used by farmers as long ago as five thousand years to clear the forest for their garden patches and to fell poles for their house roofs.

I had come to visit Mr. Doolittle in order to find out about travel regulations in the Spanish and French zones of Morocco. Now another element had been added. "Where," I asked, "did you get that?"

Mr. Doolittle picked up the axhead and fingered its smooth surface with tender satisfaction. "I dug it up," he said.

In a few minutes visas and travel were forgotten. It seemed that Mr. Doolittle and Dr. Ralph Nahon, an American physician who lived in Tangier, had excavated a cave on the outskirts of the International Zone, the smallest of the three administrative units into which Morocco was divided. This cave, which was but one of many, had yielded a rich treasure of Neolithic artifacts, including stone axes, flint knives, pottery, long bone needles, and one complete human skeleton. Before long I was sitting in the reception room of Dr. Nahon's office in the American Cinema building, the top floor of which was (and still is) occupied by Freddy's New York Night Club, and before much time had passed Dr. Nahon and I were rolling over the mountain road in the doctor's Hillman.

Tangier is always exciting because it is never twice the same; I had not been there since 1928. Tall buildings had begun to appear on the slope west of the Socco Grande, and the narrow road over the Wed el-Yahud (Jews' River) and up the Mountain was used as much by automobiles as by donkeys and mules. Spaniards, Jews, Riffians, and Arabs, in their many-colored garments, mingled as indifferently as gnus, giraffes, and Thomson's gazelles on an East African plain. Square minarets, as white as if carved from chalk, pointed to the westward-moving billows of cloud overhead. All the flowers of the Mediterranean were out at once, crawling and hanging on walls, waving from bushes, dangling from trees, and momentarily blanketing the perennial smell of stale urine with their overpowering medley of bouquets.

On top of the mountain we came to a lookout rock in which steps had been carved. From its top one could see Jebel Musa, bare and gleaming as a lion's tooth, facing Gibraltar across the eastern end of the strait; and, much nearer, the yellow sands of Tarifa, beckoning travelers eager to make the shortest crossing from Africa to Europe. Below us to the northwest stood the Cape Spartel lighthouse, silhouetted against the Atlantic, deep green as a cat's eye; the whipped gray of the strait; and the still blue of the Mediterranean.

It was hard to turn one's back on this scene. To the southwest Dr. Nahon indicated a broken beach that ran to a flat-topped headland built of green grass over gray rock, and beyond the headland another beach of silvery sand stretching as far as the eye could reach. Pointing to the headland, he said: "There are the caves."

Perched on this lofty stone lookout, surveying one of the most strategic corners of the world—so strategic that Britain holds a rock on the edge of Spain, and a city of Morocco has to be governed by a committee of seven sometimes mutually hostile powers—it was easy to realize how important this spot had been in ancient times as well. The Phœnician fleet that an Egyptian pharaoh had hired to sail around Africa had to pass through these narrow waters to reach home. The Neolithic farmers who had pecked and ground the ax now on Mr. Doolittle's desk were kinfolk of some of those who had paddled across in fragile canoes to carry agriculture and animal-husbandry to western Europe, and people of their race live on in the British Isles, France, Portugal, and Spain, as well as in the New World. Doolittle's and Nahon's discovery was the most extensive of its kind in northern Morocco. These caves deserved a close investigation.

Rolling through the canopied forest of umbrella-like Atlantic pines which covers the high land above Cape Spartel, we descended in the Hillman to the Atlantic coast road and soon reached the turnaround on the headland over the caves. Ras Ashagar, it is called—"Bald Head." A few hundreds of thousands of years ago the limestone of which the headland is formed was battered and scoured by the sea, opening up some of the lowerlying caverns to the long tongues of its waves. One cave, as large as a cathedral, is still entered and abandoned twice each day by the tides. Others are tiny cracks tempting the visitor to get out his flashlight and crawl to see what lies ahead.

The limestone of which the headland is built is of two kinds: the original rock of the headland of early Pleistocene date, and a secondary gritty deposit formed later in the cracks and bearing the fossil bones of many animals. Parts of the first kind, being both porous and hard, are perfectly suited for grinding grain. The earlier millstones, cut out in Phœnician times, were rectangular. Grain is ground to flour on them by rubbing an upper or hand stone back and forth, as with the Mexican and Southwestern grindstones. Circular pockmarks indicate the places from which millstones of the rotary type, still used in Morocco, were pecked out from Roman to modern times.

Most of the stone-cutting, however, is done inside the caves, by the light of little kerosene lamps, by men who look like gnomes. Clad in cotton shirts and baggy knickerbockers, their round heads protected by brimless knitted caps, they peck away with their small, sharp hammers, expertly circling the piece of stone to be removed, and the sound of their hammers can be heard through the stone from cave to cave. Here and there one sees a slab of roof fallen on the floor; earlier stone-cutters had pecked away too much of the underpinnings and been crushed. On the palmetto-covered ground outside, holes gaping through the red topsoil show where other roofs have collapsed. Hazardous as this business is, the gnomes work on, for the millstone market must be satisfied. Carried on mule-back and camelback over all Morocco, their product grinds grain in Fez and Marrakesh, and in the High Atlas.

These men live in Mediouna, a white village in an armpit of the mountain about three miles from the caves. Some of them claim Riffian ancestry, and indeed their numbers have needed recruits as, from time to time, owing to roof-falls, deaths have exceeded births. Wherever they came from, they nearly all look alike: short, stocky, nimble men with broad hands, round faces, snub noses, and blue eyes. Although pious Muslims, they still hold ancient and secret rites in their caves, and when a young married woman has failed to produce a baby in due time, the older women drag her to a spot on the shore where, when the tide is just right, a jet of water spouts up through a hole in the rock. Holding her over this with her legs spread and skirts raised, they make her, momentarily, the bride of the sea. Where a mortal man has failed, Neptune may succeed.

After we had visited the largest cave, Dr. Nahon led us to a rectangular hole in the highest point of the headland. This was the remains of a Phœnician tomb that he had helped excavate. From it had come golden ornaments that had since disappeared. This was an ancient place of sacrifice for the Phœnicians, and possibly for other mariners as well. When the sirocco is blowing westward through the strait, ships dependent on sail alone may spend weeks waiting to get through, and their safest course is to weather out the storm in the lee of the headland, where the cliffs rise higher than any masthead. I have seen Breton lobster boats with awkward-looking red sails take shelter there, and Portuguese and Spanish tunny-fishermen also wait at anchor, sending their crews ashore in small boats for water. During the war of independence which the Riffians waged against Spain and France in the 1920's, firearms for Abd-el-Krim's soldiers were landed in these caves, to be smuggled out into the hills on muleback in the dark of night. Many a prayer has been said in these caves, to many a god: for the wind to turn, for the roof not to fall, and for the sultan's soldiers to look the other way.

Had I been of a type easily moved to prayer, I would have uttered one myself, a prayer for an unspoiled site, after seeing the torn-up floors of these beautiful caves where the human moles of Mediouna had burrowed for millstone material, tossing aside the deposits of tens of thousands of years to be washed away in the sea. What Dr. Nahon told me about the cave that he and Mr. Doolittle had dug gave me little hope, for he said that they had cleaned all the soil out of this grotto as well. I would probably be driving my family to French Morocco in a day or two after all, for millstones and the men of Mediouna had dampened my sudden interest in unearthing the early history of this most strategic site in one of the most strategic spots in the ancient and modern world.

From the Phœnician tomb our path led to a café, Les Grottes d'Hercule, where a Frenchman with long mustaches was serving drinks, sausages, and tiny sardines fried in olive oil. Our enthusiasm somewhat restored, we moved on to the Nahon-Doolittle cave, which, unlike the others, lay under the brink of the cliff high above the sea.

While the openings on the lower level were sea caves, flooded by the lapping of waves at the base of the cliff and by the crash of surf during storms, this was a high cave, out of reach of the sea. It had been formed by the seepage of surface water trickling through the roof and dissolving limestone in its path, just as other caves, hundreds of miles from the ocean's rim, were formed.

To reach this high cave required a bit of gymnastics. Standing in the face of the cliff directly over the sea, with a roof only a few feet thick and pierced in one place by a hole through which the sky could be seen, the cave was a high window looking out over the Atlantic. In order to reach this window we had to climb down from the edge of the roof. The path leading to the mouth of the cave was narrow and steep; in some places it had fallen into the water, and we had to make little jumps to cross the gaps.

We scrambled down. To our left as we faced the ocean stretched the long beach with its giant rollers, unimpeded in their flow from America. Immediately underneath lay a jumble of rocks, and to the right the stone platform pierced for the use of the women of Mediouna: Neptune's nuptial geyser. Inside lay a deep chamber, dimly lit by the hole in the roof, high enough in some places to be crossed without stooping, and sloping around the edges down to the floor. Two fallen roof slabs of limestone, resembling seats, had been left by Nahon and Doolittle.

It was obvious that at an earlier time the cave had extended farther forward. The action of wind and rain had cut away the forward part of the floor beneath the area where the roof had fallen, and in the vertical section so produced one could see rock underlying the level of the floor of earth which Doolittle and Nahon had removed. What they had taken out was a foot or more of soft, greasy-looking black soil, as smooth in texture as chocolate cake. Some of this soil still remained in corners of the cave, to which we crawled to study it. The lip of the cave, which the earlier excavators had left bare, was not, however, composed of yellowish-gray limestone like the roof and walls. It was red, gritty, and sandy, like the surface of a New York brownstone house. Whatever it was, it was not part of the original material of the cave. It had been deposited and then had hardened. Nahon and Doolittle had stopped when they came to this hard layer, thinking it the floor. I was lucky on two counts. First, the limestone in which the cave had been hollowed out was of uneven quality, and the millstone-cutters had left it alone. Second, there was a deposit under the already excavated Neolithic level, and this had to be older. As the Neolithic could not have come to Tangier much later than 3000 B.C., what lay before me must be the handiwork of ancient hunters, for it was the Neolithic people who had first brought cultivation to North Africa, as to Europe.

I told Dr. Nahon my idea, and asked him: "Do you mind if I dig?"

He did not, and I dug my first cave, something I had wanted to do for many years. It was also my most comfortable site. Within easy commuting distance of Tangier, it overlooked one of the finest bathing beaches in the world, usually uninhabited; there we went to swim in the delicious cool surf after a hot morning's work. Up above it stood a well-equipped café with beer, bread, brandy, and sausages.

Being on a sabbatical leave and not an expedition, I had no funds with which to hire workmen, and all I could afford was the help of two men in addition to my own labor. (Later on, after the cave had begun to yield its treasures, I received some money from Harvard.) These two men were named Big Absalem and Little Absalem. They had earlier worked for Nahon and Doolittle. Coming from the agricultural village of Jibila, to the southeast of Mediouna, they lived within walking distance of the caves, and spent their spare time near the tourist parking-lot in hopes of picking up work. On my first visit with Dr. Nahon, as soon as he had stopped the car they had leaped from a place of concealment behind some palmetto bushes and greeted us with great enthusiasm.

Big Absalem (local pronunciation of the Arabic *Abd es-Salam*) was a tall man with a gold tooth and an engag-ing smile, usually dressed in a clean white jellaba with the hood down, and a white turban. Little Absalem was shorter, stockier, and stronger. His clothes were usually older and dirtier, though at home he had a better ward-robe that he saved for special occasions. While Big Absa-lem was gay and chatty, giving way frequently to flights of imagination, Little Absalem was the quieter, more sen-sible of the two. Like most northern Moroccans, either could have been taken for a European if properly bar-bered and dressed.

We began work the next day. First of all I laid out a trench, one meter wide, from the mouth of the cave to its back wall, running in an east-west direction. I did this by pounding stakes into the hard red earth and connecting them with strings. Although this was my first cave, I knew something about the principles of excavation. A cave is excavated trench by trench, rather than layer by layer. If you work layer by layer, you remove everything from a given color or type of soil, and then go on to the next one underneath. If you find only one kind of soil, then you have no way of knowing the relative age of the ob-jects you have unearthed. If, however, you dig a trench and keep the sides as vertical and clean as a wall, you have on these earth walls a record of the soils you have passed through. Such a wall is known as a *section face*.

No matter how many strips of earth you may remove later, you should always leave one face intact when you

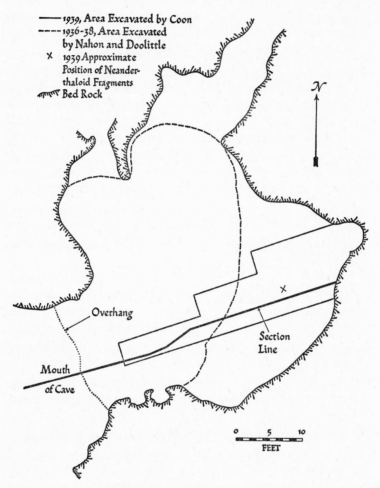

The High Cave, Tangier: plan.

have finished your excavation so that in years to come
other archæologists can see what you have done. Our
techniques improve from year to year. Nowadays we go
about searching the faces of sites dug before 1950 to pick
out pieces of charcoal for use in Carbon-14 dating. One
of these days someone will find a new mineral to analyze
for age, in sites where no charcoal was found. From the
beginning I planned to leave the south, or right, side of
my trench intact to serve as a permanent section face, for
the bulk of the soil, which could be taken out later, lay to
the north. Unfortunately, this plan had to be abandoned
because of the incursions of war and the requirements of
later digging.

This gritty red soil was so hard that in places it was
practically rock. Two things about it warranted attention.
First was the color. It is thought that cave soils turn red
during periods of relative warmth and seasonal dampness.
Such a reddening was a common feature of the Pleistocene. The second point about the soil was its hardness.
Cave soil that contains much calcium, as this cave's soil
did, will become rock-like when subjected to alternate
wettings and dryings. In the same way, calcium-bearing
water that drips from a single point builds stalagmites
and stalactites.

Had I known in 1939 these few facts about soil-deposi-
tion, which I have learned since, I could have told from
the color that the Absalems and I were digging in an
ancient, probably Ice Age soil. Ignorant as I was about
soils, I suspected this as soon as the first objects began to
turn up. These were beautiful lance points made of flint,
the product of some ancient toolmaker's consummate
workmanship, with closely trimmed, sharp edges and
points, and cleverly tanged butts. Never before had I
seen anything like this. The Absalems grinned and chuck-

led. *"Muzian, Mista Coon, Muzian bi-zaf!"* ("Good, Mr. Coon, very good.")

Dr. Nahon had spent many a week end tramping over the fields and dunes of the International Zone of Tangier, picking up flints from the surface of the ground. His be-

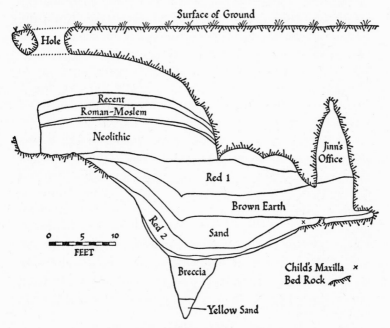

The High Cave, Tangier: section.

havior, which might have been deemed odd in a more conventional neighborhood, passed unnoticed in Tangier, where the only thing odd was to be normal. We searched his collections carefully, but they contained only one flint of the type we were now finding inside the cave. It was a tanged point that he had excavated from the soil on top of the headland near the Phœnician tomb, a piece totally unlike the tools found on the surface. If the people who had made these fine points had, like the later hunters, strewn their flints on the ground outside the cave, they had done so at a time when soil was being deposited, and the flints were deep enough to have avoided being bared by erosion.

A cave deposit containing angular stone and bone fragments that have been naturally cemented is called *breccia*. It is very tough stuff indeed, and when ancient skeletons are found imbedded in breccia, as were those of Mount Carmel in Palestine in 1932, it may take years of work by men armed with dentists' drills to extract them. The Mount Carmel skeletons were moved to the shore in blocks, hoisted aboard a ship, and carried to London, where the work with dental tools was done. Many attempts were made to discover chemicals that would dissolve the cement of the breccia without also destroying the bone, but as the two are of virtually the same composition this could not be done.

Knowing what had happened in Mount Carmel, I viewed the hardness of the red soil in the High Cave with some trepidation. To my relief, it did not become stone, and grew softer as we went down. The Absalems and I, helped to a certain extent by my two sons, removed the soil from the surface of the trench to a level corresponding to the length of a pickhead. This is about twenty centimeters, and, being convenient digging units, twenty-centimeter strips are what I have dug in cave deposits ever since.

A good pick man handles his tool as delicately as a barber wields a razor, knowing that a false stroke will be equally destructive. The standard tool in Morocco was the *pioche,* or *khaddum,* a double-headed pick or mattock with one end sharp and the other flat like a hoe. The pick man holds his tool a few inches above the surface, sharp end down, and presses it into the soil, then pulls it gently

toward him. He does not raise it above his head and
smash it into the earth as a ditch-digger would do. If he
feels something, he either pulls it out and goes down with
his fingers to investigate, or moves it gently toward him
with the pick blade. He does not use the flat side of his
tool except to remove soil already explored.

A good pick man does not break flint, fragile as it is.
He seldom does more than nick a whole pot; but few pick
men in the small world of diggers can bring bones out
whole. When one of my pick men strikes bone, he stops,
and I go in with a trowel and brushes to see what it is.
That is when the cry goes up: *"Ben Adam, Mista Coon?"*
("A human being?") The answer is usually No. Even if
it is a human fragment, I seldom admit it at once, for the
excitement that follows is contagious, and the number of
visitors, always a nuisance, grows rapidly. Then come the
religious folk who consider the disposal of human remains
their special province, and the fun begins. In the High
Cave, I did not find human remains until toward the
end of the excavation.

Most of the bones found in caves are the remains of
animals eaten by the people who lived there. As few animals are small enough to be carried easily in one piece,
what we find are the remains of the portions taken home.
Very rarely do we find tail bones. Their absence can only
mean that the tail must have been removed during the
skinning process before the animal's carcass was cut up.
We find many leg and hoof bones and many teeth and
horns, but very few whole skulls. Ribs and vertebræ are
uncommon. This evidence suggests that the cave-dwellers
ate the trunks of the animals out in the open, along with
the entrails, and brought the quarters and heads into the
cave, where they broke the skulls to get at the brains. Similarly, nearly all the shaft bones of all four limbs were
broken for marrow. This pattern, which I gradually came

to recognize in the High Cave at Tangier, I have seen repeated in other caves ever since, and other excavators
have found it as well.

As these early men were dependent on the local animals for their food, and as the animals were dependent
on the leaves and grass of the near-by forests and mead-
ows, it is possible to tell in a general way from the species
of animals found what kind of vegetation existed in the
neighborhood of the caves at the time the deposit was
formed. Then if we compare the list of animals with standard lists of those living and extinct, it is possible to determine, more or less, to what period the deposit belonged.
We must be careful not to rely too much on the presence
in any layer of animals that are extinct. No one knows
when the last of them died out. More important is the
presence of the bones of animals still alive, because paleontologists know pretty well when each of them appeared
in the different continents of the world.

When you are digging, as I was in May 1939 in the
High Cave, there is not time to find out what species of
animal each bone represents, when it first appeared on
the local scene, or when it died out. That job must be
done later by comparison with previously identified collections. Your concern at that moment is to take the bones
out as nearly whole as possible and to preserve them so
that some paleontologist or zoologist will be able to identify them later on. Naturally if you see the hoof bone of a
horse-like animal you will know that it is horse, ass, half-
ass, or zebra; cow horns are not hard to recognize on the
spot, nor is the astragalus of a sheep or goat—the small
cube-like bone which the ancients used as dice, and
which the Arabs still so use. The workmen usually can
recognize the bones of animals familiar to them, but their
ideas of ancient animals are completely unreliable. As
identifying bones is a job for specialists, we prepared the

bones that we found to send to zoologists and paleontologists.

As I have found out since 1939, such specialists do not work with every bone in an animal's body, nor with every part of single bones. Many bones are very similar in a number of animals, and the central shaft portion of a long bone is more or less the same in many species. The bones that reveal an animal are those which have to do with a special function of its body, and the two special functions that reveal themselves in the skeleton are eating and walking. Carnivorous animals have several kinds of teeth in their jaws: incisors for grasping, canines for stabbing and tearing, premolars (*carnassiers*) for cutting flesh, and molars for crunching bone. There are no grinding teeth, for the carnivore swallows his food whole, leaving the task of digestion wholly to the juices of his stomach. The teeth of dogs—including wolves—or of cats—including tigers and lions—are easy enough to recognize once you have studied a few. All you need to do is open the mouths of your pets and look in, as we did at night at the el-Farhar Hotel, where we lived.

Animals that browse—that is, eat leaves off of trees, low scrub, or even flowers—do not need much in the way of front teeth, for they can pick the leaves off the stems with their lips. Their problem is to convert this mass of coarse foodstuff into something that their stomachs can digest. For this they need four long rows of grinding teeth, two to each jaw. These teeth must be large. As they tend to wear down, they must also be long. The larger forms of such teeth indicate cattle and deer, a moist climate, and forests. Small ones of the same general character belong to goats, sheep, and gazelles, which can live on the leaves of small plants or short grass in open country and even deserts. Around the caves the jaws of sheep, goats, and cows were easy to obtain for comparison.

Animals of the horse family which graze on the high grass of prairies have to cope with a special problem that browsers seldom face. The stems of the grass that they eat, particularly when it is mature and dry, contain silica, the basic ingredient of flint and glass. Silica wears down

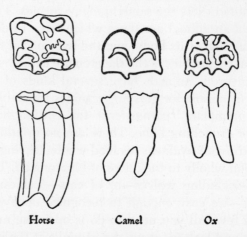

Horse   Camel   Ox

The teeth of grazers and browsers (first upper molar). The horse eats grass the year round, and dry grass stems contain an abrasive: silica. The grinding-surface of the horse's tooth is therefore extensive, and is ridged with intricate folds of hard enamel to resist wear. The high crown gives it a lifetime of wear. Browsing animals like the camel and ox eat green grass low in silica and the twigs and leaves of desert and forest plants. Their teeth are specialized for chopping this coarse food; high crowns are not needed. (One-fourth actual size.)

the enamel of the teeth. Confronted with a lifetime of silica-eating, an animal needs special teeth. They must be hard, and they must be capable of growth. Such are the teeth of the members of the horse family. They are square or rectangular, flat on the surface, intricately and finely ridged, and very long. As the animal grows older and the teeth wear down, the roots move up and the pulp cavities become filled with enamel as they approach the surface. In this way a horse's teeth can last him a lifetime. The teeth of grazing animals are not hard to recognize.

The reason why we find so much difference between the teeth of different animals is that the primary work of preparing food for digestion is done in the mouth, either when first eaten or later when brought up as a cud. A dog or cat can eat bread, and a horse can eat meat. In Siberia some of the Tungus tribes feed their reindeer on chopped-up meat, particularly the ones they ride, which need great strength. In Arabia camels are fed on dried fish. It is not so much what an animal eats which matters to the stomach, but how the food has been processed before it gets there. The teeth of different animals permit them to eat odd kinds of food which they would not otherwise be able to digest, and thus to inhabit varied kinds of country, like forests and deserts. Only one animal, the hyena, seems to have a special digestive system as well as specialized teeth. He can chew up the bones of carrion animals and swallow them. Later the lime that has dissolved in his digestive organs comes out in lumps. Being nearly pure calcium, these fecal pellets are indestructible, and we find them frequently in caves that hyenas have visited in the absence of men.

Being fairly hard, teeth rarely need treatment before packing. Some that we found in the High Cave were split and had to be glued together, and those which were still set in jaws we learned to glue into their sockets, keeping the jawbones intact by gluing on splints. It is easier to identify an animal if you have a row of teeth, rather than single ones, to work with.

The other part of an animal which reveals his identity is his limbs. Flesh-eating animals need flexible legs and mobile paws. Crouching behind clumps of bush, jumping on their prey, clawing, climbing, and holding the leg of a fallen animal with the paws while eating it are actions that could be done only by animals with four or five toes and flexible joints. While it is not easy to tell the species apart, the archæologist knows when he has found the limb bones of carnivores, be they dogs, wolves, lions, tigers, or leopards.

Browsers, on the other hand, need feet capable of carrying them off to safety when attacked by carnivores. They also need a certain amount of flexibility, for their food quest often takes some of them into forests and swamps. Their toes, which show a compromise between speed and mobility, have been reduced to two of equal size. Like dancers, they walk on tiptoe. Fundamentally the foot bones of sheep and goats differ from those of cattle only in size, but the limbs of the fleet gazelle of the desert are long and thin, as they need to be to carry him to safety on the open plain, where even the cat family has produced a long-legged record-breaking runner, the cheetah.

The grazers, which dance on single toes, are, aside from the gazelle and cheetah, the fleetest of all, and anyone who tries can tell the toe bones of a member of the horse family at a glance. As the whole weight of the body comes down on these bones, and as one leg may carry the whole load at a time, if only briefly, these bones have to be solid. Being solid, they have too little marrow to be worth breaking. That is why these bones are usually intact, while the limb bones nearest the body, the humerus and femur, are almost always smashed to pieces, and those in between, the ulna and tibia, are usually broken also. We save the end pieces of these bones, which have the smooth joint surfaces that articulate with the next section of the skeleton, because these ends also are useful in

identification. The scrap—the broken bits of shaft smashed
in the search for marrow—are counted and thrown away.
At Tangier I did not yet know this, and kept everything.

The animals whose bones were shipped back to Cambridge represented forty-two species, including elephants,
lions, rhinoceros, wild buffalo, hippopotamus, giraffe,
hartebeests, gnu, wild cattle, and guinea fowl. Looking
over the barren plain of northwestern Morocco, seeing
the bare, waterless expanse devoid of trees save an occasional scrub palm and the rows of eucalyptus which the
government of the zone had planted along the road to
the caves, it was hard to imagine hearing the rumbling of
an elephant's guts behind a bamboo clump, or looking up
at a profile of a giraffe's head against the sky, or hearing
the guinea fowl's shrill, piercing cry and the splash of a
hippo sliding into a river.

These scenes I could not yet visualize as I teased the
bones out of the red grit that the Absalems loosened with
their picks. All I did was coat them with an organic ad-
hesive known as Ambroid, patch and splint them when
necessary, wrap them in old pieces of newspaper printed
in Spanish, French, English, and Arabic, and tuck these,
properly labeled, into bags. That is one of the beauties of
archæology: you learn details bit by bit over a period of
years, until finally, if you are lucky, a consistent, if not
whole, picture is unveiled.

In the normal routine of excavation one Absalem
handled the pick and the other heaped the excavated soil
into a two-handled basket and carried it outside the cave
entrance to the open-air platform on which it was to be
sifted. The sieve that I had inherited from my predecessors was a two-handled affair. The two Absalems liked to
hold its ends and shake it between them. The earth that
fell through its quarter-inch mesh formed conical heaps,
which they later swept into the sea. This was too leisurely

a type of archæology for my taste, for it took two men to
work the sieve. If I was one of them I could not see what
was being excavated, and if not, the pick man had to
come out of the trench after each basket of earth had
been removed. So I bought a circular sieve, hung it over
the platform from the end of a pole protruding from the
edge of the roof, and took on a third workman. Now we
could have one man at the pick, one at the bucket, and a
third at the sieve, and I was free to move about and watch
all the operations.

As we dug deeper into the trench the distance from
the digging-place to the lip grew from a few feet to five
or more yards. The depth increased to more than ten feet,
and the climb became steep. This meant that we needed
more than one man on the bucket line, and as soon as I
received some money from Harvard I increased the staff
to five men. We now had a chance to reach bottom before
the expected outbreak of World War II, and even to show
the boys French Morocco as well.

We dug the red gritty layer in two horizontal units,
dividing them arbitrarily in case the bones and artifacts
should change as we went down. Luckily, the lower of
these units was softer than the upper. Under the red we
came upon what seemed to be a new kind of soil, soft,
fine, and brown, a rich, moist loam entirely different in
feel and consistency from the earth above it, and more
like the remnants of the black Neolithic soil left over from
the earlier excavation. Later geological study showed that
the red soil above it had been the same as this moist loam
when it was laid down, but had been turned red and
partly hardened by subsequent weathering. The two soils
were really one, and contained the bones of wart hog,
elephant, and hippopotamus. However, the flints in the
two levels showed a difference. Both types were made on
flakes, but the ones in the red earth had generally been re-

touched into finished form on the upper or outer surface only, while many of those in the brown soil had been finished on both sides, so that no difference between the sides could be detected. The latter workmanship was of the kind commonly found in American Indian arrowheads of a much later period.

A   **B**   **C**

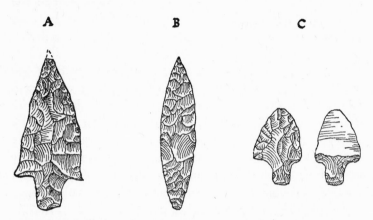

At the High Cave, Tangier, the art of making flint points from flakes was brought close to perfection. A and B were finely retouched on both sides by pressure-flaking, while C, shown in two views, was retouched on the back, creating a thin tongue for the attachment of a handle. (One-half actual size.)

Once we had begun to excavate the brown soil at the far end of our trench, we found that the back wall of the cave suddenly ceased to exist; it was but a lintel to an inner chamber that had been sealed off, probably for tens of thousands of years. This discovery caused a bubbling-over of excitement among the men. The three new workers were not so blasé as the two Absalems. I heard much talk of jinns down in the trench, and the new men, apparently frightened, left the cave frequently for reasons that one does not ordinarily ask about. At length Big Absalem, whose brow had been wrinkled in thought for some time, exclaimed: "Mista Coon! This is the office of a jinn!"

The idea of a local spirit sitting in the little cave like an Arab wholesale merchant, doing business with desk and telephone, amused the other men and relieved the tension for a half-hour or so, but muttering and eye-rolling were resumed.

Finally I crawled into the alcove, when enough earth had been excavated to let me in without upsetting the stratigraphy, and sat there with a flashlight. It was a perfect Persian dome, high and narrow, about five feet in diameter and fifteen in height. It had been formed by water dripping from the surface above through a weak spot in the limestone. I found that when I spoke in it, my voice boomed and rolled in a peculiar fashion, and so I carried on a conversation with the jinn in two voices, each one using several languages but ending up in local Arabic. The gist of the conversation was that the jinn felt a hardship in being disturbed by this intrusion, and wanted to know why we were interfering with his business. I apologized to him, but explained that we were obliged to keep on digging because we were looking for the bones of ancient monsters. When we found them we would take them to America, to prevent them from coming to life again. I explained to him that there were lots of other caves to set up his office in, and offered to pay him for his trouble. After a bit of haggling he finally agreed and departed.

This bit of tomfoolery was a complete success. Five Moors, three of them bearded, rolled on the ground, weeping with laughter. For about a quarter of an hour after I emerged from the jinn's office, as it was forever after to be called, they sat on the ground, sobbing and gasping until they had calmed down enough to go back to work.

From that moment on there was no more talk of jinns, except in jest. I am not well enough versed in psychological matters to interpret their reaction. It is unlikely that they believed I was actually talking with a jinn. Surely they knew that I was speaking in two voices. Perhaps they were laughing at my clumsy Arabic. What was really important was that I had taken the trouble to recognize their fear of the jinn and had done something rather elaborate and amusing about it. Recognition, time, and energy were the elements that laid this particular ghost. I could not have shattered their belief in jinns as a class of living beings; all I could have done was to render this particular one harmless.

In the brown soil in which we were digging at the time of the discovery of the jinn's office, we found the only complete skull of an animal which turned up in the entire excavation. It was a lion's skull, reddened by the color of the surrounding earth. The poor creature had broken off its upper right canine tooth sometime during its youth, and the jaw muscles of the right side of its head had atrophied to such an extent that the crest of bone which separates the two temporal muscles on the top had deviated to the right, to accommodate the compensatory overdevelopment of the left side. This handicap had not, however, prevented the noble beast from living to full maturity, nor from receiving honors after death. Finding this trophy carried us back through barriers of time to a scene in which these ancient men who had made such beautiful spearpoints and knives of flint may have conducted a ceremony in that very cave, perhaps using the unbroken skull as part of the décor in initiating their sons into the cult of lion-hunters. As usual, this discovery caused much conversation, in which I was asked to give explanations and did so. One can do this in a cave. In a big, formal, outdoor excavation involving city walls and temples, hundreds of men are employed at a time, and informal chats of this kind are impossible.

During the chats Big Absalem's mind soared in flights of imagination. One of the hazards of cave-digging, as of millstone-cutting, is smacking one's head on the roof when suddenly standing up. This happens rather frequently and that is one reason why the workmen wear turbans or knitted caps. Big Absalem told me one day that the men of his village are mostly tall because they work out-of-doors, while the Mediouna men are all short because they work in caves. Whenever a tall man appears in the Mediouna population, Big Absalem explained, he hits his head so many times in the course of his work that, despite the protection of his headgear, he kills himself, and only the short ones survive to have offspring. Little did Big Absalem know that after Charles Darwin had had the same idea a century earlier the whole course of scientific thought in the Western world had changed.

By the 1st of June the weather is likely to change in that part of the world, and instead of blowing steadily off the ocean the wind becomes temperamental. One day as I was standing in the mouth of the cave near the sieves, a zephyr from the south raced up the beach, like a testy jinn, and hit our sifting-platform a quick, hard blow. It picked up the dried grit left over from the Red #1 layer and drove it into my left eye. The pain blinded me. Full of solicitude, the men leaped out of the trench to help. One of the new men, Hamidu, had a remedy. Lifting a long-stemmed pipe out of his leather scrip, he filled it with *kif*—a local mixture of hashish and tobacco—and lighted it. After several puffs, he filled his lungs with it and exhaled the smoke over my eyeball. Waiting a second for the drug to take effect, he seized my head in his hands and ran his tongue over my eyeball, under the lids, licking its entire surface, and then spat.

While he may have removed the grit, the pain returned. My sight was also blurred. It seemed to me best to go to town immediately to let Dr. Nahon look at it, so I left the cave, climbed the narrow path, and ran to the turnaround, to which a number of tourists had come in taxis for a look at the caves. Several taxi loads had finished and were about to return to town. The tourists were French, off a ship that had put in at Tangier on its way to Casablanca. I approached a middle-aged couple and said, in my best French: "Excuse me, *msieudame,* I have just suffered an accident and need to see a doctor; may I have your permission to share yout taxi to town? I will pay my share."

The woman let out a little scream and placed a plump hand over her mouth. The man raised his fist and growled: "*Va-t'en,* you dirty dog of an Arab! Filthy beast!" etc., etc. He approached me threateningly. Torn between my desire to get to a doctor, and a craving to give the Frenchman a bloody nose, I turned to the next group and recognized a pretty Jewish prostitute who habitually sat around a certain restaurant in the Socco Chico. She was accompanied by a young Frenchman.

"Come with me, *monsieur,*" she said. "I will take you to the doctor."

Once we were in the cab, she asked: "What is that on your head?" and giggled.

I put my hand to my head and found that I was wearing one of the knitted woolen caps made by the Mediouna people to keep themselves from hurting their heads in the caves, and which marked me as a Muslim. Dirty dog of an Arab indeed! My eye recovered after a few days of looking like the focal point of a shirt advertisement, and thereafter I took care to remove my protective headgear when leaving the cave.

At the bottom of the layer of brown earth in which

we were digging we encountered a white crust of lime which was completely unbroken. A crust of this kind is a valuable thing. Nahon and Doolittle had found one between the Neolithic black earth and the gray soil overlying it which contained Roman and medieval Arab material. Some of both these soils, and the intervening crust, had remained in a small tunnel in the northern part of the cave; I had made a small face there, down to the top of the red, for study. The presence of the crust meant that a period of time had passed between the end of the Neolithic occupation and the beginning of the Roman. During that time a spell of wet weather had caused the crust to form. It was a seal, making the cave a bonded warehouse for the intact preservation of the Neolithic material, and preventing mixture with objects of later date. Eight years later, in 1947, it was a crust of this kind which Mlle G. Henri-Martin found in the cave of Fontéchevade in southwestern France, separating the Neanderthal-made soils above from the soils in which she discovered the two famous Fontéchevade skulls, thus proving that men of modern type were alive in pre-Neanderthal times. We took great pains to clear our trench of all soils, and to clean the faces, lest anything fall in from the sides, before breaking this new, lower crust. Under it we found orange-gray sand which had blown or been washed in from outside, and which, containing neither flint nor bone, was absolutely sterile. This reached to within nine feet of the back wall of the jinn's office. The last nine feet was composed of a second layer of red grit, similar in composition to the soil we had first excavated. We called it Red #2. As we removed the orange-gray sand, we found that it covered this Red #2, the surface of which curved, apparently to conform to the shape of the floor of the cave.

This level contained few implements—indeed, there

was little soil there in any case—and these were more or less like those in the top Red, without so many finely finished pieces. Bones there were in plenty, including those of dog, jackal, fox, cave hyena (plus his droppings), wild ass, hippopotamus, gazelle, wild sheep, wild cattle, water buffalo, rhinoceros, elephant, crested porcupine, and hare. Both the European wild boar (*Sus scrofa*) and the African wart hog could have snorted and rooted in each other's presence in the forest outside. Two things were notable about this list of fauna: not a single beast was present in any level which is not alive today, except for the cave hyena; animals of both African and Eurasiatic species were living together. Water-loving forms such as the hippo coexisted with desert types such as the wild ass and the gazelle. The climate was obviously favorable for many kinds of life, and connections were open both with Africa south of the Sahara, and with the Palestine-Syria part of Asia. As all but one species is still alive somewhere, the time was not extremely remote. The latter part of the Pleistocene was indicated.

It interested me to see that the people who lived while Red #2 soil was being deposited had knocked off a stalagmite about six inches from the floor; its broken surface lay flush with the crust by which the layer was sealed.

While scraping around in the area behind the stalagmite stub one day I came upon a small, light-yellowish piece of bone which looked like nothing that had turned up before. As I turned it over in my hand I saw that it was human.

Before we left that day I knew that it was a piece of the left maxilla (upper jaw) of a child about nine years old whose permanent incisors and first molars had erupted but had fallen out after death. The permanent canines and premolars, which had not yet erupted, were still there, sunk in the bone. These teeth were very large. For a child of the age indicated by the state of eruption of the teeth, the bone was very heavy and thick. The edge of the nasal aperture was grooved somewhat like that of an ape. Obviously I had found something of extreme interest.

Carefully packing it in cotton, I put it in a Players cigarette tin and tucked it into the pocket of my jacket, hanging from a peg. I then looked around for more. Before long I came upon a very much worn human molar tooth that, because of its condition, must have come from a second and much older individual.

I would like to be able to say that I found the child's upper jaw in its original position, brushed the dirt clear, and photographed it *in situ* before removing it. Such was not the case. I found it sitting on the surface of the Red #2 soil in a place that I had only partly excavated. How it got there I do not know. It may have dropped out of a basket on its way to the sieves, or it may have fallen from the lintel of the front edge of the jinn's office. If it came from a basket, it would belong to Red #2 level; if it fell from the lintel, to Brown. I examined it carefully for its dirt, and found that although it was fairly clean—the soil was dry in that rear section—what grains remained embedded around the teeth were reddish-yellow and sandy, a kind of material which came in Red #2. Had it come from the Brown level, it would have had some of that very fine-grained darker soil instead. By this means I concluded that it came from Red #2, but I would have been happier had I found it in a completely undisturbed condition.

That evening, sitting on the terrace of the el-Farhar Hotel, I showed the specimen to a physician. Looking at it critically, he stated categorically that it belonged to an ape. I did not argue with him; his opinion merely meant that it had not belonged to a modern type of human be-

ing, which made it all the more interesting. I did not wait
to bring it home, for fear that we might be trapped by
the threatening war and that if anything should happen
to me it would be lost. It went out in the next pouch to
Professor Earnest Hooton at Harvard, who turned it over
to a young Turkish specialist on fossil teeth, Dr. Muzaffer
Suleyman Şenyürek. Dr. Şenyürek studied it exhaustively
and pronounced it a piece of a Neanderthal child—the
second supposed Neanderthal, as far as I know, to be
identified on the continent of Africa. The first was a fragment of lower jaw found in 1923 near Diré Daoua, Ethio-
pia, by the famed French prehistorian Abbé H. Breuil.

Since that time other finds of early man have amplified and altered the North African picture. A fossil jaw,
discovered in Rabat in 1933 by blasting in a rock quarry,
was described by Dr. H. V. Vallois in 1951. Although its
age is unknown, it is probably older than the Tangier
specimen. It is a heavy, brutal, chinless lower jaw with
teeth very much like those of our child. In 1951 Professor
Arambourg, the famous French paleontologist, found
three fragmentary lower jaws in a pit at Palikao near Mascara, Department of Oran, Algeria, which are also chinless, with large teeth resembling, curiously enough, those
of Peking man found in China in the 1920's. Dr. L. Cabot
Briggs, an American anthropologist who lives in Algiers
and specializes in North African prehistory, believes that
the Rabat jaw, the Mascara jaws, and the Tangier maxilla
all represent a more or less direct line of human development comparable to Neanderthal but separately
evolved. Meanwhile, another jaw considered to be Neanderthal was unearthed in a cave called Hawa Fteah in
Libya in 1952. The Tangier child continues to grace a
small glass case in the Peabody Museum at Harvard, in
the event that anyone else wishes to attempt an identification.

Returning to work the day after the discovery, I found a third crust under Red #2, and under that a layer of yellow sand that had turned to breccia. It was full of bones as clean and white as the day the animals had died. This I had to chisel out. I went down through more than three feet of this, my trench narrowing to a hole, removing the bones as best I could. I failed to find a single implement. Soon I noticed that, unlike the bones associated with human occupation in the layers above, which had been smashed for marrow, these had not been broken at all until I did it with my chisel. In other words, they had got there by some agency other than the hand of man. As we were now a good twelve feet below the level of the outer lip of the cave, it was conceivable that the animals had fallen in and been unable to climb out again. The sand in which they lay had eventually turned to stone.

Under most circumstances I might have been pardoned had I quit at this point. However, an old admonition of Professor George Andrew Reisner, the famous Egyptologist, with whom I had taken a few courses, kept popping up in my mind: "Never quit until you get down to gebel." *Gebel* is the Egyptian form of the Arabic word for *mountain,* and *mountain* in this sense means *bedrock.* I had not reached bedrock, and I could not bear to quit. So I chiseled through the bone-laden sandstone until finally my tool fell through into a soft bed of yellow sand. I scooped this up with my fingers, finding in it a flint core from which many flakes of the type found in the upper layers had been detached. Farther down I reached another hard surface, which I soon determined to be the bottom. It was the limestone of the cave. I had got down to gebel, and could face Reisner's ghost with equanimity. So I took a Moroccan twenty-five-centime piece, a coin with a hole in the middle, and in front of the workmen I kissed it and dropped it to the bottom of the hole, saying:

Dr. Lewis Leakey of the Coryndon Museum, Nairobi, skins a Rhodesian antelope with a Paleolithic stone tool, as quickly and easily as with a steel knife.

PLATE I

Ras Ashaghar, Tangier, Morocco. Millstones and the men who cut them inside a large sea cave immediately below the High Cave.

PLATE II

The High Cave, Tangier, from the sea.

The High Cave, 1947 season. The excavation is nearly over. Two workmen are sifting earth in sieves suspended on either side of the pulley cable, over which earth was hauled from the pit. The two Americans in the foreground are picking over broken pieces of breccia for flint and bone.

PLATE III

Dr. Hencken and Mrs. Coon working on the plan of the High Cave.

The interior of the High Cave in 1947, after excavation. The Jinn's Office is to the left and rear of the measuring-rod.

PLATE IV

Bisitun, from the schoolhouse roof. The Great Rock bearing Darius's inscription can be seen on the left, the cave itself just above the trees on the right.

PLATE V

Bisitun. The cave before excavation. As in all open caves that we dug, the floor is covered with a thin, elastic layer of consolidated sheep or goat dung, laid down in winter when the caves are used as shelters for animals. Although most of it is scraped away in the spring, enough is left to protect the archæological materials underneath.

Bisitun. The cave during excavation. The workmen are removing flints and bones with knives and trowels. The boy in the middle, Ali Akbar, recited classical Persian poetry by the hour.

PLATE VI

Khavar, the *femme fatale* of the Bisitun schoolhouse, spinning wool in the garden.

Bisitun. Sifting excavated earth under the shade of a tent-cover.

PLATE VII

Bisitun. A pause in the exc
vation. Owing to the heat, v
knocked off several times ea
day for ten-minute breaks

Some of the workmen at Bisitun. The second man from the left is One-Eyed Qasem.

PLATE VIII

"Here, jinn, is your payment. Thank you for the use of your cave." With that I filled in the deep pit I had dug through the breccia, Little Absalem sealed it with stone slabs, and we were through.

We took the children to various parts of French Morocco and sailed home from Casablanca on a Danish cargo

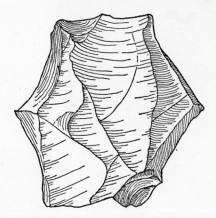

An unprepared flint core found in the yellow sand under the breccia at the bottom of the deposit. It shows the scars where flakes were struck off from many surfaces, more or less at random. (One-half actual size.)

boat that got us to Norfolk on the eve of war. I was not to see the High Cave again for eight years. During the first winter of the "phony war" Ralph Nahon continued my digging in the red and brown soils and reported almost weekly to Professor Hallam Movius and me in Cambridge, Massachusetts, over "ham" radio stations. We would receive telephone calls from amateur operators in Haverhill, Arlington, Somerville, and many other towns and cities in eastern Massachusetts who had picked up a Spanish ham in Tangier and arranged a schedule with him. The whole world of North Atlantic hams was able to hear Nahon, Movius, and myself discussing Red #1, Brown, and Big and Little Absalem over the ether, until one day the Spanish soldiers, who had taken over the International Zone, arrested Nahon's ham and both the schedule and Nahon's digging were ended. Dr. Nahon then came home, and the caves lay fallow.

After Pearl Harbor, had I been physically separated from the High Cave by a continent or an ocean, I might have been able to forget about it. However, one of the curious events that accompany all wars brought me back to Tangier in May 1942, this time alone and on leave from academic duties. My calling card said: "Special Assistant to the American Legation." The duties of a special assistant did not include visits to the High Cave. In any case, these would have been impossible because when the Spanish government took over control of the International Zone before my arrival it forbade Americans to go near Cape Spartel or the Atlantic shore.

My former workmen in the High Cave, they who had witnessed the expulsion of the proprietary jinn and his later appeasement, did not take long to discover my presence in the city. At least once a week one or another of them told me what was going on in the caves, for they were eager for the work to be resumed. First of all, I learned, the Spanish army had converted the High Cave into a stable for mules. The soldiers had leveled the remaining soil to provide a floor for their animals. Above a neighboring cave they had erected an anti-aircraft battery to shoot at our planes from Port Lyautey, and every time these devices went off they shook the roof of every cave in the neighborhood.

In 1947 Dr. Hugh O'Neill Hencken, director of the American School of Prehistoric Archæology, led a large number of experts, graduate students, and members of their families back to Tangier to solve the problems raised by the 1939 excavations. The late Professor Glover Allen of Harvard had identified the bones shipped to him, but I had been unable to provide him with a good sample of those in the breccia between Red #2 and the bottom yellow sand. More of these bones were needed.

A task of equal or greater importance was to determine the sequence of the successive sea levels produced by the combination of water-capture by glacial ice caps and the warping of the earth's crust by ice pressure during the Pleistocene. These might be tied into the sequence of soils within the cave, and might help us to date them, because when the seas were low the recession of the ocean water exposed near-by beaches and allowed the cave to fill with wind-blown sand. High seas washed around the base of the cliff, causing dampness and poor living-conditions inside the chamber, all of which was reflected in the character of the soil and the paucity of its contents. To do this very specialized and delicate work on sea-level reconstruction, Dr. Hencken persuaded Charles Stearns, a top-flight Pleistocene geologist then at Tufts College, to join our expedition. My sons, Carl, Jr., and Charles, now aged twenty and sixteen, held his stadia rods, and my wife, Lisa, worked on the plans and sections both inside and outside the cave.

While Hugh Hencken and I excavated a pair of Neolithic grottoes in the immediate vicinity, Bruce Howe took charge of the work on what was left in the High Cave. The Spanish army muleteers had done a wonderful job of mixing the soils, down through Brown, and there was little of Red #2 left. There had not been much of this soil in the first place, and even that bit had been contaminated with the materials from above. Not much remained to be done except clean out what was left, take specimens out of the sieves, and study the remains of the old trench face, which was intact in the places where we had cut through breccias and crusts. In order to get the mixed soil out as expeditiously as possible we went to the shipyards of Tangier and bought a steel cable and a pulley; then we rigged an overhead device by means of which one man at the lip of the cave could haul baskets all the way up from the hands of the shovel man and send them sliding back again empty on the pulley. This saved a lot of running and crawling back and forth over a steep and slippery path, and released the bucket men to work in the other caves.

The sieve men also had relatively little to do because the soil that came out of the inner crannies and recesses of the cave, from all levels below that of the Neolithic, was virtually sterile. This observation revealed a principle since confirmed in other caves: ancient cave-dwellers preferred to stay on the sunny side of the area immediately inside the door, for they did not like to sit in the dark. Where they sat they did their work, and dropped their refuse. The bulk of the cave's archæological content had already been removed in 1939 from the first trench, which received the maximum daylight through the entrance.

This does not mean, however, that there was not enough work left for Bruce Howe to do. My excavation had not provided him with the data he needed to determine the ages of the different levels and of their special styles of flintwork. To find out these things, he needed to chisel away at the various breccias that remained. For this purpose he employed a master stonecutter from Mediouna, one Mohammed Tuzani. We soon dubbed him Mr. Stone, a name he liked. During the course of the summer Mr. Stone removed the yellow sandy breccia through which I had so laboriously sunk a narrow tunnel, down to bedrock, cleaning out the various bones he encountered on the way. At the end of the season, in 1947, these bones were sent to Professor Arambourg in Paris for identification. As his report has not yet come in, one cannot say what animals this lowest level of the cave deposit contained.

At a certain point in his chiseling and tapping Mr. Stone broke through the breccia and came upon the yellow sand that had been sealed up in 1939. Carl, Jr., who enjoys climbing about in perilous places, went down to the bottom of Mr. Stone's excavation and retrieved the twenty-five-centime piece with which I had paid off the jinn. But the sand did not come to a bell-shaped floor as we had thought in 1939; we had tapped a side of the sand pocket and not its bottom. The sand went down in a funnel a bit to one side, and we tied ropes under my son's arms to lower him. After a little while he looked up and said: "Dad, if you can squeeze in, come here."

We hauled him up and I went down. He had removed the last scrap of sand with his fingers and opened a hole into the big sea cave down below. As I peered through this hole I saw a man of Mediouna trimming a millstone fifty feet below. I spoke to him, and he dropped his pick in amazement. What new trick of the jinn's could this be? Soon Mr. Stone's face replaced mine at the hole, and both caves rang with laughter.

This was the end of the High Cave. My 1939 face had disappeared during the war, and now Bruce Howe, in gleaning all possible information out of the disturbed soil left by the Spaniards, had removed the remains. The floor had become as clean as a whistle. Dr. Hencken and I completed our work on the Neolithic caves, and, except for sorting, packing, and labeling, we were through. The day before we left, Big Absalem led me secretly to a concealed hole in the ground, not far from the Phœnician tomb that Dr. Nahon had showed me on my first visit in 1939. This inconspicuous aperture opened into a huge cave with an undisturbed floor, unfortunately covered with slabs of roof-fall shaken down by the Spanish anti-aircraft activity.

His eyes and gold tooth gleamed with equal brightness in the late afternoon sun as he said: "Next year you dig this one, Mista Coon."

The next year found me working for a new employer and carrying my search for caves far to the east. That was the last time I have seen either Big Absalem or Tangier.

While awaiting the definitive publications of Drs. Hencken, Howe, Stearns, and Arambourg on the results of the 1947 excavation as well as on those of the 1939 discoveries, I will venture, with my colleagues' help, to summarize the meaning of this evidence.[1] At some time during the Pleistocene yet to be determined, either a glacial or interglacial cool phase when the sea level was no higher than at present and may have been lower, the cave was no cave at all but an empty, hollow pocket inside the rock, trapped like a bubble in a Swiss cheese, and incapable of being entered by anything larger than a drop of water. It was then what geologists call a solution cavity.

Toward the end of its ages-long sentence of waiting, like a captive, for release, the cave-to-be, as part of the

[1] Some preliminary reports have already appeared:

M. S. Şenyürek: *Fossil Man in Tangier* (Cambridge, Mass.: Peabody Museum Papers. Vol. 16, No. 3; 1940).

Bruce Howe and H. L. Movius, Jr.: *A Stone Age Site in Tangier* (Cambridge, Mass.: Peabody Museum Papers, Vol. 23, No. 1; 1947).

H. O'N. Hencken: "The Prehistoric Archaeology of the Tangier Zone, Morocco," *Proceedings of the American Philosophical Society,* Vol. 92 (Philadelphia, 1948), pp. 282–8.

Bruce Howe: "A Program of Excavations in the Stone Age of Northwest Africa," *Archaeology,* Vol. 2 (Summer 1949), pp. 76–83.

Bruce Howe and Charles E. Stearns: "Geology and Archaeology of Cape Ashakar, Tangier, Morocco," *Actas del I Congreso Arqueologico del Marruecos Español* (Tetuan, 1953 [pub. Tetuan 1954]), pp. 39–51.

L. Cabot Briggs: "The Stone Age Races of Northwest Africa," American School of Prehistoric Research, Vol. 18 (Cambridge, Mass., 1955), pp. 5–19.

headland, witnessed the beginnings of human history in that area well before its own first period of occupation. One day a hunter who walked on the surface of the land over this hollow promontory lost a beautiful flint cleaver, a delicately retouched implement of the hand-ax family, eminently useful for skinning animals. That this hunter lost it and did not throw it away as a worn-out tool is evident from the mint-perfect condition of the implement.

Such a cleaver is not quickly or easily made, nor is the material for its manufacture everywhere available. Why did the hunter abandon so fine a tool? Did a lion surprise him skinning a zebra and eat both? He did not simply hide it for future use, because it lay in the road bank at a depth of about eighteen inches among thousands of unshaped stones, where Charles Stearns and my son Carl, Jr., found it. After this discovery Dr. Hencken dug a trench near by, but found no others. However, later that fall Bruce Howe, who stayed on after the excavations were finished, found several others in a bed of gravels cut through by a ravine to the north of the caves, and thus established a Paleolithic industry in the Ras Ashagar area earlier than the content of the High Cave.

How much earlier it was we do not yet know. During at least two following high-water periods waves gnawed at the face of the cliff below the solution cavity. Finally they so undermined the upper portion that lay above the reach of the tips of the waves that some of the overhang fell, and a piece of the face with it, into the sea. Over the tumbled top of the pile of giant blocks which was thus created could be seen, from the sea side, the mouth of a cave. Now for the first time since its formation the solution cavity was open, and fresh air and sunlight entered its hitherto Stygian recesses. Seeking a place to dump their burdens, the winds then began carrying yellow dune sands through its mouth and dropped the grains over the funnel-like bottom of the cavity. As the sea descended still farther, animals browsing beyond the range of safe footing fell into the cave and were buried. The sands thus accumulated made a floor, which ground waters and drip from the cave roof hardened. Now for the first time the High Cave was ready for human occupancy.

Once again ice formed far to the north, and the weather around the Strait of Gibraltar grew cool enough to make this new cavern attractive to hunters. A band of human beings who were to become our Red #2 people moved onto the headland and took up residence in at least this one of the higher caves. From the modern point of view, they were peculiar-looking folk with big teeth and long faces; they were probably chinless as well. Collecting nodules of flint in the ravines, they hammered them with pebbles, striking off flakes that they skillfully snicked and knapped into spear points and knife blades. Among these people was the baby whose maxilla I found in 1939, and another was the old man who lost a tooth on the floor of the cave. Capable of killing such huge and formidable beasts as giraffes, rhinos, and lions, these people lived on intermittently in their happy refuge until the weather again changed.

No traces of fire were found in this deposit, possibly because it was later subjected to prolonged and heavy weathering that may have destroyed or washed out all traces of ash and even some charred bone. At any rate, we found no material to use for Carbon-14 dating, and must rely entirely on the geological evidence and the animal bones.

After the time of deposition of Red #2 the climate grew wetter and warmer, and as the polar icecaps melted, the sea rose to about eighteen feet above its present level in the region of the caves. Through oxidation the soil of the habitation floor turned from its probably original brown to red and became hardened. No one knows how long or even why the High Cave remained empty during this period. The sea was near, but it did not reach the mouth. No soil was deposited during this time. With waves churning in the sea caves below and spume blowing over the threshold, it must have been a damp and noisy place. If the people who roamed the countryside around Ras Ashagar in those days were as imaginative as their modern successors, they may well have peopled the High Cave with horrid and fearsome water-jinns and given it a wide berth. Perhaps in this combination of circumstances the caves farther inland, like the one Big Absalem showed me on the last day, would have been more habitable.

Another spell of lowered sea level, and of weather that was first colder and wetter and then warmer and somewhat drier, made the High Cave once more a desirable piece of Paleolithic real estate. More yellow sand blew in, smoothing out irregularities in the floor, and a limy stalagmitic crust formed over all, like icing on a birthday cake. This was followed by a thick deposit of archæologically rich brown earth. Although the next tenants left no telltale scraps of human anatomy to reveal their racial identity, there is no reason to suppose them much different from their predecessors, because the tools they made, while more highly evolved, were of the same general category. They were the creators of the Brown industry, and probably the ancestors of the Red #1 people, who immediately followed them. From the standpoint of tool-making, the Red #1 industry differs from that of Brown in detail but not in general method. Bruce Howe considers them to constitute phases of a single industry. He and Charles Stearns believe that the difference in soil color and hardness between Brown and Red #1 is due to the fact that after the second set of tenants had abandoned the cave the process of oxidation and calcification reddened and hardened the upper part of the deposit.

In any event, abandon it they did, as the weather again shifted; once more the waters rose to uncomfortable proximity to the doorway, the rumblings below increased in volume, and the spray blew in as far as the portal of the jinn's office, which again welcomed its supernatural occupant. Here he sat in his murky counting-house for many a thousand years until a day when, long after the last ice had melted and the sea had dropped to somewhere near its present level, the first Neolithic men peered into its portal. The grunting of pigs and the lowing of cattle upset the jinn so profoundly that he unfurled his bat-like wings and disappeared out of the door of the cave with a whish and a momentary shadow and current of air which the new tenants hardly noticed.

Several important questions remain to be answered about the High Cave. Exactly *what* glacial advances and retreats in Europe do Red #2, Brown, and Red #1 represent? This can probably be answered once the whole story of the sequence of beach levels found all along the Mediterranean and Atlantic coasts of North Africa has been determined. This is not a simple matter of the periodic imprisonment and release of much of the world's water in the polar icecaps during the Pleistocene. The surface of the earth is subject to continual stresses and strains that raise and lower the old high beachlines from their original positions, greatly complicating the work of geologists. On the shores of the Mediterranean the warping varies from east to west, so that what one finds out from the beaches of Lebanon does not exactly apply to Morocco.

According to one possible theory now under consideration, the thirty-to-forty-foot sea level whose waters first opened the mouth of the cave may well have risen with the melting of the world's ice during the third and last interglacial, which in Europe saw the arrival of Neanderthals. During a later stage of this same interglacial the winds off the Atlantic blew in quantities of sand, which, with their fossil animal bones, form the basal deposit of this cave. The cold snap that followed, which was the time of the basal stalagmite and of Red #2, would have been the first advance of the last ice, according to this interpretation. That was the time of the so-called Cold Mousterian in Europe, where Neanderthal men created a flake industry comparable to that of our Red #2.

Brown would then have been deposited during the second ice advance. Now, the famous Solutrean culture of Europe, noted for its pressure-flaked laurel-leaf blades, is also usually assigned to the second advance. This gives rise to another problem. According to some, the Solutrean pressure-flaking technique originated in Spain, where, in Parpalló and other caves, undated examples of it have been found. Our Brown points, though made on flakes, are pressure-flaked too. If these two industries, whose end products look very much alike, were produced on opposite sides of the Strait of Gibraltar during roughly the same glacial sub-period, could one have given rise to the other, especially at a time when the water barrier between them was particularly narrow and shallow? Or was this apparent similarity a mere coincidence? At the moment, no one knows, but the coincidence theory is the more popular among experts.

Although no evidence has been found that the cave was occupied during the time between the second ice advance and the arrival of the Neolithic farmers, we know that the Tangier zone as a whole was not uninhabited. Dr. Nahon has found hundreds of evidently later flints on the surface nearly everywhere. Others possibly similar turn up regularly in the shell heaps on the beach four miles down from the caves. This is a complex and splendid site, but it would be hard to dig, as it is located on holy ground, near the saintly shrine of Sidi Qasem, where, on Midsummer Night, ceremonies resembling some of the Greek mysteries are still performed.

By matching the flints found in these places to similar collections made in Algeria and Spain, which are associated with skeletons, we feel reasonably sure that the local people who lived in the open air of the International Zone at some period between Red #1 time and the arrival of certain Neolithic farmers were true human beings in the modern sense, big, heavy-boned, large-handed, and broad-faced, with jutting chins; they may have looked like the freckle-skinned Riffian who served us coffee in the Legation in May 1939. Some of these people moved over to Spain and eventually to northwestern Europe; after them came the Neolithic farmers, burning and grubbing their way slowly westward along the coast from Palestine and the Nile delta to the Atlantic, and in turn ferrying the strait. They also moved into the large High Cave, as well as other smaller and less attractive ones, two of which Hugh Hencken and I excavated in 1947. Here some of the Neolithic folk stayed on into Roman times, using flint and stone for tools and silver and copper coins for money.

It is now clear that the Tangier region has not played a large role in human history. The Strait of Gibraltar, never dry during the periods of low water in the Pleistocene, its current swiftest when the Atlantic level was lowest, has served more often as a barrier than as a gateway. The Arab general Tariq ibn Ziyad's dramatic conquest of Gibraltar in A.D. 711 was an exception to a historic rule, as were the earlier and less well-documented passage of Neolithic farmers in the same direction, and the putative spread of the pressure-flaking technique to Parpalló and thence to the mammoth-hunting centers of France and central Europe.

During the vast expanse of the Pleistocene and indeed the first millennia of our present geological era, the Tangier region, and all Morocco, was a backwater in which outmoded ways of life were allowed, like marsupials in Australia, to perfect themselves in isolation. Once the Neolithic farmers had settled in, their descendants remained dependent on flint three thousand years after the Egyptians, at the other end of the Mediterranean shore, had begun using metal.

The Romans jolted the complacent lives of inhabitants of this corner of Africa, as did the Arabs, the French, the Spanish communists, and the Arab League Nationalists, all in turn. Tangier is a lovely place, a flowery refuge for the odd and unwanted, but not a focal point of cultural creation. It is not there that we must look for the solution to our problem: where, when, and how modern Western man came into being.

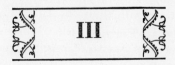

III

THE STAG-HUNTERS OF BISITUN

MY SECOND VENTURE into the world of caves was as accidental as the first. In the fall of 1948 the University Museum of the University of Pennsylvania and the Oriental Institute of the University of Chicago sent a joint expedition to Iraq to resume excavation at the vast ancient city mound of Nippur, the fabled seat of En-Lil, paramount god of the Sumerians. Fifty years earlier the powdered debris of this long-dead metropolis had yielded to the current crop of Pennsylvania excavators the major part of the world's collection of Sumerian tablets, over which cuneiform scholars have been straining their eyes ever since. My job on the expedition, representing Pennsylvania, was to study whatever skeletons might be unearthed.

In the middle of our five weeks' stay there, our expedition house was visited by the director of the Oriental Institute, Dr. Thorkild Jacobsen. Knowing of my interest in fossil men, he advised me to visit Iran, a country completely unexplored from that point of view. A little later he was followed by Dr. George Cameron, then of the same institution, who had just finished making a latex squeeze of the famous trilingual cuneiform inscription of Behistun, first copied in 1837 and again in 1843

by Sir Henry Rawlinson. This inscription, carved shortly
before 500 B.C., commemorates the military successes
of the Emperor Darius I, in three languages: Old Persian, Elamitic, and Assyrian. It was carved on a twelve-
by-thirty-foot smooth space on the face of a seventeen-
hundred-foot mountain, some two hundred and fifty feet
above the level of the road below,[1] by sculptors who cut
away their stone steps as they climbed down, thus pre-
serving the monument from future vandals. Besides the
trilingual inscription, the sculptors carved bas-reliefs of
Darius himself with henchmen behind him, and of nine
captive chiefs or kings facing him and bound with cords
around their necks. Overhead they placed the figure of
Darius' god, Ahuramazda.

This monument was more than an imperial signboard
or even the product of aerial daring and skill. It was a
cuneiform equivalent of the Rosetta stone, giving Rawlinson and others the means to break the riddle of cuneiform writing, and thus to unlock the treasure house of
Sumerian, Babylonian, Assyrian, and early Persian literature. While Sir Henry had managed to reach the inscription itself by ropes from above, he had lacked the
equipment provided by later scientific inventions to make
an exact copy, and in 1948 certain errors and uncertain-
ties still remained, which Dr. Cameron wished to clear
up. So he made an actual facsimile impression of the inscription in latex, working from the planks of a painter's
ladder perilously dangling and swinging in the breeze,
about forty times his own height above the bleak and
stony ground. As he recounted this experience to us in
the expedition house of Nippur, Dr. Cameron still seemed
to tremble.

Neither the inscription itself, nor the impressive con-

[1] No two sources that I have found agree on its elevation, figures
ranging from 500 to 160 feet. I am following Cameron, and my own
observation.

quests of the mighty Darius I which it recorded, nor George's daring aerial feat impressed me so much as his revelation that while teetering on his giddy ladder he had seen, at ground level below the inscription, a small cave, its floor apparently undisturbed by either the inscription-carvers or the myriads of travelers who had passed that way. I was eager to see that cave.

So on December 29, 1948, our work at Nippur finished, my wife Lisa and I set out from Baghdad, where we had obtained Iraqi exit permits and Persian visas, rolling along at fifty miles an hour over a smooth if narrow hard-topped road. It was a dull, gray day, damp and cold. Owing to a number of wrong turns, we did not reach the Iranian border until late in the afternoon, when, a mile beyond the last Iraqi post, we came to a building three stories high, ornamented like a movie theater and bearing the insignia of the Lion and Sun, the Persian imperial arms. Some of the officials inside wore splendid French-style blue uniforms, replete with braid, and tall peaked caps of the same materials. Other officials could have stepped right out of any college-town clothing store of the eastern seaboard of the United States. Considering that I spoke no Persian, we got through quickly. Most of them spoke French and a few—like the Iraqis, whose customs and security posts we had just passed through—knew English. They wanted to take my cameras and send them to Tehran, where I could pick them up later. I said that they were little cameras, and they passed them through.

That is one thing that I like about Persian officials: they will listen to reason. I have never tried to bribe a single person in that country and never intend to do so. If a mistake has been made, or if it appears that the strict application of a rule will cause unnecessary hardship, local officials are willing to take into their own hands the responsibility of interpreting the law, at no loss to the nation. This, my first experience with them, was an agreeable one.

It was now four o'clock in the afternoon, and growing dark. We had left the drab Mesopotamian plain, and had crossed a low ridge of sandstone. The road rose gradually. After passing several villages of adobe houses we reached the snow line. At three places before this we ran into road blocks—single-log gates swinging on posts, like railroad crossings. At each a soldier, after examining our passports, let us pass. Now, having left the plain, we were climbing between limestone cliffs that confined a long valley, and these cliffs were honeycombed with caves, high, inaccessible, and empty. Many trucks passed us, and we rode in their tracks, for the road had not been snowplowed. Soon the dark forms of trees whizzed past, many of them junipers. Before we reached the head of the valley we had seen, in our headlights, five wolves, a jackal, a long-quilled Asiatic porcupine, many hares, a herd of white-rumped deer, and many flocks of quail, accompanied by huge strutting magpies, their wings barred with white like military police.

Crossing the pass at eight thousand feet in the dark, we rode along the plateau past numerous villages, fenced in by long rows of water-loving poplars, which grow in the banks of the irrigation ditches, their limbs tucked to their sides as if in strait jackets so that the trunks can be spaced as little as two feet apart. Lights twinkled in the windows of the tightly closed teahouses. All of these things, after the dreary flatness and stoneless monotony of the Iraqi plain, stimulated us with the magic of seeing a new country in the dark of night, a country that reminded us, because of the mountains, trees, stones, and snow, of home.

Our destination was the house of the Reverend John Watson, evangelist of the Presbyterian Mission, a friend of George Cameron's. As Bisitun was within commuting distance of Kermanshah, the Camerons had lived with the Watsons while working on the inscription. At half past nine we were in the Kermanshah police station, where an officer telephoned the mission, and at ten our jeep was in a garage and we were sitting in a typical American dining-room eating an American supper while snow-flakes swirled outside the window. After a hot bath in an American bathroom we were soon asleep.

The next morning we looked out the window at a white landscape with drifts as deep as in northern New England, framed in the distance by gleaming white-flanked mountains. In the morning light the poplars stood out in sharp contrast of light and shade. It was like a colored etching, very beautiful and very frosty. The jeep was frozen. I thawed it with hot water, drove to the center of the city, and went to call on the police chief with our passports. The office was closed. It was a holiday, the anniversary of the murder of the prophet Muhammad's grandson, Hasan, so we dispensed with for-malities. Having bought some Prestone in a G.I. tin, the Coons and the Watsons set out for Bisitun. In some places the road was bare from the wind, in others two feet deep in snow. The four-wheel drive and low-range gears were very useful.

After an hour we had crossed the valley of the Gamas-i-Ab River and reached the mountain of Bisitun, a mighty slab of white limestone which stands like a bea-con at the edge of the plain, steep and clean. On the right is the village of Bisitun, with one huge ruined car-avanserai, built by Shah Abbas at about A.D. 1600 for the use of travelers but now inhabited by poor people, and several hundred houses, hedged between the road on the cliffside and a forest of poplars that border the agricultural land leading down to the banks of the swiftly flowing stream. As we craned our necks to look at the inscription high overhead, we realized the full extent of George Cameron's daring. We could see the scars on the rock where Darius' workmen, having completed the inscription, had cut away the stone below it, leaving it completely inaccessible. The jagged edge of the rock where George had hooked his ropes was seventy feet above the inscription at the nearest point—hence the wide swing of his ladder in the wind.

Walking about under the inscription itself, I could see no cave. A dozen yards up the road a torrent of water burst from a hole in the rock, running in a culvert under the road into a pool a half-acre in extent, where despite the cold the water bubbled too violently to freeze. It was this crystal-clear, absolutely pure water that fed the terraces below the village, kept the villagers healthier than they might have been, and had made this pool a standard stopping-place on the road from Babylon to Ecbatana and the lands beyond. Such a supply of water, unfrozen in winter, could have been useful also to a band of hunters living here in much more ancient times.

"I know where the cave is," said John Watson, and he led us a quarter-mile farther up the road.

Although I found it hard to believe that George Cameron had been so inaccurate, I nevertheless followed my host. Climbing over the snow-covered boulders, we arrived panting, seven hundred feet above the edge of the plain, at the mouth of a cozy cave twenty feet wide and about five feet high, with an inside length of twenty-five feet. Halfway along the right wall inside the cave a narrow side-corridor led off we knew not where, and seven feet from the entrance, on the same side, a window looked out over the plain. The floor was lightly strewn with sheep dung, and a nest of twigs and hay stood in the corner for shepherds to sleep in. Near the entrance we stepped over a wolf trap of hand-forged iron.

Although this was the middle of winter, the soil under the dung was not frozen. I scraped a small test hole twenty inches deep, through a loose sterile layer of mulched sheep dung and wood ash, to a hearth of small stones. This was good: whatever lay beneath was well sealed by the activity of sheep during the last six or seven thousand years. The cave was big enough to live in, and not too big—no predatory animals could lurk far in its recesses. It had a sunny exposure, a window over the grazing-ground of wild herds, a perennial source of water which never froze, and it was so warm inside that the ground, covered with a thin layer of animal debris, could not freeze. Its only drawback was its height above the plain, requiring a stiff scramble several times a day, but ancient hunters were probably hardier than we. I measured this cave carefully, took several flash photographs, and went back to Bisitun to eat an excellent meal of shish kebabs in the local teahouse. Although I was by no means sure that this was Cameron's cave, I was happy with it in any case.

The next day we drove on over the Asadabad Pass in the deep snow, getting stuck and nearly frozen, to arrive at the home of another missionary, the late Dr. Mary Zoeckler, in time for supper and a midnight Persian New Year party. On the way up the side of the Zagros I was too busy keeping the car on the road and ourselves alive to pay much attention to caves, but we saw none comparable to Bisitun either then or on any of the many occasions when I have driven that road since. *Bisitun,* in its original form, *Behistun,* means *The Place of the Gods,* and so it seemed to be—a rock as high and white as Gibraltar, as sharp and smooth as a lion's fang, yielding at its feet enough clean water to slake the thirst of an army; a rock, furthermore, not too hard to house a cave. How the ancients came to worship there was easy to understand.

Six months later, on June 30, 1949, we returned to Bisitun—this time from the east, for we had left the jeep on blocks at the National Museum in Tehran. Our party now consisted of six persons: Lisa and myself; my son Charles, who was now eighteen; David Elder, aged fifteen, the son of the Reverend John Elder, of the Presbyterian Mission in Tehran; Mr. Habibollah Samadie; and Asadullah, the Lion of God. David was the interpreter. He had been born in Iran and spoke Persian as well as English; his only problem was how to translate my blunt Anglo-Saxon monosyllables into polite Persian. Sometimes he just said nothing, which was probably the best course of all.

Mr. Samadie was an official of the Iranian government sent with us as official representative of the Department of Antiquities. We spoke French together, and here again our vocabularies did not exactly match, for his French was exceedingly polite while mine had been learned in Morocco talking principally with Foreign Legion and Arab soldiers. I am afraid that I taught him a few words that he might not ordinarily need. Asadullah was an exceptionally handsome young Persian from Hamadan, the son of the cook of one of the missionaries. A convert to Christianity, he had attended the high school at Hamadan and was trying to earn money to put himself through the University of Tehran. He had joined the expedition as cook, temporarily following his father's profession.

During my first few days with Mr. Samadie he seemed extraordinarily incompetent at pronouncing my name. Instead of saying Coon in the regular way, he would stammer a little and come out with Cowan, or Co-own, or even call me Mr. Carleton, using my first name. As these attempts seemed to embarrass him I asked the missionaries at Hamadan what was the trouble, and before long learned that in Persian *Coon* means *rectum,* a word that Mr. Samadie could not bring himself to pronounce. I also learned that the name *Payne* means *excrement.* Once when Mr. Coon in Hamadan telephoned Mr. Payne, the executive officer of the Mission in Tehran, all circuits were connected at once. The operators all along the line were prostrated with laughter, while Mr. Payne and I conversed on a clear line.

By the time we got to Bisitun, however, this misunderstanding between Mr. Samadie and me had been overcome and I had resigned myself to the need of disguising my name, a subterfuge that, in time to come, alternately made us trouble with permits and let us through security barriers on the strength of sheer embarrassment. I can never make fun of a person's name, nor can I fail to understand the Persian requirement of a little clean deception in such matters to grease the social machine.

The Department of Antiquities in Iran, as in most Middle Eastern countries, is a branch of the Ministry of Education. Therefore Sammy (as we came to call Mr. Samadie) had brought with him a letter from Tehran to the head of the Department of Education at Kermanshah, and he in turn assigned us the schoolhouse to live in. Because the school children were having summer vacation it was comparatively empty. I say comparatively because one front room was inhabited by the schoolmaster, a tall, thin, sensitive man who was delighted to have Sammy and Asadullah to talk with; the other front room was occupied by the school janitor, a very old man with a magnificent hawk-like nose and long white mustaches, and by his wife, who had suffered a psychic trauma when someone told her, as a joke, that her husband had taken a second wife. Since that time she had been unable to speak, and she communicated by gestures alone. The woman whom the joker had named in this tragic jest inhabited the corridor. A tall, thin, stately, and once beautiful Kurdish widow named Khavar, she looked about fifty. She wore a russet-colored nightgown-like dress, full of holes, through one of which the attenuated tip of a pendulous breast occasionally protruded. She was the janitor's assistant. When not otherwise occupied, she spent her time spinning wool.

Asadullah set up the kitchen in one classroom, Lisa and I took over a second with our camp cots, and Charles and David requisitioned a third, while Sammy moved into a front room with his new friend, the schoolmaster. As soon as we had established ourselves I set out eagerly to revisit the cave. Outside the schoolhouse we passed a stand where a young man sold cucumbers and played his short-wave radio; he was listening to the Voice of America as we passed, and saluted us smartly. Next came the teahouse where we had eaten shish kebabs with the Watsons in the winter; this had now moved out of doors, and guests lounged comfortably on settees perched over a babbling brook, part of the irrigation system of the village. Beyond this bubbled the famous spring, from which the maidens of Bisitun were filling their shapely jars, mushroom-like copper vessels, and ugly oil tins. Some of them had started to walk home with these containers perched on their heads, and as I looked at the top of an oil tin, over it I saw an opening in the rock.

Running up to it, I found myself in a second cave. This must be Cameron's grotto, for it could easily be seen from the face of the inscription, while the one that John Watson had showed me lay around a corner and much higher up. This, the Cameron cave, had been filled with snow last winter. I placed myself in the role of a Paleolithic hunter and followed the well-known law of least effort in my thinking about the cave. Why in the world should I run up and down that seven-hundred-foot slope of limestone blocks every time I wanted a drink of water, and make my wife or wives and children do the same, when I could live on the ground floor and get my drink by a minimum of exertion? How would I like to drag the carcass of a horse, stag, or other animal up that slope? No, I would not like any of these things. Unless the terrain were infested with hideous enemies from whose presence I had to conceal myself, I would live in the lower cave, and if such enemies did exist, the upper cave, exposed as it was and permitting movement only downward, was strategically untenable.

People have often asked me how I select caves for excavation. The answer is very simple: I merely imagine myself a primitive man, which is not very difficult, and look for caves that are better than others in respect to size, shape, exposure, protection from the elements, view of pastures on which game could have grazed, and source of water. In many parts of the world such first-class caves are still occupied by human beings, who have to be ejected by some legal means before excavation can begin. In all respects save one the lower cave of Bisitun filled the bill. That respect was that it was small, being no more than twenty feet long or wide, and small caves are usually shallow. However, not knowing so much about caves then as I do now, I took a chance and decided to dig at once.

The next morning, July 1, I hired four men and began, laying out Trench A, an area eight meters by two meters (twenty-four feet by six feet), on the right side of the floor, which ran into a crevice to the rear. This crevice was, of course, the solution cavity through which a stream of water, comparable to the existing springs, had once flowed. After the water had been diverted elsewhere, people had (as I supposed) begun to live in the crevice, and its floor had risen until its roof was now only two feet high. That people had also lived out front in the sun-

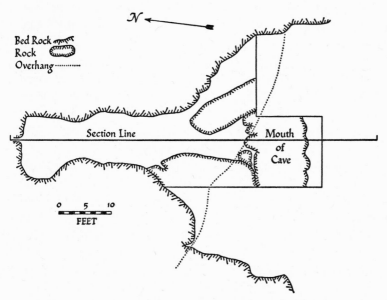

Bisitun Cave: plan. Only one trench was dug in this cave.

shine was evident from the presence of a fan of earth and stones, known to geologists as a *talus slope,* strewn with sherds and flints. The foot of the talus reached the road right opposite the bus stop on the Baghdad-Tehran route. As work went on, the bus passengers soon discovered our presence and we had a visitor problem. Crowding one another on the lip of the dig, they kicked dirt and small stones onto the workmen below, and before the excavation was over I had to take drastic steps to keep them at a safe distance from the edge.

The trouble with digging caves in different countries or parts of a country is that new men must be trained each time, and as soon as a good crew has been got together the job is finished. The city-mound archæologists in Egypt and Iraq employ workmen whose ancestors have been archæological excavators for as many as four generations, and who move about from site to site with different expeditions. Compared with the surfaces of city sites, the area of a cave floor is small and the amount of material per square meter of earth great. The stratification of a cave is laid down on a smaller scale, the light is often poor, and quarters are crowded. Despite ladders, pulleys, and other devices, the problem of soil-removal may become a bottleneck when disposal fails to keep pace with the digging. Under these conditions one needs good men of even temper who will not quarrel, for a blow with a pick or even a harsh word suddenly spoken may cause a man to fall into a deep trench, and it is easy for an angry man to kick stones of various sizes down onto a rival's head. The morale of a submarine crew is needed in a cave.

How to find such men in a particularly poverty-stricken village without knowing more than a few words of Persian—actually, the men of Bisitun spoke Kurdish, and Persian was only a second language to them—was a problem. One of the men, Ali Akbar, had worked for George Cameron. While ladder-flitting was no training for digging, it did give him an excuse to make himself appear superior to his fellows. He was a troublemaker whom I eventually had to fire. Then there was a father-and-son combination: Qasem, a one-eyed man from another village, and his son Abbas, who was clearly too young to do strenous work. I kept him on, however, when Qasem told me that the boy's stepmother was cruel and he did not dare leave the two in the house together. The presence of this boy created a disturbance because the other men complained that he was being paid disproportionately on half-wages. The fourth worker was a boy of about seventeen named Abdul Ali, a bright-eyed lad with an aquiline nose and a marvelous memory for poetry. Although illiterate, he used to entertain us by reciting Persian classics, dozens of lines at a time, including Hafiz and Firdusi. It was his oft-stated ambition to marry Rita Hayworth and tour Europe with her in a jeep.

On that first day the school janitor squatted at the edge of the trench, joining in the conversation. He told us a tale of a dervish who had kidnapped a woman from her husband and brought her to this very cave, where he abused her constantly until one night, when he was exhausted, she asked his permission to go outside to relieve herself. Being too tired to go with her, he tied a long string to her wrist and held the end. Once outside she tied her end of the cord to a bush and escaped to rejoin her husband, who ran back to the cave and engaged in mortal combat with the dervish. I never heard the outcome of this tale, either because it was considered too immoral for my ears or simply because the narrative was interrupted by the arrival of Asadullah, who announced that the kitchen roof had fallen in on his Primus stove. I halted the work, arranged for the repairs with an itinerant Assyrian carpenter whom I found on the road, and was back again in a few minutes. Too late for the punch line.

Stimulated by his success as a teller of tales, the janitor volunteered to serve as night watchman at the cave, and I hired him. He failed, however, to keep this job for more than a single night, owing to his many-faceted ability as entrepreneur. At noon the next day Asadullah suggested that we eat lunch in the cool, shady garden in back of the schoolhouse, where a small tile-lined pool of running water produced a pleasant atmosphere. As we rounded the bushes into this shady nook we surprised three couples busily engaged in an active phase of love-making. They had brought a complete *Rubáiyát* equipment of rugs, blankets, food, and drink out from Kerman-shah in a taxi, paying the old janitor for the use of the premises. As the highest ranking representative of the Ministry of Education present, Mr. Samadie dispersed this fun-loving group and reprimanded the janitor sharply. His feelings ruffled, the old man resigned his post as night watchman immediately and retired in sullen hostility to the passive company of his speechless spouse.

I took on in his place a short, thick-set man who smoked opium, and added to the digging staff two muscular Kurdish brothers, one of whom looked Irish and the other like a Scots Guard, as well as a fat man with a round face and bulging eyes, whom we called Banjo Eyes. These four were excellent workmen. This second day did not, however, end without further incident. When I got back to the schoolhouse to relax by the pool in the late-afternoon sun, a blood-red jeep stopped at the front door and two large, sinister-looking men dressed in good European clothes walked through the corridor, stepping over the pallet of Khavar, the janitor's assistant, and confronted me. They were licensed opium-distributors, whose business it was to provide addicts with their rations. They had come to Bisitun to sell opium, and, according to them, the Kermanshah representative of the Ministry of Education had told them that they could live in the schoolhouse: we must get out, or share our quarters with them. Mr. Samadie valiantly defied them, but to no avail. I therefore stood up and stretched myself to an inch or two beyond my full height, so that I looked down on the tops of their heads. Clenching and un-clenching my fists, I said, with an attempt at dignified belligerence: "If you do not leave quietly, I will throw you out."

As no one was willing to translate this, I repeated it in as many languages as I could think of, with appro-priate gestures. Somehow or other they understood, and left. Soon we heard the jeep engine start and the tires grip the road bed. The two men drove about fifty yards down the road to the teahouse, in which they took up residence, and from which they later cast evil glances at me as I passed to and from my work at the cave. As if the day had not been full enough, as soon as dark had fallen a busload of Kurdish Jews stopped in front of the schoolhouse to disgorge its occupants, male and female, dressed in Western garb, who sang loudly to the music of guitars and accordions as they danced wildly in rings, holding hands, in the middle of the road, in the glow of the headlights. I fell asleep before they had fin-ished.

Despite the interruptions of the first two days, I was still able to keep the work moving at the cave, and I was keenly interested in what we found in it. I was appre-hensive lest we should find it filled with the angular rub-ble produced by stonecutters' picks, for there had been quarrying here as well as inscription-carving. At Tangier, Hugh Hencken had excavated a small cave down to the floor only to find it completely filled with this debris. I had no wish to repeat his experience. Scraps of this kind there were in the top twenty centimeters, along with old bricks, a G.I. trouser button, and pieces of a brown bot-tle in the base of which was stamped: "NOT TO BE RE-FILLED." In the second level no more bricks, bottles, or buttons appeared, their place being taken by a few sherds of black-burnished pottery, a tiny flint core used in post-glacial times for the production of miniature implements called microliths, several scraps of ordinary flint, and some bones of sheep or goat. I was happy to see no more stonecutters' chips. This meant that at the time of Darius I, about 500 B.C., the surface of the cave stood at only twenty centimeters below its present height. What lay under it had to be older than 500 B.C.

By the end of the second day we had cleared out sixty centimeters of this upper, or black, layer. Its contents included some coarse pottery of the kind made from the time of Darius to the present for carrying water or storing liquids; two sherds of burnished ware with red stripes, which I later learned was Assyrian (a few centuries older than the Darius period); and a few dozen worked flints. The flints were of two kinds: microliths matching the tiny core, which could have been postglacial; and flakes of the kind made by Neanderthal man in Europe and similar to the industry of Red #2 in Tangier.

All of this material had been disturbed at one time or another between the end of the glacial age and the arrival of the inscription-carvers, as well as by an occasional overnight guest symbolized by the story of the amorous dervish. The presence of the flake implements, which could have been left behind when an older floor had been eroded, cheered me greatly. Here was the handiwork of Neanderthal man, comparable to the implements found by Dorothy Garrod in 1928 one hundred and twenty miles to the northwest in the same mountain range, in the cave of Iraqi Kurdistan known as Hazer Merd. As far as I knew then, Bisitun was the easternmost stratified site of this kind yet found. Russian reports on the cave of Teshik Tash in Soviet Uzbekistan, which contained the skeleton of a Neanderthal child, were not published until 1949. When we were at Bisitun I had not seen it.[2]

It was also interesting to see that no Upper Paleolithic blade tools were to be found in the level over the rich deposit of flakes. Reputable archæologists, at a loss to find the cradle of European Upper Paleolithic culture,

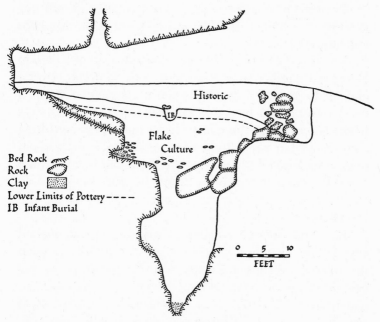

Bed Rock
Rock
Clay
Lower Limits of Pottery
IB Infant Burial

Historic

Flake
Culture

0   5   10
FEET

Bisitun Cave: section.

had postulated that it might lie in the archæological void of Iran. Bisitun, the first Ice Age cave dug in that country, failed to confirm these hopes.

[2] For a review and critique in English, see H. L. Movius, Jr.: "The Mousterian Cave of Teshik-Tash, etc.," American School of Prehistoric Research Bulletin 17, 1953, pp. 11–71.

On the third morning we arrived at last at the bottom of the black soil and reached an ancient floor—the surface of the undisturbed Ice Age deposit, which was red and gritty and fairly hard. It resembled in all these respects the Red #1 layer at Tangier, and was possibly of the same age. Its color, due to oxidation, indicated that it had lain exposed for a long time before the end of the last glacial period, after which sundry Mesolithic, possibly Neolithic, and metal-age folk had built fires, kept animals, and slept on it.

We had just succeeded in cleaning this off, and in laying out another trench in order to make our area wide enough to go down deeper, when a commotion stopped us. A ten-year-old boy, robbing birds' nests of their eggs in the cracks along the cliff wall, let out a blood-curdling scream not ten yards from our excavation and then ran toward us, his right hand extended. He had poked it into a crack, where it had been bitten by a snake, probably *Vipera lebetina*, whose venom can be deadly to a child of his size.

His hand began to swell, and several things happened very fast. His mother, who had been at the well, dropped her oil tin with a splash and went into a dramatic sequence of actions symbolizing grief. A tall, thin woman like Khavar, she first spread her arms wide apart as if crucified, then moved her hands in a circular motion in front of her as if winding yarn, and then grabbed me by the shirt with one hand and pinched the folds of my skin with the other. Each time I shook her off she went through the same three-scene act again. Meanwhile Lisa, Charles, and Asadullah piled the boy into the jeep and conveyed him at top speed to the American hospital in Kermanshah, with Charles at the wheel. Having found kinfolk to lead the woman to her house, I returned to my work.

By eleven o'clock, in time for Asadullah to prepare lunch, the snakebite expedition returned. Its members reported that, as the American hospital had had no antivenom, they had taken the boy to the government hospital, where the doctors had asked them to leave him. Presumably the boy would recover. During the afternoon nothing of great interest happened, for I was enlarging our digging-area in the cave by carrying Trench A to the eastern rock wall. The solution crack was already beginning to narrow, and working-space was cramped.

As soon as I arrived back in the schoolhouse more trouble arose. The old janitor collapsed in the corridor and lay there on his back, waving his hands and feet feebly about, while drooling and babbling. After we had brought him back to his senses by sponging him with water and by massage, he sat up scowling and upbraided us, saying that the smell of our food cooking had overpowered him. Although other elements may have entered into his condition, the immediate cause was a combination of hunger and the charcoal fumes from Khavar's brazier, which were blowing in his direction.

Actually, he had a legitimate complaint. The holy month of Ramadhan had begun, during which the faithful must fast from dawn to dusk, taking into their bodies neither food, drink, nor smoke. Each year this month, being lunar, begins eleven days earlier than it did the year before, and in 1949 it fell in the very longest days of the year, which made it particularly irksome. In 1947 we had passed through several weeks of Ramadhan in the Caves of Hercules, and most of the workmen had fallen ill; almost none were able to get through to noon, when we knocked off. Here in Bisitun, however, I had thought little of it because all the workmen ate lunch and drank water throughout the day, except one, Qasem the One-Eyed, who was a stranger. Although the workmen were

Kurds, they were also Shi'a. Now, the Shi'a sect is the official religion of Iran, to which most true Persians belong, while most Kurds are Sunnis, like desert Arabs. Our workmen, village Kurds, differing from their fellows of the mountains in religion and from the Persians in language and customs, fell between two stools and ignored the fast. It had not occurred to me that the janitor would observe it, and this was my error. After this we tried to keep the kitchen smells away from his aristocratic nostrils.

But that was not the last of our interruptions. During the following night David heard a noise in his room. It was a scratching, metallic sound, but as it was only a little noise he paid no attention to it and went back to sleep. In the morning he found a drowned mouse in his washbasin. The same thing happened in our room, but after a while Lisa got up and searched for the source of the sound with a flashlight. Thus she discovered her mouse swimming around and tossed it out the window, water and all, and it survived. In the morning this combination of happenings so impressed everyone that at breakfast I began searching my memory for an earlier version of such an omen.

The closest parallel I could find was Herodotus' account of how the Scythian king, whose bas-relief figure hovered over us on the rock with a rope around its neck, had sent a herald bearing gifts to our own Darius of Bisitun when that emperor was lost, like Napoleon, on the vast steppes of Russia. The gifts consisted of a bird, a mouse, a frog, and five arrows. The herald left the interpretation of these symbols to the Persians, one of whom offered the following version, translated by a brother of Sir Henry Rawlinson: "Unless, Persians, ye can turn into birds and fly up into the sky, or become mice and burrow in the ground, or make yourselves frogs, and take refuge in the fens, ye will never make escape from this land but die pierced by our arrows." [3]

Despite the proximity of Darius' larger-than-life-size figure on the cliff above our heads, we could find no exact application of the omen of the mice to our present situation. For the moment, we relegated it to the back of our minds, because the snakebite boy had reappeared. He told us that he had been discharged from the hospital on the preceding evening and had come home, but now his hand and forearm were hideously inflamed and infected. Back in the jeep he went, again under Charles's guidance, to the American hospital at Kermanshah, this time in all likelihood to have his arm amputated.

Despite this latest interruption, I began work on time and had the pleasure of excavating some beautiful flints from the reddish earth in which we were digging. *Flint* is technically an inaccurate word to describe the material from which these implements had been flaked. Mineralogists prefer *chert* as a general term, but some of the Bisitun pieces were not exactly that. They were chalcedony, of many colors: red, white, green, blue, and in some cases milky and translucent. One piece that we found was chalcedony on one side and chert on the other, with a transitional zone between. So handsome were these pieces that they were almost jewelry. The thrill of discovering something of high æsthetic quality, not as individuals but as a small group of initiated cave-diggers, gave the workmen as well as me a deep feeling for these pieces. In the face of this feeling, snakebites, fallen roofs, and quarrels over who kept the fast and who did not were soon forgotten.

Sometimes One-Eyed Qasem was in the pit. As he

[3] *The History of Herodotus,* translated by George Rawlinson (Everyman's Edition, New York, 1910 etc.), Vol. I, p. 338; Vol. IV, pp. 131, 132.

handed each piece up to me he cleaned the sleek dirt off
its shiny side, his single orb also sparkling. At other times
he was relieved by Ali Shah, the Irish-looking one of the
two brothers, who placed the flints, like a clutch of pea-
cock eggs, on his cloth cap to hand them up to me, his
big teeth bared in a grin. When his brother, the one who
looked like a Scots Guardsman, followed him below, he
too used his cap, and finally One-Eyed Qasem did likewise. These caps became symbols of their new profession of flint-finding, and at the end of the dig I bought
them all new headpieces so that they could preserve their
flint-cushion caps as family treasures to show their pos-
terity.

As we dug downward, the sides of the cave expanded
until I came to believe that we were uncovering the opening of a lower cave, as in the jinn's office of Tangier. In
that case the amount of earth to be moved might be increased immeasurably. As I have since found, this is Il-
lusion Number One in cave-digging: every concavity in
the rock wall is a potential secret cavity. Most of them
flatten themselves out, as this one did.

As far as stratification was concerned, two possibilities
faced us: either the deposit in the Bisitun cave was all
of one piece, or we would be obliged to deal with several
cultural layers possibly culminating in hand axes. I gave
the men long lectures on the subject of changes of soil,
but we found none of a dramatic nature. Gradually the
coarse red turned into a sleek brown, as it had in the
High Cave, and in the brown the implements were commoner than before. In fact, they were stuffed like plums
in a pudding, and the men ceased all work with the pick
and excavated with trowels, packsaddle needles, and
their fingers. What they were now finding was a series of
caches where someone had tucked away whole toolkits
of perfect implements. Not a piece was broken.

Along with the flints we removed thousands of splinters of bone which rang like cymbals when struck with the blade of a knife. Very few of these bones were articulating ends, and teeth and horn cores were also rare. Most of them were plain splinters shattered by some hungry people to extract the marrow. About two thirds of the ungulate bones were those of the red deer, or stag, the Asiatic equivalent of our wapiti or elk. About one third were those of horses. It would seem, therefore, that before ax-wielding people had cut down the forests in this neighborhood the hunters of Bisitun had their choice of two hunting-grounds: the forest behind them, teeming with stag, or the plain in front, grazed by herds of horses. From the standpoint of protein intake their standard of living must have been as high as that of the average American, and well above that of the modern occupant of the village of Bisitun. In a nutritional sense, therefore, one might say that the civilization of Bisitun has deteriorated since the end of the Ice Age.

I think that the men in the cave felt this, for they were villagers by force of circumstance rather than by heredity or inclination. As they saw all these bones come out they could see what they were, for every Kurd is a zoologist in this respect, and they realized how much better off had been their predecessors, who, as far as they were aware, were also their ancestors. Some readers may doubt that these illiterate workmen understood what they were excavating, and may think that their work with me was as vacant of intellectual stimulus as sewer-digging. I am sure, however, that these cave-diggers were just as receptive of new ideas as the rest of us, and that I succeeded, with little effort, in communicating to them the feeling, if not the exact knowledge, of what we were doing.

Their situation was rendered doubly dramatic by the

contrast between what went on in the cave, where they experienced the joy of finding flints, uniting all of us in the pit as mystically as chanting does a company of dervishes, and the stark poverty of their home environment. They were tenant farmers who did not own even their tools or the oxen with which they plowed their landlord's fields under the supervision of a *katkhoda*, or landlord's agent. They rarely got enough to eat, and their poverty brought on daily frictions and incidents of which I mention here only those which were related directly to our work. In fairness to the Persian government it must be said that the Shah himself is taking active steps to alleviate the burden of poverty in villages like Bisitun.

When we finished the cave in Bisitun these men volunteered to leave their homes and follow me wherever I might go, but I could not take them. I had seen how the others felt about Qasem the outsider. To introduce a whole crew of old retainers into a new village might inflame the locals to the point of violence. And another thing: in my daily conversations with these men I was learning not Persian but Kurdish, a language that in most other parts of the country would be about as useful as Chinese.

While this work-group of friends was forming in the cave, another clique was taking shape in the schoolhouse. This consisted of Mr. Samadie, Asadullah, and the schoolteacher. As all the landlords who owned portions of the village lived either in Kermanshah or Tehran, these three—aside from the telegraph operator, who could not leave his key—were the only mutually accessible Persian-speaking intellectuals in the place, and they all lived in the same building.

Before our arrival the schoolmaster had been starved for someone to talk with. The cucumber boy with the radio was eager but untutored, and lit-

tle intellectual satisfaction was to be had from conversing with the elderly janitor or Khavar. Now, with Mr.
Samadie and Asadullah available, he found himself in
the middle of a small circle of educated people who spoke
the same language in more than one sense and who could
discuss together all the problems of the great world outside of Bisitun and even outside of Iran, particularly including America. While they had learned much about
America from books and movies, they could see that Lisa,
David, Charles, and I did not look much like the Deer-
slayer, Simon Legree, or Uncle Tom, nor did we live like
Hollywood stars and starlets, any more than did the missionaries with whom Asadullah was familiar. So they constantly turned to us for information to use as substance
for their discussions.

Although these sessions sometimes took place on the
narrow platform outside the cave, this was an awkward
place, and furthermore Asadullah usually had business in
the kitchen. When I failed to see any of the three on
Thursday afternoon, July 7, their absence made no impression on me. At four thirty that afternoon, a half-hour
before closing-time, with a workless Friday ahead of us,
I was down in the bottom of the trench with One-Eyed
Qasem, excavating beautiful flints by hand from a special
cache that some hunter had secreted under an overlying
rocky shelf, when I heard unusual noises, just as David
and Lisa had on the night of the omen.

Climbing quickly out of the pit, I saw Mr. Samadie,
panting desperately, collapsed on the ground in front of
me. He was clad in his underdrawers only, and his pink
skin—for, like many upper-class Persians, he is as fair-
skinned as a Scandinavian—was fiery red from sunburn,
while his feet were lacerated and bloody.

"Asadullah," he gasped "is in the water."

My mind was full of flints. As far as I was aware, Asa-

dullah was in the kitchen creating delicious shish kebabs
for our supper. It took a moment or two for Mr. Samadie's
appearance and message to make sense to me, from water to mouse to Asadullah, and then I was off. In part
people told me what had happened, speaking in various
languages—I could never say exactly which; in part I
learned it from their gestures and glances out over
the vast plain to the snaky course of the river, the
Gamas-i-Ab, flowing swiftly toward the Persian Gulf,
chewing away slices of bank and grinding them in its
watery crop to deposit them as mud and gravel on the
fetid plain below. In what seemed an hour but was probably only a few seconds I was out of the trench and running, and all the men with me, most of them ahead of
me, toward the river, more than a mile away.

Poor Mr. Samadie, who had made the course once
and was exhausted, nevertheless plodded bravely along.
So far had Charles and David outstripped me that when
I arrived at the bank I saw them naked, plunging and
diving in the swift stream, searching for Asadullah's
body, while the lanky schoolteacher, still in dripping
shorts, coursed up and down along the bank searching
for some trace of it. Meanwhile, a gendarme had arrived
from the post just below the cave, and matters were now
in his hands.

For what seemed to me a very long time Charles and
David continued to dive and swim about, exploring
the subterranean portions of clumps of reeds, and being
themselves carried short distances downstream as they
ventured into the swift side of the river. They were growing tired, and I shouted at them to come out. In horror
I pictured myself facing the Reverend John Elder as well
as my own conscience; I cupped my hands, waded out,
and did my best to persuade them to desist. The Persians
present tried to help me, as did Lisa, who had by now

arrived in the jeep, not knowing what had happened. Unfortunately, the gendarme's attempts had the opposite effect. He beckoned to them to come in, but he did so in the Persian fashion, by pushing his hand away from his body. Charles thought he meant that they should *not* come in but should keep on diving. David, who had seen a bus plunge into a stream the year before and had revived some of the passengers by artificial respiration, did not want to give up until the time limit of possible resuscitation had been passed.

Finally the boys crawled out of the water, cold and silent, and as they lay on the bank recovering their breath, their places were soon taken by eight strong swimmers brought there by the katkhodas of Bisitun and the village across the river. The gendarme, who had sent for these men, had by now succeeded in creating order on the riverbank. As soon as he was replaced by another man in uniform, the gendarme mounted the jeep. Leaving the swimmers bobbing up and down, we drove back with him over the hummocks and irrigation ditches to the village. In the gendarmerie building a long inquest took place. Asadullah's effects were listed, and Mr. Samadie, the schoolmaster, the local opium-inspector, and I had to affix our signatures.

This inquest brought out the facts of the drowning. After their luncheon the three members of the intellectual club of Bisitun had decided to go wading in the river. Asadullah had therefore asked Madame for permission to bathe, which was his exact word, and she had granted it. Not thinking of the distant river, she had believed that they intended to paddle around in the enclosed pool at the spring, where the water is nowhere more than four feet deep. She also did not know that not one of the three knew how to swim.

And so it had happened. Three young men of good

family, good education, and high ideals stripped to their trunks and stepped into the inner and slower side of a snow-fed mountain torrent. One of them, bolder than his companions, stepped out too far and the water caught him. Despite his magnificent musculature, he did not know what to do, and was soon out of sight. There had been no other witnesses. The schoolteacher had run up and down along the bank, searching everywhere, while the inspector had raced across the hot, flinty plain on his bare, pink, and soon bloody feet. Then we had come, and the gendarme had been with us. He had seen the rest.

My next job was to notify the missionaries at Hamadan, who could break the news to Asadullah's family and make the necessary arrangements. I sent them a telegram, which could not go out until morning as the service was closed for the day. Then I stopped a car and gave a colonel riding in it a note to be delivered by hand. The next day was Friday, and the telegram did not go out at all because the office was closed. The colonel also failed me. As soon as I could, I got through to the Mission on the local telephone and delivered my message.

It was now the middle of the morning. With the others I walked over to the riverbank to watch the rescue attempt, which was continuing in full force and had taken on the structure of a ceremony. Now that Charles and David were standing beside me instead of being in the water, I was able to look at the scene and setting with more detachment than I had possessed on the previous afternoon.

On two sides of the eastern horizon rose high chalk-colored mountains, walling in a wide plain that was partly green and partly brown, depending on the presence or absence of irrigation. In the middle flowed the curving stream, fifty feet across. Although its surface was deceptively smooth, the water flowed very swiftly, bursting into nodes and ripples on the outer sides of the curves. Its dusty banks were lined with a crowd of over a hundred persons, men, women, and children, clothed in garments of many colors and standing silently as they watched the water.

Had any of them wished to communicate with one another they would have had difficulty making their voices heard, for the katkhoda or landlord's agent of the village across the river had produced two gypsies, one blowing a *shawm*, a primitive oboe played with a double reed, and the other drumming. To play the shawm one must put the whole reed inside one's mouth and puff out one's cheeks like a pair of apples; the sound that results is very loud, penetrating, and continuous, like that of a bagpipe without drones. As I closed my eyes I felt myself back in Gibraltar in the early fall of 1942, watching the fabled Ceremony of the Keys, and hearing the skirl of the pipes and the roll of the drums of the massed pipers of the Black Watch, those of them who had survived after they had piped the rest of the British army into their boats at Dunkirk.

The swimmers had come back again. Like aquatic ballerinas, they dived and popped up again in perfect rhythm to the beat of the gypsy drum. A huge water snake, lured by the strident notes of the shawm, thrust its black head out of the water in midstream and swam swiftly with the current out of the area of commotion.

"You see?" said the khatkhoda, standing by my side, "the music brought out the snake. There is a big fish down below there holding Asadullah's body in its jaws. When it hears the music it will have to open its mouth, and the body will float to the surface. That is why I brought the gypsies."

"That is not true," said Mr. Samadie heatedly. "Actually, it is a piece of jagged rock that is holding the body, not a fish at all, and the vibration of the music will jar the rock and shake the body loose."

Personally, I subscribed to neither theory, but agreed with Charles and David that the body had been carried far downstream; that was the place to look. I therefore offered a reward of five hundred rials, equal to twenty days' pay, to anyone who would find the body, and we returned to the schoolhouse. The chief of the gendarmerie, who was a most agreeable man, told me not to worry, that he would take charge of everything, including the payment of my reward and the guarding of the cave. But with all his kindness, firmness, and effort, he could not do everything.

The presence of so many foreigners—and our numbers had doubled with the arrival of an automobile from Hamadan—as well as of city folk from other parts of the country, along with the fact that it was Friday and no one had work to do, built up to fever pitch the excitement caused by the drowning. A crowd gathered outside the schoolhouse, a noisy crowd filled with the imminence of some new event. As always happens at such times, people who thought that we owed them something made haste to collect, as if afraid that we would depart in a puff of smoke, and those who had been nursing things to say to us felt it necessary to say them at once.

First the gypsies forced their way in, claiming that of the two hundred rials I had given the katkhoda to pay for their services they had received only fifty. Then the carpenter whom I had hired to build a coffin, and who had done an abominable job with old pieces of boxes, demanded two hundred rials over the one hundred I had already paid him. Then Ali Akbar, George Cameron's ladder mate whom I had hired at the cave, burst in, raising a hullabaloo because I had paid the youthful Abbas, son of One-Eyed Qasem, a day's wages when the boy had been sick. We ejected these people and I also fired Ali Akbar, and we were managing to hold our own when the crowd began muttering ominous things.

First of all, the schoolteacher had killed Asadullah because the handsome young newcomer had stolen the affections of his secret lover, Khavar, whose allure had already driven the janitor's wife mad. Then it was Mr. Samadie who had murdered him for his wrist watch— this item had not turned up at the inquest and its absence had been noted. Huddled in a corner of his room, his cheeks tearstained and his face gray with justifiable fear, the schoolteacher cowered, motionless and soundless except for an occasional sob. Equally upset but putting on a braver front, Mr. Samadie was trying to answer the taunts of the multitude, which he was not afraid to face, but we hauled him inside and shut him in a room. Before my eyes I had a wonderful example of what happens in a Neolithic-style village when something goes wrong, and of what happened in Salem, Massachusetts, in the days of the witch trials. When a tightly knit group of people is disturbed, scapegoats must be found. Khavar being a widow and Samadie and the schoolteacher being outsiders as well as the only witnesses to the tragedy, these three were natural victims.

Before matters had gone much further the gendarmes took over. The drowned boy's father, who had come down from Hamadan with other members of his family, was too stricken to show any emotion. At our urging he left this howling rabble to take a walk with his younger son, and several hours later we found the two of them pacing thoughtfully along the riverbank. His chief fear, he told us—and he seemed relieved that he could now find words with which to speak—was that his son's body would be eaten by birds, like the corpses of Zoroastrians.

Much power lay in the father's hands, for his signature was necessary to release Mr. Samadie and the schoolmaster from arrest and trial.

The next morning I arose at five and commenced work as usual. One of Asadullah's uncles had replaced his nephew as cook, the rest of our party had gone to Kermanshah in the jeep, and the schoolmaster was safe enough in his room. During the early hours of the working-day the piping and drumming continued by the riverbank and we could hear it faintly, as from a distant glen, as we removed flint after beautiful flint from the rich soil with trowel, brush, and penknife.

At ten o'clock a tall, bony man, dressed wholly in black, appeared at the lip of the excavation, along with the katkhoda of the village across the stream. The tall man was the katkhoda of a village two parasangs (twelve miles, more or less) down the river. The body had floated ashore in his area. As the jeep was in Kermanshah, we had to wait. I notified the gendarmerie and resumed excavation, finishing the morning's work at twelve, when the jeep returned.

Charles and I hooked on the trailer, threw in the coffin and a couple of mats, and departed, with a gendarme, the tall katkhoda, and three of Asadullah's uncles. After we had driven ten miles down the main road we turned off to the left over a trail that finally led us to a summer village made of poles and mats, occupied by a band of semi-nomads who had left their winter village of mud houses to spend the hot weather by the river. They had laid Asadullah out on a door, tied his two big toes together, and built a canopy of poles and rugs which covered all of him except his feet, which they had sheltered with a posy of flowers. Owing to the temperature of the water, his body was fresh and undecayed. Luckily for Mr. Samadie and the schoolmaster, it was also un-blemished.

One of the uncles collapsed and had to be supported by a second one on the ride back; the third held the body in the open coffin to prevent the head from banging about. After we had returned we ate a hasty lunch and I left the care of the body to the boy's father and broth-ers, going at once to the cave, where I worked until five. Then we heard someone shouting at the foot of the talus slope; it was the katkhoda, who wanted four men to dig the grave.

This grave-digging was a disagreeable business. The workmen did it with the utmost reluctance, for they had heard, since the drowning, that Asadullah was a convert to Christianity, one of those persons of whom it is said contemptuously by Muslims: "He has become an Arme-nian."

With the jeep I hauled the stone slabs with which the grave was to be lined and covered, and we finally got everything ready for the burial. Then word came that I had to drive four parasangs (twenty-four miles) and back on the Hamadan road to fetch a major and his staff from the nearest administrative post. All was not in order with the burial permit, and these officials had to view the body, which was already drawing flies in a back room of the gendarmerie. I viewed this ride with the same reluc-tance the workmen had shown toward grave-digging. On the way back, there were seven people in one jeep, and I was very sleepy.

On this ride Mr. Samadie was exceedingly ashamed of me. I had gone directly from stone-hauling for the grave to jeep-driving for the major, who was a well-dressed, well-groomed, and well-mannered officer, very much a gentleman. I had embarked on this journey without bathing or changing my clothes. In fact, I had not had a real bath since arriving in Bisitun, because I had refused to buy a big forty-dollar tin-lined bathtub in Kermanshah as Mr. Samadie had requested. If I had known him better at that time I probably would have bought it, for I have seldom if ever seen him make a serious mistake, and he was the last man in the world to urge me to useless extravagance. Anyhow, had I followed his advice and bought the tub—this conclusion was but faintly implied and never stated—he and Asadullah would not have had to go to the river to get clean.

Aside from this unspoken reprimand, there was the much more obvious and immediate matter of my attire. At the moment I was wearing an old and dirty G.I. officer's shirt with a pair of torn khaki trousers which Khavar had patched in three places, and one of the patches was hanging loose. Tired as I was, I could still read the sequence of thoughts going through Sammy's most active mind. As a rule his mental equipment worked more quickly than mine and he could anticipate my statements, but on this occasion fatigue seems to have been on my side. Perhaps it was our mutual fatigue that made the connection.

What he was thinking, my built-in mental radar told me, was that the major was an important person without whose help we would never get this unfortunate mess resolved; that he, Sammy, was technically under me in status, but was at the same time the official representative of the Department of Antiquities, which was under the Ministry of Education; and that my sloppy dress was a disgrace to him, to the Department of Antiquities, and to the Ministry of Education. Thus, my undignified dress might impede the speedy termination of the proceedings for which the major was now on his way to the Bisitun gendarmerie. Why did I have to be so eccentric?

Then, suddenly, the picture brightened. Almost asleep at the wheel, I noticed an object in the middle of the road which was too big to bump without previous identification. It looked like an overturned basket. It was a tortoise, and a very big one. I jammed on the brakes, stopped the motor, and got out. Picking up the tortoise, which weighed about twenty pounds, I carried it across the road and set it on its way to the river. When we had started off again, Mr. Samadie was as happy as a flatful of clams, bubbling and chatting with animation as he quickly explained to the major and the other four passengers in the crowded jeep what a saintly character I was to manifest such concern for one of God's lowliest creatures. Being a saint, I could afford to be eccentric in small matters such as bathing and wearing the right kind of clothes. The day was saved—or, rather, the night.

One further hitch in the procedure occurred when the Hamadan authorities expressed dissatisfaction with the circumstances of the drowning, and Mr. Samadie and the schoolmaster had to be grilled a third time. On July 13, six days after the tragedy, another man drowned in the river. This was too much for our inspector. Although Asadullah's father had generously signed a statement absolving him of all suspicion, his nerves were understandably shattered. After convincing him that he had done more than his duty toward the Department of Antiquities and the Ministry of Education, as well as the University of Pennsylvania, I persuaded him to return to Tehran. When two westward-bound carloads of Seventh Day Adventist missionaries came to see the cave, I persuaded Sammy to ride with them to Kermanshah to get passage on a Tehran bus. The next day he reappeared briefly at lunch to pick up his suitcase, and he soon disappeared in a cloud of dust in a bus loaded with homeward-bound school children. The Department of Antiquities has never reproached me for this action. For all they knew, I might steal all the flints and bones in Bisitun, but they trusted me. Their trust has been neither abused nor unrewarded.

At the expense of appearing callous, I am able to state that the entire episode of the drowning failed to stop the work at the cave for more than a total of a few hours. It happened on Thursday when work was nearly over, and the next day was Friday, on which we would not have worked in any case. On the day of the recovery of the body I took a long lunch hour and knocked off early for grave-digging and fetching the major. The efficiency of the missionaries from Hamadan and of the boy's relatives, as well as of the government, made any further activity on my part unnecessary.

On that fatal Thursday we had gone through the reddish, rubbly soil that formed the top layer of the flint-bearing material and were working in a soft brown soil nearly free of stones. The situation was similar to that in the High Cave when we had passed from the lower portion of Red #1 into Brown. Here the transition seemed more gradual, and I could detect no conspicuous change in the types of implements. These were confined almost entirely to spear points and single-edged and double-edged knives. The walls of the rocky crevice were narrowing in. Here and there we found a cupboard-like cavity, and this was bound to be full of perfect implements, left there by a hunter who had failed to return from the chase or who had offered them to the spirit of the never-freezing spring, along with splinters of the marrow bones of elk and horse.

We continued digging until Sunday, July 17, when at a depth of 6.5 meters (about 22.5 feet) Qasem finally struck bottom. For the last two days he had been excavating with a spoon, as the crevice had narrowed itself down to a slit. The stratigraphy of Bisitun Cave held no complications. The soil changes were gradual, and the flints were more or less the same all the way down. What changes could be found from meter to meter could most readily be explained on the basis of a gradual evolution, over a continuous time span, of tool-making in the hands of a single and skillful people who perfected an art that they had brought to Bisitun without further invention.

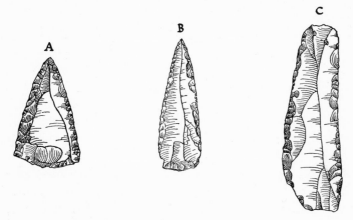

As at Tangier, the Middle Paleolithic flint-workers of Bisitun approached perfection in the manufacture of flake tools. Their principal types were points (A and B) and knives (C). (One-half actual size.)

Later I measured the butts of the spear points and found that the hunters had recognized an optimum thickness for hafting. If the butt was too thin the point would break easily, and if too thick it would make a clumsy joint, impeding penetration into the animal's body. Furthermore, from strip to strip I found a constant ratio between the number of single-edged and double-edged knives. These tools must have had separate uses, and the hunters were methodical people who knew what they needed and made it. They were no fools.

Although we cannot be sure exactly who these hunters were, we did find two small pieces of human material which give us a clue. One was an upper median incisor tooth, the other a section of the ulna, the longer of the two bones in the forearm. Both were characteristically Neanderthaloid. These hardy people were, therefore, men of a different race from our own, one which can no longer be seen in unaltered form anywhere in the world.

Like the people of the High Cave of Tangier who lived during Red #1 and Brown times, they existed at some part of the last glacial sequence, but more than that it is impossible to say. There was not a trace of fire in the cave, but we did not excavate far enough forward to be sure that no hearths had existed. No Carbon-14 dating was possible. Judging entirely from the excellence of their craftsmanship, which improved as one went upward level by level, the hunters of Bisitun were able to perfect their tool-making skill gradually without outside interruption and without the stimulus of new ideas produced by meeting people of other races and cultural backgrounds. The achievement of perfection takes time. As the blade-users of Europe were already making tools more varied and advanced than these in a technical sense during the first cool interval of the last glaciation, this could not be their place of orgin. Even if the entire Bisitun sequence were squeezed into the time span of the first ice advance, still the virtual absence of burins and the low proportion of blades to flakes would put this region out of the running. What we needed was a cave with blades and burins in the time of the first advance of the fourth ice sheet. Bisitun appeared to have been off the main line of history.

In a geographical sense our work in this cave was complementary to that at Tangier. In both places people of Neanderthaloid, if not fully Neanderthal, racial type lived on frontiers of the Paleolithic world past the time when, in certain other places, men of our own race had begun making a large variety of tools, using blades instead of flakes, and sowing the seeds of later civilization.

The boundaries of the center of Paleolithic inventiveness were beginning to take shape. Both Tangier and Bisitun have been famous highroads of history. Across the Strait of Gibraltar migrated the ancestors of some of the Neolithic peoples of western Europe, and later the Romans crossed the strait frequently between their colonies of Iberia and Mauretania. Tariq and his Berbers crossed them to conquer Spain, and the Spaniards reversed the process. Through them sailed many a fleet, from that of the Phœnicians who circumnavigated Africa for an Egyptian pharaoh to that of Eisenhower and Mark Clark at the time of Operation Torch in 1942. Bisitun was a vital station on the post road from Ecbatana to Babylon, with a branch road leading southeast to Persepolis. It was important enough to Darius I to be chosen as his imperial signpost, and today every bus that passes between Baghdad and Tehran goes through it.

During the time of the last glaciation both Tangier and Bisitun were rustic refuges inhabited by already outmoded types of humanity. In historic times, to the contrary, they were gateways of travel, because the historic peoples who passed through them had ships and horses. A barrier to Ice Age hunters can be an Iron Age man's highway. Bisitun and Tangier had taught me a valuable lesson in geography.

Bisitun was not, however, the end of our Neanderthaloid experience in Iran in 1949. During the rest of the summer and early fall our team dug two more caves, though neither of them produced results that could warrant adding them to the list of the seven most significant ones with which this book is chiefly concerned. After finishing Bisitun we explored the eastern side of the Zagros Mountains in the region from Mahabad to the Russian border, and excavated a cave called Tamtama in the country of the Shikak Kurds, just north of Rezaiyeh and a few miles from the Lake of Urmiya. In Tamtama we found only seven pieces of flint, not one of them clearly worked.

Then we went all the way across Iran to Mashhad, down along the Afghan border to Zabol at the mouth of the Helmand, and back up the Mashhad road to a village called Khunik. Here we excavated a beautiful rock shelter, but it was an upside-down site. On the surface we found fine flints like those of Bisitun, but as we went downward we came to potsherds of modern type, and finally pieces of iron and a modern skeleton.

This is what had happened: Around A.D. 700 the rock shelter was bare. Some people newly converted to Islam, perhaps Arabs, moved in, building their houses just outside and throwing their debris inside the overhang. Eventually they moved out, and their houses crumbled. As their descendants cut away every tree and bush from the mountain behind the shelter, and as their sheep and goats methodically removed all the grass year after year, the rock above became bare. An earthquake broke off the roof of a smaller cave higher up, whose fill was washed out by the water running down the denuded slope. This cave had been the home of hunters in the last glacial period, and the fill had contained their tools and weapons; these were now deposited on the floor of the rock shelter, sometime between about A.D. 1000 and the present.

Although these were only second-rate sites, the first because it contained so little and the second because its stratigraphy had been destroyed, they nevertheless have given us some information. In Tamtama the pieces of flint, though unworked, had been struck off their cores in a fashion comparable to that of Bisitun. This suggests that the same kind of people inhabited both places, though the Tamtama folk left no indication of an equal sophistication in the tool-making tradition. Of the two, Bisitun was the more attractive place to live during a period colder than at present, because it would have been warmer than Tamtama.

Khunik is important because it lies on the Sarrakhs Corridor. If any important Paleolithic movement had passed through the corridor, one might expect to find traces of it, and they still may be found. But this is doubtful, because the Khunik industry, while similar to that of Bisitun, contains even more sophisticated techniques without any evidence of mass-produced blade-making or the manufacture of burins. Khunik, in other words, was another place where Neanderthal man, or whoever it was who made these implements, lived on and on, long enough to perfect his tool-making to its natural limit without innovation. That is not what one would expect to find in a corridor of frequent travel. Boxed between Bisitun, Tamtama, and Khunik, the Iranian plateau ceased, in 1949, to look like a good place to search for the origins of the European blade-makers, but this interpretation could be wrong.[4]

[4] C. S. Coon: *Cave Explorations in Iran, 1949* (Philadelphia: University Museum Monographs; 1951).

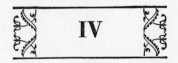

IV

BELT CAVE AND THE CASPIAN SHORE

ALTHOUGH OUR WORK in 1949 made it appear unlikely that the Iranian plateau was an Upper Paleolithic breeding-ground, another part of Iran held and still holds distinct possibilities of that nature. This is the Caspian shore region, part of it below sea level, which is divided into the three provinces of Gilan, Mazandaran, and Gurgan. To the northeast it opens without barrier onto the Turkoman steppe; to the northwest it can be reached from the southern Russian steppe by a narrow route around the eastern end of the Caucasus Mountains, and it is connected with the shores of the Black Sea by the Transcaucasian trough. Geographically speaking, it is not a part of the Middle East at all, but a southern extension of the northern Eurasiatic realm.

At the time we first decided to go there I had not reasoned this out. It was limestone that I was thinking about as Lisa and I took our jeep ride in the snow over Asadabad Pass, between Bisitun and Hamadan, on New Year's Eve, 1949. During that ride I had noticed that at the crest of the plateau the limestone core of the mountain range gave way to red sandstone, and that all outcrops visible under the snow were of the latter material. Sandstone weathers more quickly than limestone, and caves found in it tend to be of recent formation. After consultation with Dr. John Frame, the surgeon of the American Mission hospital in Hamadan, I found that the nearest limestone beyond the Bisitun area was to be found at the northern rim of the plateau and in the foothills of the Elburz Mountains along the Caspian shore, where Dr. Frame, whose father had been a surgeon before him, had been born. This country, I was told, was covered with thick forest and drained by swift streams; it was filled with game, including tigers, wild boars, and elk; and its climate was mild enough to permit the growth of citrus fruits, tea, and palms.

The combination of heavy rainfall, mild winters, and possible caves made me think of a number of similar places in the world, such as southern France, Spain, Italy, Lebanon, the Palestine coast, and the Crimea, in all of which the remains of an old friend, Neanderthal man, have been found. Therefore I secured a letter from the Iranian general commanding the Hamadan area to the general in Resht. Armed with this and several other documents, we started out on January 3 from the Presbyterian Mission compound in Hamadan at a temperature somewhere between ten and fifteen above zero in deep snow, and arrived late that night at Qazvin, a small city that had once been the capital of Iran, only a hundred and fifty miles to the northeast on the Tehran road.

Finding the principal hotel filled with Shi'a pilgrims on their way to Kerbala in Iraq, we spent the night in a second-rate Armenian inn run by a man who had relatives in Boston. He served us the most delicious shish kebabs I had eaten up to that time, which was before I experienced the culinary perfection of Hagop's in Aleppo. During the ride from Hamadan we had got stuck several times in the snow, and each time been rescued by kindly villagers or Armenian truck-drivers, some of whom joined

us at the inn. In the morning a bucket of water standing
a few inches away from the oil stove in our room was
frozen solid. There was no chance of the snow's melting,
and the more the trucks rutted the roads, the worse it
would be for jeep travel in any direction.

It was lucky for us that our inn was also a truck-
serai, its courtyard filled with heavily loaded giants
whose drivers were busy draining and refilling their radi-
ators. After consultation with them we soon solved our
transportation problem. Leaving the trailer and most of
its contents with the innkeeper to be picked up later,
we drove the jeep onto a truck that I had rented for the
purpose. It was simple enough. On the outskirts of Qazvin the truck drove down a gully, backed up to the bank,
lowered its tailboard, and on we drove. Sitting in a vehicle on a vehicle, we left for the shore, bundled up in all
our clothing and sleeping-bags against the zero weather,
like tourists in the top deck of a transcontinental train.
From our frigid perch we could look down on everyone
we passed, and no one thought to look up high enough
to detect our presence.

This luxurious ride lasted for thirty-six kilometers.
During the first part our truck plowed through drifts
both on and off the road, cutting across cultivated fields
wherever the highway was blocked. There was much
traffic crawling in both directions: buses, trucks, and one
jeep containing the port commander of Bandar Pahlevi,
the Caspian lake port of Resht. We met him just above
the snow line coming toward us and wished him luck.
Perhaps he got through on his own wheels; perhaps he
followed our example.

During this part of the ride we had a curious feeling
of being on the moon; the ground seemed smooth and
curved, with mountaintops below our eye level, and flat
streamers of pearl-colored cloud floating motionlessly

even lower down, below the peaks. Then almost before
we knew it we had left our convex world and entered a
concave one. Our truck rolled down a gorge, the road
following the bed of the Sefid Rud, which, flushed with
melted snow, roared and raged and spumed after the
age-old fashion of mountain streams, polishing for the
millionth time the shiny gray rocks in the upper borders
of its bed, which it reached only at this time of year.
Spray blew onto both our upper and lower vehicles, where
it instantly froze on cold glass and metal.

Before long our breath ceased to come out in steamy
puffs, and the snow lay behind us, except for dirty patches
breaking the linear symmetry of rice stubble in soggy
terraces. All of us now began looking for a place to un-
load the jeep, for the going was good. The road, built by
the Russians during World War II, was broad and beautifully engineered, but it had never been paved and the
surface was rough in spots. We could find no such place
as the gully at Qazvin, but finally backed the jeep off
the truck onto the porch of a country inn at a small village, where our unprecedented maneuver caused much
commotion.

We were soon on our way under our own power, from
an altitude of seven thousand feet to our destination below sea level. We might have driven through a paper
curtain into another continent, so different were the landscape, the architecture, and the clothing of the people.
The steep sides of the gorge were now covered with forests in which beech trees predominated, mingled with
some holly, box, and other broadleaf evergreens and a
few hemlocks. Where the slope permitted, the land was
terraced, principally for rice, and for all kinds of familiar
fruit trees such as apples, pears, plums, and cherries. In
one place we also saw a grove of olive trees. The style
of houses had changed abruptly from the rectangular,

flat-roofed, clay-walled upland form to wooden construction with steep roofs covered with thatch or metal. The men who inhabited these houses wore round black caps, heavy homespun jackets of the wool of black sheep, white woolen trousers bound at the ankles, and rawhide buskins with the hair left on the skin. Ruddy cheeks, thin noses, blue or gray eyes. Where were we now? We might have been back in the Balkans, in Albania, Yugoslavia, or even farther west, in the Tirol. All this we saw where the valley of the Sefid Rud was wide enough for cultivation. In some of the narrower places we passed dozens of caves, their open mouths inviting us darkly, like lonely women looking out of windows.

Unfortunately, the trip through the snow had been slow. We had seen the last of it only after four in the afternoon. The sun sets early on January 4 at 37° north latitude, which is also the latitude of Richmond and San Francisco. Soon we found ourselves riding through utter darkness in a cold, pelting rain. At ten we reached the outskirts of Resht, where we filled out forms in a police post; then we searched the nearly deserted streets of the watery city for a place to sleep, until finally we came to rest at the home of the Reverend John Browning, whose saint-like wife took us in though her husband was very ill. Badly as I felt about disturbing this household late at night, I hope that I made up for it later by bringing a little cheer and chatter from the outside world to the bedside of a brilliant, witty, and self-sacrificing man. He has since passed away.

During the two days spent in Resht we met the dozen or so other members of the American and British colonies and called on the principal government officials, who gave us credentials for a trip along the whole Caspian shore to Gurgan, as well as much excellent advice about where to look for caves. On Friday, January 7, we set out on a ride through a landscape that might have been created by Lord Dunsany. The first half of the day's journey took us through the so-called jungle, the heavily forested narrow plain sandwiched between the Elburz Mountains and the sea. The day was warm and sunny. We rode past patches of melting snow, shiny white mountain peaks, forested slopes, huge trees fantastically pruned for firewood, a dense undergrowth of shiny green privet, and rushing streams spaced about a mile apart and spilling into the sea enough potential water power to rival the rivers of Connecticut.

Then we came upon houses in the forest with high, thatched gables like those of New Guinea, granaries on piles, long-horned zebu bulls carrying loads on their backs, little men trotting with shoulder poles laden with vegetables, strange-looking shepherds in heavy brown suits, their heads crowned with huge caps of brown fleece, like the bearskins of Buckingham Palace guards; some also wore square felt cloaks with wings at the shoulders. We passed duck-hunters carrying flintlocks, other men busily hollowing poplar logs with adzes to make dugout canoes, while still others were nailing planks together to make a kind of punt. Then came terraced rice paddies as tidy and geometrical as if painted by Grant Wood, a series of tea plantations, and a span of thirty miles of sheer forest, wild and unspoiled. Then orange groves appeared, and we bought from a roadside stand a giant lemon of a kind called *badrang*, eight inches long and six wide, mostly rind, and used for candying. Next we passed a huge tea plantation laid out by a prime minister who had passed a law that at least half the tea drunk in Iran, which is a lot of tea, must be grown there.

For the second half of our journey the road ran beside the sea. Here the shore was one long sandy beach covered with pebbles. Not a ship was in sight, though we saw three boats rowed by fishermen. At the mouth of every river were fish weirs, built to trap the caviar-bearing sturgeon that spawns in these streams. At Ramsar we came upon a royal pavilion and a large, luxurious hotel, where we lunched on squab, steak, and white wine. This establishment was filled with rich Tehranis who had fled the cold of the capital, and who were playing cards in the lobby completely indifferent to the fresh, wine-like air outside and the incredibly beautiful scenery, in which mountains and seashore, snow, ripe oranges on the limb, and palm trees were combined. Our journey ended at dusk when we came to a modern hotel at Challus, equipped with real baths, flush toilets, and hot water.

The hotels of Ramsar and Challus and the silk factory in the latter city, along with other modern buildings and paved streets, stood out in sharp contrast to the Neolithic appearance of the Gilaki country (the Resht region), particularly to anyone who had studied European prehistory. The houses looked very much like the reconstructions of the pile dwellings unearthed in lake bottoms in Switzerland, which dated back to 3000 B.C. The clothing, the dugout canoes, and the whole feeling of the wood-working reminded me of ancient objects recovered from the peat bogs of Denmark, in which organic materials had been preserved intact. This impression was heightened when I saw a team of oxen dragging a wooden sled over the road. This was a so-called summer sled, for use without snow, of a kind found in the tomb of Queen Shubaid at Ur of the Chaldees, dated at about 3000 B.C., and also used by the ancient Egyptians. Today it can still be seen in such remote places as the valleys of the Caucasus, the Basque country, and the island of Madeira, where its use has survived from ancient times.

Physically the people looked more European than any others I had seen in the Middle East, both in their facial features and in their clothing. Many of them particularly resembled northern Albanians, a people whom I had studied in 1929 and 1930, and I soon saw one reason why. In Albania mothers strap their babies into cradles, which they carry about with them as they go to market or to their work. Although the infants' heads are not bound, the immobilization of their shoulders forces them to lie on the backs of their heads. As a result, the heads are flattened in infancy, and this condition is retained throughout life. As soon as I saw a pair of young mothers carrying their babies in such cradles, I knew why these people looked so much like Albanians.

We had come to the Caspian shore in search of Paleolithic cave sites, but it was now apparent that this rich and pleasant strip of country had something else to offer both the prehistorian and the student of living cultures. Here was a surviving culture closely linked to the origins of European civilization, lived in by people of European physical type, in the one part of Iran which has had enough rainfall to preserve the forest on which its technological aspects depended. The same environmental factors that had made the Caspian shore both the industrial heart of modern Iran and its scenic showplace, had also let this culture live and retain its essential features.

There could be no question of this culture having come from Europe. The whole trend of history had gone in the opposite direction. Many writers had claimed that Europeans had derived their Neolithic culture from the arid lands of Palestine, Syria, and Iraq, from the so-called Fertile Crescent of arable land surrounding the eastern, western, and northern flanks of the Arabian desert. I had always found it hard to believe this because the European Neolithic was a forest culture in which wood-working played a prominent part, and in which agriculture was carried on in small patches of soil cleared by ax and fire, rather than on semi-arid open plains.

A half-century ago an expedition led by Raphael Pumpelly had excavated two ancient mounds at Anau in Merv Oasis in what is now Soviet territory, and in them they had found early Neolithic remains. Without precise means of dating such as we now possess, they had calculated the age of their earliest levels on the basis of pottery styles, proportions of domestic to wild animals in the bone collections, and similar means, arriving at a date of about 6000 B.C. Since their time, as more sites were excavated to the south of the mountains bordering the Turkestan plain, archæologists had formed a habit of debunking Pumpelly's dates and reducing them by two or three thousand years. As I saw the situation on the Caspian shore, however, it occurred to me that Pumpelly might, after all, have been right. The Neolithic culture of the Old World might have begun north of the mountains, rather than south of them. At least, a search for Neolithic remains could be added to our original objectives.

These thoughts darted about through the connective fibers of my brain as I guided our jeep over the muddy road eastward out of Challus. I asked myself why it had taken me so long to think of these things. The Caspian shore was not an unexplored tributary of the Amazon; it was a well-traveled modern place, written up in such accessible periodicals as the *National Geographic*. I had read about it, people had told me about it, and I had been taught about Pumpelly and Anau twenty-five years previously, but nothing that I had read or heard conveyed to me the connected body of information which stared me in the face as I saw, heard, smelled, and totally sensed the essential quality of this place. Now that the idea had penetrated my thick skull I concentrated on seeing all that I could without wrecking the vehicle.

As we rode eastward the coastal plain widened. In the eastern part of Gilan, the province of which Resht is the capital, it is quite narrow, in some places no more than a mile wide, but in Mazandaran, the central Caspian province, it reaches a breadth of twenty-five miles along the banks of the Talar River. Here are situated the cities of Babul Sar, Babul, Shahi, and Sari. While Babul Sar is a seaside resort, the others are centers of industry, with textiles in the lead. In this region most of the forest had been felled and replaced by fields in which cash crops such as tobacco, cotton, and green vegetables for export, particularly romaine, were growing. Furthermore, most of the houses were now of brick or clay, with roofs of tile.

Beyond these cities the plain narrowed again to about twelve miles, and the highway was joined by a railroad track that ran from Tehran through the Firuz Kuh Pass and down the Talar valley to Shahi and Sari, and then along the landward side of Asterabad Bay to Bandar Shah, a seaport built by the late Reza Shah and now rendered too shallow for ships of useful draft because the level of the Caspian, for some unknown reason, has been sinking. At Surak, the next town beyond Sari, both the road and the track left the higher ground and ran along the rich black-soil plain at an altitude of thirty to fifty feet below sea level. At this level an old beach could be plainly seen alongside the road.

To the left, the Caspian side, we could see numerous earthen mounds studding the plain. Some of them were irregular or elongated, covering several acres; these were apparently the sites of ancient villages, possibly Neolithic. Others were small, trim, and cupcake-shaped, in certain cases crowned by a modern building, usually an *imamzadeh*, or saint's tomb. These circular mounds may have been erected as tombs for metal-age nomadic chiefs who wintered in this warm and fruitful place. In 1931 Dr. Frederick Wulsin had excavated one of them, Turang Tepe, for the University Museum. Out of similar mounds Russian archæologists had extracted, during the nineteenth century, great treasures in golden jewelry, the ornaments of Scythian kings.

This was manifestly a meeting-ground between the European-like culture of Gilan and the nomadic culture of central Asia. Of the trucks that we met on the road a good proportion were driven by somewhat slant-eyed men wearing wheel-shaped black karakul hats. These were Turkomans of the Yamut tribe, settled just east of Gurgan. The commonest type of horse-drawn vehicle which we passed was a high two-wheeled cart of pure Mongolian type, and the men who drove them were physically Mongols. They were, I discovered later, Kirghiz who had fled across the Soviet border and who were now employed by the Persian road department to haul gravel.

To the right the road skirted a low range of hills, the foothills of the Kuh-i-Shah-Jehan, a spur of the Elburz Mountains, behind which lies a fertile sheltered valley known as the Hazer Jerif, or "Thousand Fields." In it Mazandarani farmers and foresters, similar to those of Gilan, live in peace, away from the dust and noise of motor roads. These foothills form a kind of mesa which splinters out toward the shore in fingers, and the slopes of these fingers are covered with scrub forest. All these slopes are alike, steep and broken into a series of steps. Although unable to see the underlying rock, I knew that this formation indicated limestone.

By this time the sun was setting blood-red into the Caspian, casting long shadows in front of the jeep. Soon that stage of twilight arrived in which headlights are almost useless. It was then that we came to a stretch where the road ran close to the edge of one of these projections, at a place where the vegetation had been removed and the rock exposed, as I later learned, by blasting for building-material. I stopped the jeep and got out. In the dying light, with the help of a pocket flash, we found a number of small caves. Although not one was large enough to be excavated, still there could be others. This might well be the place we had been looking for—warm in winter, watered by a neighboring stream, lying between the fish-filled Caspian and the game-filled forest of the Kuh-i-Shah-Jehan and the Hazer Jerif, with swamps and lakes near by, the resting-grounds of ducks and geese on their annual pilgrimage to Siberia. This could be our site, but there could also be others farther along. On the rest of our ride to Gurgan, where we slept, it was too dark for further search.

It was October 7, one day short of eight months, before we passed that way again, and this time we were looking for the site. As previously related, we had spent the summer of 1949 digging Bisitun, Tamtama, and Khunik, and searching for sites elsewhere on the plateau. Because the Caspian shore is uncomfortably hot and humid in summer, we had saved this part of our work until fall. On October 7 we got a late start from Challus, and once more failed to reach the place that I had earmarked for possible caves before dark. The reason for our delay was a curious one. At Challus, in the morning, I sent Paul Schumacher, who had joined our expedition after Bisitun, to gas up the jeeps at the pumps. We now had two jeeps, the blue one in which I had traveled the previous winter and had used at Bisitun, and a yellow one which belonged to the University of Chicago and which George Cameron had used during his inscription-copying session at Bisitun.

As Paul drove the blue jeep to the pump in the town's

only filling-station, a soldier drove another jeep directly in front of him, squeezing in to be served first, nearly wrecking both jeeps in the process. Being an old soldier, Paul took down the number of the soldier's jeep and asked him for his serial number. The soldier refused to give it. As soon as his vehicle had been filled he dashed off. It was shortly after this that I came out to the front of the hotel, where the sounds of a ruckus were to be heard. About a dozen people had collected there, including the hotel proprietor, our inspector Mr. Samadie, an interpreter named Ahmad Tabrizi whom I had brought from Tehran, a number of Europeans, and several army officers.

The center of the stage, however, was held by Paul, just returned from the filling-station. Paul was being tongue-lashed by a Persian lieutenant colonel, who was trembling with rage. It turned out that a party of United Nations observers and various newspapermen, headed by a gigantic Swedish officer in plain clothes, was being escorted by the lieutenant colonel to Gurgan to investigate the latest of a series of border incidents along the Russian frontier. It was the lieutenant colonel's official jeep that the soldier had been sent to gas up. The soldier had reported Paul's interest in his serial number, and this, combined with the idea that anyone else should be served ahead of him, had touched off this Olympian wrath.

"Vous avez insulté un soldat!" screamed the lieutenant colonel, stamping on the ground.

Unfortunately, I then intervened, in my best Moroccan French, asking: *"Mon colonel, qu'est-ce que c'est cette affaire des insultes?"*

After he had let out another stream, I said: *"Bien sur, mon colonel, ce n'est pas sérieux? Vous blaguez, mon colonel?"*

"Blackie, *alors, je suis un* blackie, *ha?*" bellowed the officer.

I soon realized my mistake. The somewhat slangy French verb *blaguer,* which means to kid, was not a standard item in the refined schoolboy French that Persians of the upper class are taught in Tehran. The lieutenant colonel thought I had called him a *blackie*—that is, a Negro. The current Russian radio propaganda, to which this officer had apparently been listening, had been dwelling at this time on the plight of the Negro in America. According to the Persian-language broadcast from Moscow, the Negroes were still enslaved and every self-respecting white American capitalist lynched at least one of them each morning before breakfast. As I looked at the colonel I saw that his skin was a little darker than the Persian average, and his hair somewhat curly, though he was in no sense Negroid.

If he had been angry at Paul, he was six times as angry at me, and I watched him to see if he would have a stroke. When it came to the point where I would soon have to choose between swords and pistols, the tall Swede, who had been hard at work smothering a smile, finally broke into the lieutenant colonel's semantic wave length and pleaded with him until he had persuaded him to desist.

At length they departed, driving slowly and halting frequently alongside the road, while we followed them at a distance. I would have passed their procession early in the day had not Mr. Samadie, who had recently been in a serious jeep accident, persuaded me not to, for fear that the soldier driving the lieutenant colonel's jeep would smash into us and wreck us all as we went by. That is why, for the second time, we did not arrive at the region of the caves until it was too dark to look

around. We kept on ten miles farther to the town of
Behshahr, where we took rooms for the night in the Hotel
Tabaristan.

This delay wasted three more days. The hotel proprietor and other local people told me that there were no
caves of any size at the place I had earmarked, but that
some splendid ones were to be found to the east, along
the road to Gurgan. These we failed to locate. On the
11th we were back in the hotel, where I was forced to
spend another day, this time in bed. Driving over the
Challus Pass the day before the Colonel Blackie incident,
I had chilled my left shoulder in a snowstorm, and now
I could not move my left arm.

Thanks to the local doctor, the next morning I was
up early and back at the wheel, convinced that the caves
we sought were ten miles west of Behshahr, and so they
were. For the first time we passed the limestone outcrop
in full daylight, and then rode past a stream, arriving at
some tobacco fields.

A village stood two hundred yards inland from the
road; facing the village and the stream, on the sunny
side of the outcrop, was a beautiful arched sea cave.
Both jeeps were immediately abandoned as everyone
raced across the fields to the cave. There we surprised
two families of dervishes from Sultanabad who had come
to the shore for the winter season. One man was cough-
ing with tuberculosis, one woman was nursing a baby,
two dogs began barking at us, and two donkeys, tethered
in the back of the chamber, were craning their necks to
see what all the rumpus was about. Although the dervishes had spread some straw about, and scuffed the surface making hearths, they had not damaged the deposit.
There it stood, a perfect floor, fifteen feet above the
stream bed outside. Before the sun had set, the dervishes
had been lured out—donkeys, dogs, babies, and all—to

take up more sumptuous residence in a tobacco shed at the expedition's expense. The villagers would not take them into their houses for fear of fleas.

That day I hired five men from the village, which was named Turujan. As the dervishes went back and forth removing their few possessions, my new employees cleaned off the floor, down to the top of the more permanent part of the usual layer of sheep manure, the bedded compost in which individual pellets have lost their identity and been merged into a springy carpet. The cave was named Ghar-i-Kamarband, or "Belt Cave"—why I did not discover. In references to this cave which have since appeared in archæological literature the shorter, translated version has been used.

During the delay caused by the gradual evacuation of the dervishes we spent our time studying the position and dimensions of the cave. Facing northwest, it overlooks a broad expanse of the Caspian plain. Immediately to the west of it runs a small, intermittent stream, which has built a raised fan of gravel out onto the plain. The point where the road crosses this fan, about two hundred yards north of the cave, is the most elevated part of the roadbed in that neighborhood. The level of the cave floor above the Caspian Sea turned out to be sixteen meters, or about fifty-three feet.

Between the road and the sea we could see two ancient mounds of the village type, the bases of which could hardly have been more than twenty feet above present sea level. As these mounds might well have been begun as early as 3000 B.C. (a conservative estimate), it was clear that the floor of Belt Cave had been above sea level since that date at the latest. The ancient beach lying to the north of the road represented an earlier highwater level of unknown age. At the time of its formation Belt Cave would still have been dry. Although I knew little about the history of the Caspian sea levels, it was obvious that only the highest of them could have disturbed this site.

The walls of the cave are built of white limestone laid in nearly horizontal strata of varying widths; we obtained successive readings of 70, 30, 20, and 50 centimeters (28, 12, 8, and 20 inches) for the thicknesses of the strata

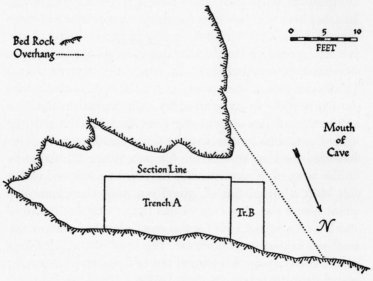

Belt Cave: plan.

within easy reach. This limestone contains well-preserved marine fossils which look like the chambered nautilus, but which actually proved to be an ammonite of the genus *Perisphinctes,* the index fossil of the Jurassic period. Limestone of this age is valuable building-material because of its fine grain and straight line of cleavage. Fifteen years previously the contractors building a cotton factory at Behshahr had dynamited the face of this

whole cliff. Although they had removed part of the overhang in front of the cave, they had not damaged it seri-
ously and had not disturbed its floor at all.

Between the cleavage lines of the limestone strata we
saw flattened disks and biscuit-like sheets of amber-colored flint, most of which had been broken off as if by
people seeking tool material. With this supply close at
hand, so close that it could be obtained without going
out of doors, early men could have left implements in the
floor beneath us. The cave chamber was thirty feet long
by twelve wide by seventeen high—architecturally an impressive room, which I was eager to make more impressive by lowering its floor.

Besides cleaning up after the dervishes that afternoon,
our five men hacked a road in through the brush from the
highway, and the next morning we drove the two jeeps
up to the mouth of the cave. Now we had nine men. The
foreman was Parviz, a lithe, blondish man with bad eyes
but indefatigable energy and a natural power of leader-
ship. Next to him in the hierarchy came Abbas, a former
employee of Dr. Erich Schmidt at the classic Neolithic
and Bronze Age site of Tepe Hissar in Dameghan on the
Iranian plateau, and therefore an experienced archæologist. Abbas claimed to be village carpenter of Turujan,
and in this capacity he put handles in our picks and
shovels and built frames for our sieves, which we carried
rolled up on top of the trailer loads when moving about;
later he constructed ladders as the trench grew deep
enough to need them. Akbar, Parviz's brother-in-law, was
a huge, pink-faced, blue-eyed, snub-nosed ox of a man,
powerful, loyal, and simple. Three of the others were *sayyids,* or descendants of the Prophet, on which account
they wore blue turbans.[1] Although the other men always

---

[1] The green cloth, which they were entitled to wear, was said to be
too expensive for them.

spoke to them deferentially, using their titles in the most informal conversations, the sayyids were as poor as the rest, or poorer, and did the same work.

I laid out a trench on the sunny side of the cave, long enough to give us working-room and wide enough to permit passage along the southern side to the rear. In

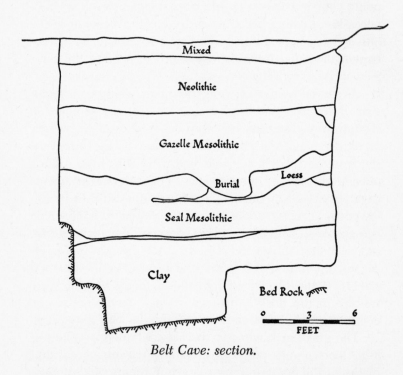

Belt Cave: section.

the back we would have a good face; in front we would leave the best material, which is always found in that position, until we had finished Trench A and thoroughly familiarized ourselves with the stratigraphy. Parviz and Abbas immediately demonstrated their skill as excavators. They are the two best pick men I have ever employed except for Murat, another Schmidt alumnus, who joined us a few days later, and who was their peer. As they were good companions as well as intelligent men, I tried to take advantage of their presence by talking with them. This they made easy for me by using simple words and speaking slowly. I was now beginning to understand rudimentary Persian, a very different thing from carrying on polite conversations with educated people, which was unnecessary anyhow because most educated Persians speak either French or English. It was with the class in between, the minor officials, that I really needed the services of an interpreter.

As these men took out the first twenty-centimeter strip, I realized that we faced a complicated problem in stratigraphy, because this thin layer showed a variety of earths from one end of the trench to the other. At the front end, black soil that had drifted in from a bank outside encroached some twenty centimeters over our excavating-area. Moving backward, we found this to be followed by a meter, more or less, of yellowish soil, which turned out to be a *lens*—a thin, discontinuous layer of intrusive material. Beyond this we came upon a fine, grayish soil, composed of a mixture of brown earth and wood ash. In it the blackened remains of many hearths were visible. In the back half of the trench, some five to ten centimeters of peated manure still overlay this gray earth.

The gray earth was pay dirt. It contained a wealth of flint, bone, and pottery, including twenty-three flint blades of the finest and most delicate quality, and of Neolithic type. The potsherds seemed to represent various periods from what could have been Neolithic to modern wares, and the bones were those of domestic animals, particularly sheep, goats, and cattle. By the time we had finished this first level, which in most caves is unproductive, we were aware of our good fortune. We had found Neolithic remains right at the very top of the deposit, and would not have to remove meters of more recent materials such as Islamic, Achæmenian (First Persian Empire), or Bronze Age, to get at the implements, pottery, and animal bones that we needed for the solution of an important problem. That was: what part had the Caspian shore region, in which so many early European-type cultural survivals were to be seen, played in the origin of the Neolithic of Europe?

In the second twenty-centimeter strip, now all in gray earth, we found two Neolithic *celts*—small, jewel-like axheads of polished stone, one of them of jade. Not a single trace of metal appeared here or at any point farther down. In the second level a few sherds of more modern type still appeared in the front of the trench, but in level #3 all of them were of a single type, a coarse, thick, mealy, ill-fired ware, made by hand without the potter's wheel, rubbed with ocher, and burnished with pebbles. It did not resemble in any way the usual Neolithic pottery of the Fertile Crescent and Iranian plateau, which is thinner and harder and either solid gray or painted with geometric or animal designs. Mr. Samadie, who had studied pottery in the Tehran museum and on other digs, had never seen anything like it. It appeared to be a true early Neolithic ware.

We excavated five levels on that first day. The next day was Friday, normally a day of rest, but the men wanted to work and we had no objection. In level #6 it was soon apparent that we were moving below the pottery horizon; only eight pieces came out, and those in the very front, where the strata sloped downward and outward a little under the dune. In #7 Parviz found near the front of the trench a perfect limestone globe, about six inches in diameter, pierced with a hole drilled conically from both ends, presumably with a stone drill, and lipped at both openings. A second pierced stone of inferior workmanship soon followed it. Much speculation ensued as to the purpose of these objects. Some said they were loom weights, others net-sinkers, still others anchors for boats. I did not find the answer until many months later, when Dr. Robert Braidwood, of Chicago, who had done much digging in Neolithic sites in Iraq, visited the University Museum. They were, he said, digging-stick weights. When one was hafted on a pointed stick, a foot or eighteen inches above its tip, an early root-digger or farmer could press the point into the soil by treading with his bare foot on the globe's upper surface. We examined the globes with this in view, and, sure enough, the surfaces were polished from such use.

Level #8 was entirely without pottery, and we found no more in this trench except one spook in level #10. A *spook* is a potsherd or other specimen that is found in an apparently undisturbed level in which it does not rightfully belong. Its presence can be explained in several ways: by the action of roots—and roots went down four meters in this cave; by falling down the hole of a prehistoric burrowing animal, such as a mole vole or small rodent; or by slipping down along the rock wall of the side of the cave, where air spaces sometimes occur, probably owing to water action. At any rate, the presence of spooks is interpreted statistically. One or two may be forgiven for being in the wrong place, but if too many turn up, then either they indicate a disturbance, as where someone has dug a grave through several levels, or else they really belong in the place in which they are found and must be interpreted as trade objects or part of the local toolkit of that period.

In levels #8 through #10 we not only lost the pottery, but also most of the fine flint blades, particularly the ones that show polish on the cutting edge when turned about in the light. This polish is an overlay of silica granules deposited on the surfaces of flint blades used as reaping-knives. Silica is found in the stems of all grasses, including cereals. Millions of years before, the teeth of the horse family had become adapted to the rapid wear that a diet of silica-bearing stalks imposes, and in Neolithic times the flint blades that early farmers used for cutting these stalks were polished in the process. Whenever these polished blades turn up, one may be reasonably sure that the people who made them were farmers. Food-gatherers who collect wild-grass seeds have no time for reaping and threshing, for wild grasses spill or eject their seeds the moment they are ripe, and people must be present with sticks and baskets to gather as many as they can at that moment. Cultivated grains hold their seeds in the glumes or pods until they have been reaped. In levels #8 to #10 we had no certain indication of agriculture, but plenty of evidence of animal husbandry, for the bones of the four standard barnyard animals, ox, pig, sheep, and goat, continued down, with ox and pig at the top and only sheep and goat at the bottom.

In two days we had found in Trench A an early Neolithic industry that had pottery, following, without soil change or interruption, a still earlier Neolithic that lacked it. Whereas the ceramic Neolithic people had reaped grain and herded cows and pigs as well as sheep and goats, the pre-ceramic Neolithic people, who can have been their immediate ancestors, had been simple herdsmen, pasturing only sheep and goats. This was the first time to my knowledge that this cultural transition had been recorded. I did not believe then, however, nor do I now, that these folk were the inventors of pottery, for what they used, though crude by later standards, was too stylized and too good to have been invented on the spot at the time this deposit was laid down. The technique must have evolved elsewhere. Neither can I believe

that these people were the Old World's first farmers or
first herdsmen. Finding a "first" is an exciting thing, and
it is easy to delude oneself into believing that one has
done so. On a simple statistical basis, if one site and
one site only is dug in an area thousands of miles in extent in which some trait or combination of traits may
have been discovered, it is too much to ask of the law of
chance that the first archæologist who digs a hole in the
ground should locate the exact site where the invention
took place.

The floor of level #10 was also the bottom of the
Neolithic soil. Although the color of the earth did not
perceptibly change, its consistency did, as Parviz immediately noticed. Whereas the upper soil had been soft and
loose, and had contained a few large stones, this new
earth was harder to excavate, owing to the presence of
many small chips of limestone. In this respect it resembled the Paleolithic-bearing soil of equal depth at Bisitun. There was also a change in the soil's contents. The
flint yield of the previous afternoon had been mostly
scrap pieces, but now we began to remove implements
that belonged to a new and distinct industry. Exotic
honey-colored flint pieces came out in the forms of retouched blades, backed blades, and snub-nosed scrapers
of the type used for cleaning the flesh from the insides
of skins. This was not a Neolithic assemblage at all. It
had to be either Paleolithic or Mesolithic—at the time I
could not tell which. Later we found that it was Mesolithic, which is a term covering the various industries
used by hunters between the end of the last glaciation
and the beginning of agriculture, roughly from 9000 to
5400 B.C., the dates varying in different places.

Most conspicuous among the animal remains were the
horn cores of an animal then unknown to us. Later on,
in America and in England, it took me much time and

consultation with zoologists to identify it. It turned out to be *Gazella subgutturosa Güldenstädt*, the goitered gazelle, described as follows by Mochi and Carter: "General color pale sandy with indistinct side band. In winter the color paler and the coat much thicker. Female either lacking or with poorly developed horns. Derives its name from the swelling of the larynx in the male during the breeding season. From northwest Iran and Asia Minor east to the southern Gobi Desert." [2]

Although no goitered gazelles graze, as far as I know, in the neighborhood of Belt Cave today, the presence of their bones in level #11 and below does not indicate a climate radically different from that of today. It might have been a little colder then than now, and it was certainly drier, for the nearest border of the grasslands on which the goitered gazelle could have grazed is now at least forty miles to the northeast of the cave, on the Turkoman steppe east of the Caspian Sea. It is conceivable but hardly likely that the principal food animal of these Mesolithic people would have been carried over forty miles for every feast. The border of the steppe must have been much closer at that time than it is now.

All the horn cores were abraded at the tips, indicating some use. As the cores were shaped exactly like the picks that Parviz and Murat were using, and as the Persian word for pick, *kolang*, is a cognate of the old Indo-European root for *horn*, as in Latin *cornus*, I concocted the theory, which I can neither substantiate nor disprove, that these people used the horns of the goitered gazelle for digging, just as Bushmen and their women in the Kalahari dig with oryx horns today. The Mesolithic people ate the rest of the animal, as was evident from the great quantity of their bones.

[2] Ugo Mochi, and T. Donald Carter: *Hoofed Mammals of the World* (New York: Charles Scribner's Sons; 1953), plate XVII. Quoted by permission.

In the Neolithic levels the bones of sheep and goats bore a high ratio of immature specimens: twenty-five per cent in the pre-ceramic and fifty per cent in the

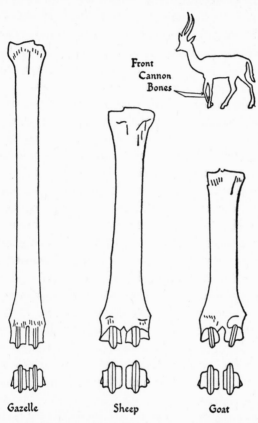

Front Cannon Bones

Gazelle   Sheep   Goat

Sheep, goats and gazelles: the front cannon bone. How to tell the sheep from the goats is an old archæological problem. Although most bones of these two species are closely similar, the metacarpal, or front cannon bone, is always longer in proportion to its breadth in sheep than in goats, both wild and domestic. The front cannon bone of the gazelle is easy to distinguish from both by its long, slender gracefulness. (One-half actual size.)

ceramic. This meant that the animals were domesticated, because hunters rarely kill the young. The gazelle bones were nearly all those of mature animals. Furthermore, the domestic animal bones were white, fatty-feeling, soft, and light, whereas the gazelle bones and those of the other wild animals were brown, hard, glossy, and heavy.

The reason is that wild animals always arrive at a state of natural balance with the other elements in their environment, over periods of thousands of years, through nature's version of the trial-and-error process. By a rigid process of natural selection, the plants that wild animals eat have acquired their present sizes, shapes, leaf colors, and ways of flowering. They have thus become perfectly suited to the local variations in temperature, rainfall, wind velocity, and other meteorological features, to the local soil composition, and to the activities of animal species, including the bees that fertilize them and the hoofed creatures that derive sustenance from their stems and leaves. During the same period the local animals have been just as rigidly selected by nature as the plants, and adapted especially to the nutritional qualities of their plant foods. The relationship between animals and plants is like that of an eland with the bird that sits on his back, removing insect pests. Wild grasses are never overgrazed and the wild animals that live on them are sleek and in good flesh, as anyone who has visited an African game park knows.

When man began breeding animals he started with a poor lot anyhow, the ones that he was able to catch and tame. As time went on he began selecting them for qualities which had nothing to do with the balance of nature, but which suited his own needs. Thus, he bred animals that yielded exaggerated quantities of wool, milk, and fat; animals with thick fleeces, pendulous udders, and chubby bodies, caricatures of their wild cousins that still browsed the forests or leaped from crag to crag in the mountains. These unnatural beasts had developed nutritional requirements different from those of their free-ranging ancestors, and as they were also confined by herdsmen to smaller pastures than before, they upset the delicate balance between plants and animals which had hitherto obtained. Overgrazing led to soil-erosion, and in some parts of the world with less rainfall than the Caspian shore, man-made deserts came into being.

Meanwhile, the meat that the herdsmen ate came to differ from the hunter's fare. Animals living under domestication tend to have slender bones, tender flesh, and much fat. The body type that they have achieved under human interference with natural laws is exactly the one that in man himself is most prone to degenerative diseases, particularly, coronary attacks, linked to high cholesterol content, and in this sense the Neolithic farmers ate food inferior to that of hunters. This change in body type was reflected in the special appearance and texture of the bones of Neolithic animals, which I soon learned to distinguish from the Mesolithic bones of wild animals by a simple sense of touch, as anyone could. The Neolithic bones feel greasy and light, and the Mesolithic ones polished and heavy.

The Mesolithic hunters apparently used bows and arrows. We knew this because we found many beautiful small backed blades of flint which could be gummed to the tips of arrows as barbs. Along with their staple diet of goitered-gazelle meat these hunters ate quantities of swan, goose, bustard, and grouse, and hunted with the domestic dog. The possession of the bow and the dog gave Mesolithic man a great advantage over his Paleolithic predecessors, who had to hunt in groups in which some men would do the dog's work of driving and flushing game toward the killers. The hunter's task was made immeasurably easier by substituting the bow for the spear. A bow, in fact, is superior to a muzzle-loading gun in that it can be loaded much more quickly and makes no noise to frighten the game. The men who lived in Belt Cave during the period represented by levels #11–#21 must have been prosperous and well-fed by any standards.

Of these levels only #11–#17 were pure representatives of this culture. In #17 some yellow soil, as fine as wind-blown loess but laced with coarser grains,[3] began to appear in the front of the trench, and contained almost no artifacts. At the back of the trench in level #19 another soil appeared, this time of powdered ash, which indicated the presence of many fires. These fires had consumed the wood completely, leaving almost no trace of charcoal.

We had now excavated downward not only to a soil change, but also to a change of floor slope, indicating, like the transition from level #10 to level #11, a time gap between periods of occupation. Before I had a chance to find out much about this new cultural horizon we had a little trouble with our new interpreter, Ahmad Tabrizi. He was an Azerbaijani Turk who was deeply interested in all sorts of religious and social problems, and an avid reader of scientific literature. He had temporarily left his post as editor of a Persian-language magazine in Tehran to come with us in order to learn something about our work, and I was glad to have him along because he spoke all the languages and dialects that we were likely to encounter.

Unlike most white-collar men in that part of the world, Ahmad was happy to work with his hands, and was full of energy as well. Now and then when the men on the shovels and buckets were flagging he would take a

[3] Whether or not this was wind-blown, as it seems, is still controversial.

shovel or a bucket in hand and set them an example of speed and energy which I sometimes had to curb. On this occasion he started a round of what Paul and I came to call his Stakhanovism in level #17, which was finished, including the sifting, in the record time of forty-five minutes. I did not mind this as much as I might have because he did not particularly influence the pick men. Also, we were at the bottom of a culture level, where, as is usually true, nothing of any consequence was coming up. But he was still steaming ahead and champing at the bit in level #19, despite all my warnings to him to slow down.

While this level was being removed, one of the pick men uncovered the distal end of a human humerus in the long face of the trench. I ordered all work stopped, and leaped down into the trench to take out the burial myself with trowel, dental pick, and brush. Before I could get there and just as I shouted "Stop!" Ahmad reacted with lightning rapidity by grabbing a shovel from a workman and thrusting it through the soil over the protruding armbone as if spearing a hippopotamus before it could get away. To my horror, I saw that he had cut through a human skull.

Why he had done this I could not imagine, nor did I give the problem much thought. Lisa and I went to work immediately, but I then discovered that my left arm, which had been chilled on the Challus Pass and had been growing worse during the last few days, completely refused to function. I could not open or close my fingers. A shot of vitamin B-12 would have fixed it, but we had no B-12. Lisa and Abbas took the skeleton out as I watched anxiously, keeping Ahmad at bay. He gazed at the scene of disinterment with rapt attention, for the sight of human remains seemed to fascinate him.

What we had found was a burial of a twelve-year-old girl, her bones painted red with ocher. After the flesh had been stripped from or had rotted off her skeleton, she had been interred with her head nestled, upside down, between her thighs. My chief concern at the time was to make sure that all of the pieces of the skull, broken by Ahmad's hysterical action, were recovered. Luckily, most of them were, and it has since been reconstructed by Dr. J. Lawrence Angel of the Jefferson Medical School in Philadelphia. The damage done was not irreparable. The young lady was of European type, with strong traces of Neanderthaloid features in the region of the mouth, features that can probably be duplicated here and there among living Europeans. A number of other human bones and teeth were found, but nothing that could be restored with equal success. These people left scraps of their fellows lying around in the floor on which they worked, and casually built fires over them in some cases. I would not go so far as to say, as has been said of some Mesolithic remains in parts of Europe, that they were cannibals, only that they were careless and callous in the disposal of human remains.

The skeleton came out of a pocket of intrusive soil, a grave dug by the goitered-gazelle hunters through the older floor of the gray-earth people. These were also hunters, specializing in the capture of two species: the red deer, which still roams the forest on the slopes behind the cave, and the Caspian seal, which still swims in waters within sight of its door. Quite clearly, theirs was a different climate from that of the goitered-gazelle people. The forest and the sea were both near, the grassy plain farther away. Fishbones of the Caspian rudd, a still existing species, were also plentiful, indicating a preoccupation with the sea, which might have been lapping on the stones of the beach a few hundred yards away.

As in the cultural levels above, the flintwork was primarily a blade technique, but the implements differed in type. A multitude of end-of-blade scrapers attested a preoccupation with the preparation of skins, and many beauifully retouched geometric blades, perfect for arrow barbs, gave evidence of the use of the bow. Furthermore, the men in this level made chisels or primitive axheads out of staghorn by grinding the antler and polishing it. This anticipated the technique used in manufacturing stone axes several millennia later.

They also had dogs. One bone that we found was a complete muzzle, with front teeth and nasal aperture. It was that of a very big dog. After I got home I carried it about in my pocket, seeking to find its match among the living. One day during the Christmas holidays of 1949–50 while I was walking down Everett Street in Cambridge, Massachusetts, on my way from the Peabody Museum to my brother's house, I saw a gigantic St. Bernard standing in the snow on someone's lawn. I called the dog, and he came to me in friendly enough fashion. First I shook his hand, then I opened his mouth and quickly placed my muzzle from Belt Cave alongside his teeth. It was a perfect duplicate.

At the bottom of level #25 we came on sterile clay underlying the ashy soil of the seal-hunters' deposit, and as the floor of this cultural layer sloped toward the rear, we did not expose its course along the entire trench until we had finished level #27. At the back of the trench we struck the rear wall of the cave, which at this depth was sloping forward, a fair indication that we were approaching the rocky floor. We were now four meters, or about thirteen feet, down, and the sterile clay held little interest for the workmen, who were eager to get the job over with. Furthermore, they were tired. Although I paid them enough so that they could eat well, many of them had large families and needed the extra food money for their children's clothing. Actually, they were not accustomed to so much regular, sustained effort. Fatigue sets in among the workmen at every dig at about this time, and the men of Turujan were better than most.

Parviz was more tired than the others, not only because of his responsibility as foreman, but also because he was acting as night watchman, sleeping in the cave with an antiquated muzzle-loader to ward off robbers and tigers. Of the two the tigers were the more to be feared, for they had a habit of dragging their victims into caves to consume them at leisure. We had found the bones of a wild boar in a small cave around the corner, left there by a tiger not long before, and while we were digging, a tiger ate a cow a mile or two up the stream.

That day another workman, whether accidentally or otherwise I do not know, dropped an empty bucket on Parviz's head, which triggered him into a short frenzy. After staggering about for a few seconds he threw a pick at the offender, luckily missing him. Under the circumstances I did not fire Parviz for this, as he promised me not to do it again, and he kept his word. Whatever we were to find in the immediate future, it was clear that the season's work was approaching its end. That we were in a deposit of natural clay was just as well.

Much of this clay was *varved;* that is to say, it had been laid down in thin, regular layers. Geologists in Scandinavia and in some of the northern states of America, such as Minnesota, have found thick deposits of these varves in ancient lake beds, where they were laid down in early post-glacial times. During the flood time, streams brought muddy water into lakes, and in winter this water froze. Each year as ice formed, the particles of mud that had been held in solution settled on the lake bottom, creating one of these layers of clay. The same thing must have happened in Belt Cave at a time when either the sea level had been high, or else a natural dike of some sort had turned the local stream into a small lake. It also must have been cold enough in winter to cause this precipitation. In Scandinavia geologists count the varves in each deposit, and as no two layers are of exactly the same thickness, they can plot individual sequences. As the thickness of a varve is an index of annual rainfall, sequences from different sites in the same rainfall area can be pieced together, and a long chronology of hundreds of years established.

In Belt Cave we had nothing to tie this sequence to, and could only note the presence of varves for future investigation. For our immediate purpose they indicated that the floor of the cave had been under water, which explained why no one had lived in it at that time. However, the entire bed of clay was not varved. In places this neatly layered deposit had been scoured out and refilled with coarse, unstratified clay. Its presence could only mean that after the water level had fallen, the stream outside the cave had become swollen in the spring rains and, deflected by a bar of gravel outside, had whirled into the cave, biting into the varved deposit, churning the layers into a homogenous solution, and dropping them again into the cavities from which they had been so forcibly removed. Only after this series of violent water actions had ended did the cave become habitable. If anyone had lived in it earlier, his remains had been washed out long ago.

On October 19 we struck bottom at 5.60 meters. This is about eighteen and a half feet, three times my height, which is as deep as a trench eight feet wide can afford to be, even when one wall is cave rock and the other firm and dry. Had we been forced to go deeper, I would have been obliged to take away the south face.

During the last two days of the excavation we moved forward into Trench B, an extension of Trench A reaching

2.50 meters toward the mouth. We removed only the Neolithic material from this trench, finding more polished-
stone axheads, perforated stone globes, and pottery.
When we came upon human arm and leg bones, which
indicated the presence of burials, I filled the earth back
in again, for we were in no position to excavate skeletons
that year. The men were too tired and so were we. It was
growing cold, and the passes to Tehran would soon be
blocked with snow. Another season's work had by now become obligatory.

On October 21 some of the men guided me on a
search for other caves. First we visited the cave of
Rustem Qala'a, in back of the village of the same name.
There we found that dynamiters had ruined a magnificent
open-faced grotto situated more than one hundred feet
above the plain. As the plain was equally high over the
Caspian, this cave may have been above the later and
feebler flood levels of the last glacial period, but as the
deposit had been washed out, this question had lost its
importance.

Then they led me on a mad scramble up the face of
a cliff that I had trouble negotiating to another cave called
Ghar Kollareh, the word *kollareh* having no meaning
they knew. There had been no blasting here, and the cave
was within commuting distance of the hotel in Behshahr,
but it was a very rough climb to make four times a day.
Still, the floor and talus were strewn with recognizable
flints and pottery of the same kind we had found at Belt
Cave. On the way back in the jeep, while I was debating
the possibility of excavating this at a future date, Parviz
and Murat asked me why I did not dig the big cave next
to Belt.

"What big cave?" I asked.

"We will show you," they said.

And so they did. Not more than a hundred yards

from Belt, on the way to the road, they showed me a hole in the rock just under the lip of the mesa. This rock had been opened up by the same blasting operation that had truncated the front of Belt Cave. As I looked inside with my flashlight, pigeons and bats brushed against me on their way out. Here was an immense cave, higher up than Belt and thus perhaps higher than the Caspian high water level, with a floor at least fifty feet long and over fifteen feet wide. The men poked a small tree trunk down the hole and helped me inside. There I landed ankle deep in a soft cushion of bat dung which threw off a rank, pungent smell. I have smelled that exact odor only once elsewhere—in a kitchen in New Caledonia where flying foxes were hanging before being cooked.

Moving in the direction of the cliff face, I found the original entrance. It was completely plugged up with earth. This cave had been sealed, up to the moment of blasting, for a very long time. I asked the men its name, and they told me Otu or Hotu, a word for which I could get no satisfactory meaning. Once they told me that it meant *flatiron* because a stone in it looked like a flatiron, which was more or less true. Another said that if one shouted *Ho!* in it the echo of his voice would say *Tu!* This was, of course, utter nonsense, and was probably invented on the spot. In any case, I decided then and there that, come hell or high water, I would return and dig it.

And so I did in February 1951. This time Mr. Samadie was again along, as was Ahmad Tabrizi, but Paul Schumacher had been replaced by two people, Louis Dupree, then a graduate student at Harvard, and his wife, Anne. They had just finished digging a cave of their own in Afghanistan. We still had the now aging yellow jeep, but had been obliged to surrender the blue one to other museum workers in Iraq. In its place I had purchased an old World War II ambulance in Tehran, or, rather, a vehicle composed of parts of several such ambulances through the normal Middle Eastern process of vehicular cannibalization. This ark was driven by Yed Allah, a youthful driver whom I had recruited in Tehran.

This group did not, however, all arrive at once. Mr. Samadie came by train, while Lisa, Ahmad, Yed Allah, and I crossed the Firuz Kuh Pass in the ambulance, leaving the yellow jeep for the Duprees, who had been held up on their way out of Afghanistan. The four of us who had ridden in the ambulance were not in the best of condition when we arrived at the Hotel Tabaristan on the evening of February 25, for we had spent two nights sleeping in our vehicle, trapped in the snow. Nevertheless, on the 26th I located Parviz, and on the 28th we were back at work.

We arrived at 8:45 a.m., three quarters of an hour later than our old starting-time, to find that the men, impatient at our tardiness, had begun work, clearing rockfall from the area in front of Belt Cave. The 1949 pit was nearly clean, so solid were the faces that we had left. I went back into Hotu and tried to estimate the position of the mouth. "It is a three-hundred-sheep cave," said Abbas, who had crawled down with me. The measure of any cave in that part of the world is the number of sheep it can hold in the winter. Three hundred is a big one, comparable to the Hazer Merd ("one thousand men") cave in Kurdish Iraq, which Dorothy Garrod had dug. Not knowing the formula for converting sheep space into man space, I cannot compare them accurately, but, having been in both, I can say that hers was the larger. This one, however, had one advantage over any other cave I had ever been in. For a very long time its mouth had been completely sealed.

Parviz divided the men into two gangs, one to remove

the disturbed soil and rock from the dune in front of Belt Cave which had been formed by blasting, and the other to bore into the hillside to find the entrance to Hotu. Neither was a delicate operation. Meanwhile, the other men busied themselves hacking down wild pomegranate trees to enlarge the driveway to the caves and make a parking-space. It is illegal to fell trees in that part of the country, and that is why the villagers climb the beeches and other large trees, with their razor-sharp billhooks, to lop off limbs for firewood. Now that we were there to protect them from the landlord's wrath they could lay in a season's supply of firewood under the guise of road-making.

The spirits of the workmen were at a high pitch. Spring was in the air, and though fog blanketed the hills every morning, the pomegranate buds were bursting. As the scarlet petals unfolded and the sweet scent of their pollen perfumed the air, the buzzing of bees could be heard. Craving vitamins after the gloomy winter, the workmen began munching great heads of romaine which their wives and children brought to the cave, and two of the largest and most muscular of the men, Sayed Ali Akbar and Gulbagu, put on an impromptu wrestling exhibition in front of Belt Cave. To my mind this is a dangerous sport, for the trick in Persian wrestling is to grab the other fellow under the crotch and throw him, but they did not seem to hurt each other. In this scene I was aware of an essential difference between the personality and culture patterns of Persians and Arabs. Persians love sports and do not mind tossing one another around. Most Arabs whom I have known will touch one another only in love or war. I could not imagine seeing two Arabs wrestling in this manner.

Late Saturday afternoon we reached the undisturbed Neolithic deposit in our new trench, Trench C, in front of Belt Cave. On Sunday morning we unearthed a male Neolithic skeleton, the limb bones of which we had seen and covered up again in 1949. Ahmad, whose preoccupation with the dead I had forgotten over an interval of two busy years, joined Parviz in the task of cleaning this skeleton *in situ*, removing the earth from each bone with brushes while leaving everything in place. They did a splendid job. That night the yellow jeep rolled in, bearing Louis and Anne Dupree and Mr. Samadie, who had gone back to Tehran by train to meet them. On Monday the squad opening Hotu broke through the hillside into the cave, and on Tuesday, at Belt Cave, we found the skeletons of a young mother, holding a baby in her arms, and of a small boy, lying next to the male skeleton we had found on Sunday.

Ahmad now had an original idea; he told it to all of us, and it seemed to me that Mr. Samadie approved it, though he may have been simply being polite. Ahmad wanted to remove this family group of skeletons as a single unit, to be exhibited in the Tehran Museum. While this would make it difficult for me to study them, I still could do it, and with some misgivings I agreed. Therefore Ahmad became very busy digging around the skeletons and under them in order to pour a plaster base to hold them inside a wooden frame that had not yet been made.

That night when we got back to the hotel we learned that Prime Minister Ali Razmara had just been shot by an assassin. As might be expected, this news caused some disturbance in the town, an industrial center, where the news coming in over Radio Tehran was broadcast over a public loud-speaker. It also disturbed us because the victim had been a man of great competence and integrity in whom our government had placed much confidence. Not knowing what to expect next, our white-collar Persian staff was much more upset than we were.

When we arrived at the cave the next morning, however, we found that the workmen had not even heard of the assassination, and when told about it they showed little concern. They were village people whose lives were bounded by the confines of their tobacco fields. They were much more concerned by their own local rivalries, and by the endless conflict between themselves and the people of the town, Behshahr. We were soon to see a perfect case history of the latter type of trouble. Ahmad, who had been working on the skeletons all of the previous day, had failed to remove them, and I had covered them with sacking and straw. Now they were bare once more while he was fussing over them, and they were in danger of being stepped on by the men carrying buckets of earth from the trench to the sieves. Then Ahmad departed in the ambulance with Yed Allah, leaving them unprotected. Later he returned with Baba, a carpenter whose shop was across the street from the hotel in Behshahr. From the back of the ambulance Baba produced several pieces of polished wood, with which he proceeded to build a coffin-shaped frame to place around the skeletons.

At this point Abbas appeared, trembling quietly in an effort at self-control, and said: "Why do you bring a city carpenter out here to the village? I am the carpenter here."

All the men in Belt Cave heard this and the word soon passed to the Hotu people. A hush fell over all. Had they begun clamoring and shouting, I would have considered this just another episode in a sequence of normal disturbances with which it was my business to cope—part of the day's work and no more. But this silence was ominous; it was loud.

Samadie told me very quietly in French, which Ahmad could not understand: "It was just such a little thing that caused the Imbrie incident."

He was referring to the murder of an American consular officer in Tehran by a mob of religious demonstrators in 1924, an incident that both sides have chosen to play down. That so scrupulously correct and polite a man as Mr. Samadie could bring himself to mention such an embarrassing thing to me was proof enough that events had begun to take a serious turn.

Once tension has arisen in a small, closely integrated group like this over some ill-understood situation, it takes very little in the way of an issue to bring it to the breaking-point. Although I did not know it then, Abbas was no carpenter at all, but a barber. He was only pretending to be a carpenter so that I would let him do the carpentry work needed about the caves, and all the men knew this. Nevertheless, they supported his pretense because he was one of them. The tension had arisen for two reasons. First of all, the skeletons had remained exposed much longer than it was considered fitting for the remains of dead people to be seen, and they had been looked at not only by the men of Turujan, to whom they rightly belonged, but by many townspeople who had come out on bicycles and in horse-drawn cabs to gaze at them indecently. On top of this, a town-dwelling carpenter, who had no business in their territory, had been hired to make a coffin, and finally the townees were planning to take away the precious skeletons in their fancy fabrication.

Parviz, who had been quarreling with Abbas over some minor point of prestige within the last few hours, was now standing grimly at his side, ready to decapitate Baba with a billhook. Akbar, Parviz's strong but simple brother-in-law, was watching his leader for a signal.

To claim that I thought out all of these things in a fraction of a minute would be a gross lie; I merely felt them and acted. I packed Baba and his mortuary masterpiece back into the ambulance with orders to Yed Allah

Belt Cave, 1951 season. Scene from inside the cave, showing the area from which the Neolithic skeletons had been removed.

PLATE IX

Belt Cave, as we first saw it, inhabited

PLATE X

Belt and Hotu caves, seen from the Caspian shore road. Belt Cave is at the lower right of the limestone cliff, and Hotu higher up, in the center of the picture. Above the mouth of Hotu is the crack in the roof through which the cave was discovered.

PLATE XI

Earth-removal, Hotu. Passing bucketfuls of earth up the ladder from Trench D, on its way to the sieves. Buzurg (lower left) watching.

PLATE XII

The mouth of Hotu at the end of the dig.

Coon (left), Dupree, Murat, Samadie, and Abbas looking into Trench D in Hotu.

PLATE XIII

Hotu, Trench D. Excavating the Mesolithic skeletons. The men at the upper
left are removing earth left in a precarious position by the cave-in. The string
below them marks the bottom line of Trenches A and B. Iron Age, painted-
pottery, and Neolithic strata may be seen in the face of the cut behind the
ladders. The center of activity is Trench D, at the bottom, where the Mesolithic skeletons are being excavated. The total depth is 40 feet.

PLATE XIV

Abbas working on the skulls of the two female skeletons (#2 and #3) found in Trench D at Hotu. At the upper right are the shin-bones of Skeleton #2; their position shows how she tumbled backward when she was killed by stones falling from the cave's roof.

PLATE XV

Panorama from the top of the cliff above Hotu. On the work [...]
can be seen Mrs. Coon seated at a folding table sorting bo[...]
Mrs. Dupree washing flints at the basin; a workman carry[...]
earth; and three dervishes at their screens. Beyond are the [...]

PLATE XVI

ition ambulance, a pomegranate orchard, tobacco fields, and
he upper left, the tobacco sheds in which the Belt Cave der-
es had been relocated.

The orphan Sayed Hashim and Mrs. Dupree washing flints.

Screening earth from Hotu. The man seated at the screen is the dervish Medod.

PLATE XVII

Hotu. A visiting boy in Mazandarani costume, with homespun suit, buskins, and the traditional billhook.

The Caspian shore. Wooden-framed, thatch-roofed houses in Gilan. These structures are reminiscent of Neolithic houses excavated in Germany and Switzerland.

PLATE XVIII

Loading our broken trailer onto a truck, near Ghorband in Afghanistan.

PLATE XIX

Afghanistan. View of Shibar Pass, over the Hindu Kush Mountains.

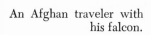

An Afghan traveler with his falcon.

PLATE XX

Kara Kamar Rock Shelter seen from the plain.
Note the expedition jeep in the right foreground.

PLATE XXI

ara Kamar. The rock
elter before excavation.
rench A is staked out on
e usual goat-dung floor.

Kara Kamar near the end of excavation. Trench D, which was mostly rock, is at
the left; then comes Trench C, the deepest part of the cave, in which most of the
implements were found. Trench B is the narrow excavation at the right.

PLATE XXII

Syrian desert. A pile of burned animal bones at Kherbet Umbashi, dated about 3000 B.C. The animals may have been sacrificed to a volcanic fissure to stop the flow of lava.

PLATE XXIII

to drive them home and under no circumstances to bring them back again. I then told Ahmad in front of the men that from now on skeletons were outside his province. After drifting about awhile with a silly smile he suddenly became interested in zoology, taking one of our best specimen boxes over to Hotu, where he caught a bat; for the rest of the day he crooned over his fluttering captive.

As soon as Baba had gone I removed the skeletons, as I should have done after photographing them. They were the remains of pathetic, half-grown youngsters apparently fated to produce a family while immature themselves, and somehow or other all had died at once and been buried without the usual Neolithic grave furniture. As their bones were very thin and fragile they came out in a poor state, despite all our efforts to preserve them. Our usual method is to coat them with a vinylite plastic called Alvar, dissolved in acetone, or with Ambroid thinned with acetone, and then to soak them in an Alvar solution later. These bones were so wet that neither mixture would penetrate. Uncoated bones would crumble as soon as they dried, and the coated ones would crumble under the plastic shell. Despite these difficulties it was possible to see what racial type these people were. They were small, delicate people of an old northern and central European stock, with small faces and straight or snub noses, closely resembling the so-called Danubians who brought Neolithic culture to Europe from the east about 3000 B.C.

That afternoon, under the skeletons, I found a beautiful four-pronged bone fork and a piece of obsidian traded in from some distant point, perhaps from the much-exploited deposits near Lake Van in Armenia. We also found, directly under the skeletons, caches of two kinds of seed; one, closely resembling sesame, is as yet unidentified, and the other was a so-called pigweed that still grows wild on the sides of the rock. The question arose as to whether these seeds had been carried by the woman in a bag, or whether they were hidden there in more recent times by ants. Abbas held the latter opinion, saying that once when he was digging a well in Russian Turkestan he encountered such seeds four meters down. Although I have shown these seeds to several botanists, I still do not know the answer.

After the removal of the skeletons the work in Belt Cave proceeded systematically, and we found exactly the same stratigraphic sequence as before. Our 1951 excavation amplified the collections made in 1949, and let us carry our face forward to the mouth of the cave. In 1949 we had removed the underlying clay to the floor level in only a small part of the trench, and I had left with some question in my mind that there might be a culture-bearing stratum lower down and forward. There was not. The Seal Mesolithic was our lowest cultural level.

Also, at the time of the 1949 expedition we had known nothing about the Carbon-14 method [4] of determining the dates of deposits, and had therefore failed to collect charcoal for this purpose. Luckily, we had sent all of the animal bones home. As many of these had been charred, we were able to send valid samples of this material to Dr. Willard F. Libby, the discoverer of the Carbon-14 method, at his atomic-research laboratory in Chicago. He published a series of four dates, ranging from 6054 B.C. to 8160 B.C.; one of these—6135 B.C. ± 1500 years—was the oldest date for the Neolithic then known. Unfortunately, we could not depend on these dates because of the general inconsistency of the sequence; also, the dates for the

---

[4] All living matter contains radioactive carbon. After the death of any organism, this element gradually becomes inert, at a constant rate. Dr. Libby's method, which has since undergone some changes, is to measure the degree to which this change in atomic structure has progressed. At present our limit of determination is about 43,000 years. See Willard F. Libby: *Radiocarbon Dating* (Chicago, 1952).

principal cultural levels failed to indicate the considerable passage of time which the stratigraphy required. One of our primary purposes in re-excavating Belt Cave in 1951 was to obtain fresh samples, of charcoal rather than of bone, since charcoal is believed to be a more reliable material.

During the second season we therefore collected large charcoal samples from hearths at all levels, placing them in glass bottles purchased at the pharmacy next door to the hotel. These bottles bore the label MALE FERN EX- TRACT, a substance whose use baffled me until I discovered later, after much inquiry and many evasive answers, that it was worm medicine. Abbas and Murat in particular became ardent charcoal-collectors, picking it up in tongs and placing it in tinfoil to avoid contaminating it, and the sieve men saved every fleck of it. We got much more than we needed, so that several runs could be made, in more than one laboratory, if warranted. Later it was analyzed in our own laboratory in Philadelphia, where the following dates were obtained: [5]

CERAMIC NEOLITHIC

(*3 samples*)   7,280 ± 260 B.P.[6] =   5330 B.C.

PRE-CERAMIC NEOLITHIC

(*2 samples*)   7,790 ± 330 B.P. =   5840 B.C.

GAZELLE MESOLITHIC

(*2 samples*)   8,570 ± 380 B.P. =   6620 B.C.

INTERVENING YELLOW SOIL

(*1 sample*)   12,275 ± 825 B.P. = 10,325 B.C.

SEAL MESOLITHIC

(*2 samples*)   11,480 ± 550 B.P. =   9530 B.C.

These dates made sense both internally and when compared to those from other Neolithic and Mesolithic

[5] Elizabeth Ralph: "University of Pennsylvania Radiocarbon Dates I," *Science*, Vol. 121, pp. 149–151 (February 4, 1955).

[6] B.P. means *Before Present,* the present being assumed to be A.D. 1950.

sites. Our ceramic Neolithic was still the oldest so far found in the world, though how long it will hold that title is questionable. Its date, more than two millennia older than the oldest Neolithic of Europe, clearly indicates that the Caspian shore may indeed have been a Neolithic breeding-ground from which some of our ancestors moved westward into northern Europe. At least, it may have been part of such a breeding-ground. The date for the pre-ceramic Neolithic falls earlier, as it should. Although the probable errors of the two samples overlap by some eighty years, the order of dates is that of the stratigraphy, and there can be no question that herding was earlier in this area than pottery, and probably also earlier than agriculture. The Gazelle Mesolithic is separated from the Neolithic by a clean gap in time, as the condition and slope of the floor between them indicated, and the Seal Mesolithic is also similarly isolated. The only inconsistency in this series is the date of the yellow soil found in the front of the cave between the two Mesolithic layers. Although older than that of the Seal Mesolithic, it falls inside the latter's range of probability.

If I might venture to interpret this series, I would say that the varved clay at the bottom of Belt Cave, which is as old as 10,000 B.C., was laid down at a time when the high level of the Caspian, possibly as high as eighty-five feet above its present surface, had fallen off and the mouth of Belt Cave was open to the air.[7] By 9500 B.C. the cave had become dry enough for habitation, and it was occupied by hunters who mainly killed seals, on or near the shore, and who had already acquired two of the principal assets of Mesolithic life: the bow and arrow, and the dog. For some reason they departed, and after about

[7] H. L. Movius, Jr.: "Late Pleistocene (4th Glacial) Conditions and Paleolithic Settlement in Soviet Central Asia and Western Siberia," *Actes du IV Congrès International du Quaternaire* (Rome, 1953), pp. 3–20.

three thousand years other Mesolithic hunters, pursuers of the goitered gazelle, occupied the cave, which was now situated in a much drier countryside, one in which the grassland of the Turkoman steppe came within a few miles of their door. Then again the cave was abandoned and herdsmen moved in, eventually to become farmers.

The excavations at Belt Cave had told us nothing about Neanderthal man, or about the origins and dispersions of the Upper Paleolithic blade-making peoples of Europe, but they had given us a basis of knowledge of the Mesolithic and Neolithic peoples and cultures of the region. As we were working in an archæologically unknown area, as far as these periods were concerned, any information that might be found was useful, and this cave seemed to have turned up more than its share. It was still possible that caves containing both Neanderthal and Upper Paleolithic materials would yet be found along the Caspian shore. For all that we knew at the time, Hotu, which was higher up on the hillside than Belt, might be such a cave, and we turned to it with high hopes as soon as we had reached bottom in the first site.

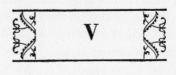

V

HOTU

On March 14, 1951, in the afternoon, we began work in Hotu, which had finally been opened up so that a man of average stature could walk in and out without bending more than his neck to avoid the overhang of the roof. The soil removed from the face of the cliff had been spread into a broad fan, on the edge of which our three sieves were set. My first job was to lay out Trench A for excavation. Placing myself, as usual, in the position of an early man seeking the best spot to live in, I studied the orientation of the sheltered area. The axis of the cliff face ran northeast by southwest, with the bulk of the mountain blocking the morning sun. The axis of the cave, however, ran north and south, at an angle of forty-five degrees to that of the cliff face, so that the north wall was thirty meters long (about a hundred feet) and the south wall only twenty meters (about sixty-seven feet). During the afternoon the sunlight entered without obstruction across the tobacco fields of Turujan and the Caspian plain, and visibility was better on the north side than on the south, as was also the case in Belt.

Any sensible early man would spend his cave-dwelling time on the north side, about twenty meters from the back of the cave, ten in from the southern edge of the entrance.

There he could find the best compromise between light and shelter. As this was the likeliest spot in the cave, I avoided it when I laid out Trench A. It would be better to dig it after the soil sequence had been established in a less felicitous area where, in the uncertainty of the first

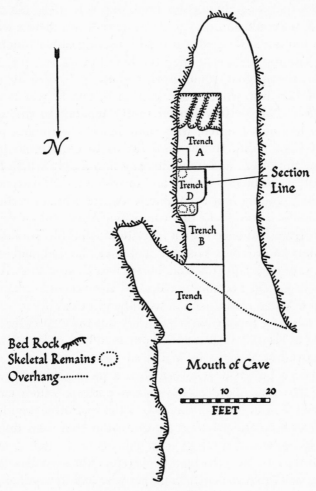

Hotu Cave: plan.

round, we could do less harm to the contents and to the stratigraphy. We divided the floor longitudinally into a northern strip three and a half meters wide and a southern one a meter narrower; then we laid out a rectangular area in the northern strip, five meters from the back wall and extending an equal distance forward. In this sixteen-and-a-quarter-square-meter area, one side of which was rock, we could afford to go down at least five meters without too much danger of a fall-in, barring an earthquake.

The top level contained the bones of ox, ass, pig, red deer, sheep, goat, some birds, and the paw of a dog, as well as a few wheel-made potsherds, one of which was glazed. This pottery looked pretty modern to me, and also to Louis Dupree, who knew much more about pottery than I did. It was hard for us to understand how modern pottery had found its way into a cave which had been so thoroughly sealed, and in which a thick carpet of loose bat dung had been able to collect without disturbance. As if to add to this confusion, Abbas now told us that Hotu had once been a favorite hideout for Turkoman raiders and robbers. His maternal uncle, he said, had once crept in here and stolen six horses and three camels from the brigands. For this brave deed the Khajarite shah of that day had rewarded him with the gift of a rifle.

Leading three camels stealthily out through that solid plug of stratified earth which our men had so laboriously removed seemed to us a feat so miraculous that it deserved a far greater reward than a mere rifle. Although we found no more of the glazed pottery, which could have fallen in through the hole in the roof after the blasting, or through whatever aperture the bats used during their nocturnal comings and goings, Louis and I continued to be puzzled by Abbas's story for several weeks. One day the Azerbaijani engineer who had dynamited the cliff visited us. He told us, among other things, that not all the stone had been used in building the cotton factory at Behshahr; the stone in front of Hotu, being flawless, had been taken to Tehran on flatcars and used in erecting the Parliament building. When I asked him about Abbas's story of his uncle and the Turkomans, he stated firmly that Hotu had not been open at all before the dynamiting, and that he had never seen it until he had blown off the small piece on top which had led to its discovery; the cave of the Turkomans was another cave very near by which he had buried by his blasting. By the time we had received this information we had ceased to worry about Abbas's story because we had reached pay dirt, the contents of which made his tale completely impossible.

It occurs to me now that Abbas volunteered this story at that time in a rush of energy which followed an emotional incident. He had come to me after the lunch hour to tender his resignation, on the grounds that one of the workmen, Buzurg, had grossly insulted him. What Buzurg had said was deemed too shocking to be repeated within wave length of my delicate ears, and I still do not know what it was. Buzurg, whose name means *Big*, really was the biggest man on our team. Tall, heavy-boned, and lumbering, he was also ragged and bleary-eyed, for he was our one opium addict. His children, unlike the other men's offspring, were ragged too because of the drain on the family budget caused by opium-buying.

Rather than lose Abbas, I toyed with the idea of firing Buzurg, whose services were not indispensable, but Parviz intervened.

"You must keep him on," he said. "With all his faults Buzurg is a useful man. The time will come when you will see what I mean."

Having faith in Parviz's judgment as well as in his power of prediction, I followed his advice, and we all pleaded with Abbas to remain. It was after he had agreed to swallow his pride, and needed some way to restore his self-esteem, that Abbas had decided to tell me the story of his uncle's prowess.

The fact that his uncle had been a Turujanite was a useful bit of information, because it helped to clarify the principal rift between the workmen, which was coming out into the open now that the greater town-versus-village crisis had been resolved with the departure of Baba and his coffin. This rift, which I had not seen before, lay between the one-hundred-per-cent Turujanites and the men like Abbas who had come from Dameghan, a large town on the Iranian plateau. At some time in the past a number of Turujanite families had migrated to Dameghan in search of work, and had set up a Turujan colony there. Now and then a Dameghan-born colonist would come back to the home village, like a Boston-born Irishman returning to his parents' native homestead in County Cork or Galway along with his fancy American ways. Hence the basis of the disturbance.

What made the crisis worse was the fact that the Dameghan men had worked for Erich Schmidt, than whom no better trainer of pick men ever excavated a mound, and the two of them, Abbas and Murat, were constantly in the trench with me, conversing with the boss on intimate terms, while poor chaps like Buzurg were employed lifting buckets to the lip of the trench or carrying them to sieves. It did not help matters any when on the next day I hired another Schmidt alumnus named Sayed Nosrallah, whose expert services I badly needed.

We were excavating Iron Age material, with which these men were familiar. Not only did they know how to take out big pieces of broken pottery, consisting largely of legs, tubes, and long spouts, without breaking them any more than they already were, but they could tell Louis and me what levels the potsherds corresponded to in

Tepe Hissar, the large mound near Dameghan which Schmidt had excavated for Chicago and Pennsylvania during the 1930's. Having these three men on our team was really a great advantage. Although we were a little disappointed to find such late stuff in the top levels, we felt that if we were to run into whole pots, gold ornaments, or other very delicate objects that turn up in metal-age deposits, we had the staff to clean and remove them professionally.

By the night of the 16th we had gone down eight levels and were still in the Iron Age. On the 17th, which was St. Patrick's Day, the sun rose big, sharp-edged, and bright red in a fine clear sky over the smoky shoulder of the mountain east of town, with a row of stubby, mutilated beech trees silhouetted along the crest. Most mornings in Behshahr the sky is white with billowing clouds, or gray with mist, and the air below sea level is humid and heavy, in great contrast to the thin, dry atmosphere of the plateau. Today, instead of feeling fat and smelling wet, the air was light and dry.

Exhilarated by this atmospheric change, we all found something green to wear, and drove out to the cave in high spirits, to be greeted by a solemn gang of workmen. Parviz announced that he was going to call a strike at noon because the new man from Dameghan, Sayed Nosrallah, had called him dirty names. Gulbagu, one of the locals, had been about to kill Sayed Nosrallah when Parviz ordered him to spare the miscreant's life. Then Sayed Nosrallah had told them that he had a pistol and a permit to carry it, and he would shoot them all. Unless I fired Sayed Nosrallah, Parviz said, the work would stop at noon.

I called Sayed Nosrallah up and asked for his side of the story, which, of course, was that he had minded his own business and had said nothing at all. As these two accounts were beyond reconciliation and as witnesses for both sides were at hand, I saw no point in protracting an endless argument. Louis and I simply told Parviz that Sayed Nosrallah would stay on, and that if the men quit we would go down to another village, Georgi-mehal ("The Georgian Place"), to dig Ghar Kollareh with a team of Dameghanis plus the Georgi-mehal men.

As Parviz well knew, this was no idle threat. We were in Iron Age stuff, which was far less interesting than the Neolithic and Mesolithic material unearthed in Belt Cave. As far as either he or we knew, we might reach the bottom without finding anything earlier. Ghar Kollareh was a fine site with flint implements actually visible on its fan, and the Georgi-mehal men, descendants of immigrants from the Caucasus, were a tough and strong bunch. Their headman had been loitering around Belt and Hotu, trying to urge me to leave Turujan and go to his place to work.

Parviz gave in, but that was not the end of the Dameghan-Turujan conflict. The first round had been Abbas versus Buzurg, the second Sayed Nosrallah versus Parviz. Now Murat, the third of the Dameghanis, fell under fire. Parviz demanded as a final concession that I relieve Murat of his overtime job as assistant night watchman and appoint a local, Sayed Ali Akbar, in his place.

From the beginning we had arranged to have two men on night duty in the cave, first in Belt and now in Hotu. Their job was to protect the tools and sieves, ladders, and other equipment such as tripods, tapes, and surveyor's rods which we did not want to carry back and forth every day. One man was not enough because of the tigers. Parviz was the number-one night watchman and Murat number-two. Theoretically, each would remain alone for an hour or two at a time while the other went home to eat supper or visit with his wife, but, according to Parviz, Murat was an arrant coward. Whenever Parviz wanted to leave the cave, Murat insisted on having a boy stay with him. This craven behavior of Murat's so disgusted Parviz that he could no longer stomach the thought of sleeping in the same cave with him, and must have as his companion a stalwart young braggart named Sayed Ali Akbar, who could help him kill tigers; Murat, confronted by a tiger, would simply collapse with fear and be eaten.

Murat's story was that Sayed Ali Akbar had been prowling around the cave every time Parviz left it, making scratching noises and growling like a tiger to frighten him. Murat had a cataract on one eye and was a head shorter than Sayed Ali Akbar, but he quietly stated that he could lick Sayed Ali Akbar even if both his, Murat's, feet were cut off at the ankles, and he seemed ready to try to prove it. Murat had been a katkhoda, or landlord's agent, in a village outside Dameghan, and that is a job which requires courage, discipline, and resourcefulness. While I could not fancy Murat, or any other of my men in that cave, in the role of coward, I had talked Parviz out of one ultimatum and could not make him back down on a second one immediately afterward.

We smoothed down Murat's ruffled feelings and went back to work. Sayed Ali Akbar, who was on the bucket line, broke into song, and regaled us all with lengthy lyrics in Mazandarani dialect which must have contained obscenity, local references, or both, because the men laughed at them and I could get no one to translate them even into ordinary Persian.

What interested me most about the Dameghan-Turujan quarrel was that each of the men involved, when considered singly, was a rational, reasonable, and, as far as I knew, honorable person. I doubted if any one of them understood the issue over which they were quarreling, or realized when he was lying. I was greatly relieved that the immediate surface issues had been talked out and that the struggle had entered a quiet phase, because we could not afford any more trouble between the men at this point. While all this had been going on we had excavated Trench A down to a depth of 2.60 meters, or nearly nine feet, which is too deep for grudges, quarreling, or even fooling. In Belt Cave, Parviz had received an empty bucket on the head, and this incident must not be repeated.

With this in mind I tried to spend as much time as I could in the trench, but there were many interruptions that took me out of it. Anne Dupree sat at the mouth of the cave just to the left of the sifting-platforms, washing potsherds in a large basin. As the water was very cold it had to be heated over a fire, for she had her hands in it all day long. Louis and I had to take turns coming up to see what she was getting. Lisa sat at a folding table near by, sorting bones; I had to go over these to separate the identifiable pieces, which were to be kept, from the scraps, to be thrown away after being counted. Then Lisa had to wrap and bag the bones, and the pottery had to be bagged as well. Despite this hectic work at the mouth of the cave, Louis and I managed it so that one of us was always in the pit.

On the 19th, while I was outside counting bones, a fourteen-year-old boy appeared, wearing clean but threadbare clothing. He had walked all the way from Dameghan, where he had heard about our dig. He was a poor orphan, named Sayed Hashim, and he was hungry. I fed him and put him to work at the basin washing sherds with Anne. As she spoke Persian well, she soon found him to be a most polite and intelligent boy, and the two of them became fast friends. My fear that the arrival of a new, though junior, Dameghani might cause another crisis was soon allayed because the sieve men adopted Sayed Hashim as one of their own.

These sieve men all belonged to a dervish order called Khak-sar, or "Dirt-head," referring to their practice of throwing dirt on their heads in their ceremonies as a gesture of self-abasement before the Deity. They received their pay in common, entrusting it to one of their number whom they had selected as treasurer. With part of the first week's installment he had bought a wrist watch, and the others called to him at frequent intervals to ask him the time. Sayed Hashim was just what these childless devotees needed to keep them happy. On him they lavished paternal affection, taking him to their chapter house after work each day, and thus a new crisis was avoided.

While the excitement of Sayed Hashim's arrival, introduction, and first efforts to make himself a member of the group was going on in the sifting-and-washing area, our driver Yed Allah tried to set up a rival show, boasting to these rustic villagers about the marvels of Tehran. So full of his own importance was he, and so eager to steal the limelight from Sayed Hashim, that he failed to notice that Anne was talking Persian fluently with the newcomer. The professor, he boasted, meaning me, was a fool. The New Year's holiday, No Ruz, was coming up in a few days, and he would demand time off to visit his parents in the big city. He would also demand a month's advance pay, which I would be silly enough to give him, and then he would go to Tehran and not come back.

In due course Anne reported this conversation to me, and, sure enough, that evening after supper Yed Allah appeared, hat in hand, making exactly the proposition he had said he would.

"That is fine, Yed Allah," I said quietly when he was all through. "Here is exactly what I owe you. Take it, go to Tehran, and do not come back."

On the advice of the hotel proprietor I replaced him with a small man with a tiny bald head named Bizar, which means *without preoccupation,* or better, if less literally, *bored with life,* an appellation given him by his fellows because of his bored expression. In accordance with the same system Baba, the carpenter, had derived his name, which means *grandpa,* from his fancied senile appearance. Despite the coffin trouble, Baba and I were still good friends because I had hired him to make the boxes in which the finds were to be transported to Tehran. As these boxes were carried only across the street from Baba's shop to the hotel courtyard, and never to the caves, no crisis was created by their manufacture, even when Parviz and Abbas, who visited me in the hotel sometimes on Fridays, saw them.

Bizar was not only an excellent driver but a good mechanic as well. Furthermore, he knew every other driver along the Caspian shore from Gurgan to Astara, and whenever a member of that fraternity got into trouble the others stopped to help him. Once I had hired Bizar, my vehicular problems, which had been many, came to an end.

Wednesday the 21st of March was No Ruz, the Persian New Year's Day. This ancient Persian solar holiday is wholly unrelated to the moon-bound Muslim calendar of festivities, which crawls, eleven days at a hitch, around the year. No Ruz is the vernal equinox, the first day of spring. It opened with fog, which the warm sun soon burned away. At breakfast time Sammy appeared carrying a tray containing the seven symbols of No Ruz, as sacred as the yule log, mistletoe, and Christmas tree are to us. These are seven substances or objects whose names begin with S, as does the word for green, the color of spring. They were: two apples, a cup of malt, some special sweet cookies, some green shoots that looked like chives, some garlic, vinegar, and hyacinths. In each household the offertory tray containing the seven S's is placed in a position of prominence, where it remains untouched for twelve days; on the thirteenth day of No Ruz the green shoots are thrown out, as the ceremonial period is over.

On Friday—the men had chosen to work that day to make up for No Ruz, and only the pious old Abbas failed to show up—our luck turned at the cave. At 4.80 meters, or sixteen feet, which is a long way down in a dark cave, we came to a change of soil, under which we found quantities of painted pottery and many fine flint blades. We were now in the Neolithic, and the Iron Age deposit did not reach the bottom after all. It was, however, a different kind of Neolithic from what we had found in Belt Cave. Painted pottery is a special kind of earthenware common to the Neolithic of other parts of the Near East. Pumpelly found it at Anau in Russian Turkestan, and many others had excavated it in mounds in all the countries from Pakistan to Turkey, including the Iranian plateau region. Many studies had been made of its variations in color and design, and the dates of its occurrence had been carefully worked out on the basis of linkages with historic sites, particularly in Iraq, though in 1951 these had not been confirmed by Carbon-14 analysis. Here in Hotu we not only had a new lot of painted pottery to study in terms of details of manufacture and design, but also plenty of charcoal with it for dating. We now had a means of discovering the relationship between the Caspian shore Neolithic and that of better-known archæological provinces of the Middle East.

On the next day we came to the bottom of this level at five meters (about sixteen feet eight inches) from the surface, and immediately under it found only soft, unpainted Neolithic pottery of the same type that we had excavated in Belt Cave. This definitely proved that the software was older than the painted ware, as we had

suspected at the end of the 1949 season but had been unable to demonstrate. We were now so far down that all
the work was being done by the light of pressure lamps,
which burned kerosene and gave good illumination,
though they heated the confined area of the trench and
used up much oxygen.

In this new soil, which was sticky and gray compared
to the loose brown material in which the painted pottery
had been deposited, we found polished-stone axes,
polished-stone chisels, and flint sickle blades shiny from
grain gloss. There was a brief alert when we thought we
had come upon a burial, but it was a false alarm. Lying
side by side in the soil were two huge human thighbones,
brown and shiny, polished from much handling. As they
were completely alone, they were not part of a burial at
all. All I could think of to explain their presence was that
the ancient inhabitants of the Canary Islands, who were
Neolithic people, had consecrated their kings by holding
just such a pair of bones over their heads, and that pairs
of thighbones were also used in the rituals of some of the
Nilotic tribes of the Sudan. Perhaps the kings of Hotu had
been similarly initiated into office. Who knows?

The top of this early Neolithic deposit was also the top
of a number of roof slabs that had fallen in during some
ancient cataclysm, possibly an earthquake. As we dug
downward by the light of our lamps we found them lying on their edges in a row, like a set of books neatly
placed on a shelf. How far they extended toward the back
of the cave we did not know, nor do we yet; toward the
front they took up two and a half meters' space, or one
half of our digging-area in Trench A. This made a very
narrow area for excavation, but at the same time it gave
our trench two rock walls instead of one. As we had gone
down through the painted-pottery levels we had cut a
series of steps into the front wall of the trench, both to

facilitate the passing of buckets and to provide an escape hatch in case of trouble. This operation had made much work in the sifting-washing-bagging area because the material from the steps had to be assigned to its proper trench levels, but it was worth the effort, if only from the point of view of relieving claustrophobia down below. Now that we were working in half a trench we were happy that we had gone to this effort.

At 3:10 p.m. on March 26, the day after Easter Sunday, at a depth of 7.15 meters or twenty-four feet, we came to the bottom of the Neolithic deposit and reached an entirely different kind of soil, a coarse rubble filled with angular pieces of limestone of the kind we had found in other caves. They had been chipped off the walls and roof by water action, for water, when it gets into cracks and then freezes, expands and breaks off small pieces of stone. As it rarely freezes at Turujan nowadays, the period during which these chips were broken off must have been colder than at present. This rubble reminded me of what we had found in the upper part of the Paleolithic deposit at Bisitun, and also of Red #1 in the High Cave at Tangier.

This soil was full of flint, including some big, coarse implements and some pieces that appeared to have been rolled by water so that their corners were rounded. The bones looked quite different from those above, and some of them were fossilized. Not a scrap of pottery was to be seen. This was, of course, what we had been looking for, but it had taken us twenty-four feet of digging in a damp, dark, dimly lit hole to reach it. We kept going down in it for two more days, through a complex series of rubbles and sands laid down in narrow, irregular bands, until we had reached a point where we were too cramped to examine the soil sequence properly and where also it would be foolhardy to excavate farther. Not only did we have

our own lives to think about, but we were also responsible
for those of our men, and Parviz was getting nervous.
We stopped, therefore, at 8.50 meters (about twenty-
eight feet nine inches) and left this most interesting deposit for the future, covering the bottom of Trench A
with gunny sacking to catch whatever might fall into it.
Meanwhile, we had laid out Trench B, a seven-meter
strip immediately in front of Trench A. This took us to the
very edge of the overhang of the roof.

We excavated Trench B steadily until the 9th of April,
following the lines of the soil changes which had been revealed by our earlier work in Trench A. Although it contained no surprises, Trench B yielded a valuable addition
to our collection of painted pottery and soft undecorated
Neolithic material, as well as to the Iron Age wares higher
up, and our charcoal samples were greatly increased. On
the 9th of April we again reached the rubble under the
Neolithic, but in the meanwhile many things had happened. Parviz, who had been breaking rock in front of the
cave to facilitate the passage of the bucket men, had
pointed out that if we made a face over twenty feet deep
at the very lip of the cave it would not only cut out light
but make the problem of soil-removal unnecessarily difficult. He therefore proposed that we create a third trench,
Trench C, five meters forward in the open air. We began
this trench while still in the Iron Age levels of B.

Shortly after the work on Trench C had begun, when
I was up on the sifting-platform sorting bones, a dark-
skinned young man wearing Arab clothing appeared, looking for work. With two gangs operating at once, we had
plenty to do and could use another pair of hands, particularly such large ones as this youth possessed. I spoke to
him in Arabic, to his apparent joy. He told me, in that
language, that he was a native of Kerbala in Iraq, the
seat of one of the three great Shi'a shrines, the other two

being in Najjaf in Iraq and Mashhad in Iran. He had gone on a pilgrimage to Mashhad, and was broke. He was working his way home. The money he would earn would carry him another station on his way.

The kindly dervishes, who had already taken in Sayed Hashim, also made overtures toward Ibrahim, but they seemed to be having linguistic difficulty and asked me to interpret for them. This I did, to the best of my ability. From that time on Ibrahim became their second guest, with whom they seemed to find a way of making themselves understood by nods, gestures, kindly smiles, and here and there a word.

Seeing Ibrahim with the others gave me a chance, day by day, to compare in a direct fashion the personality patterns of Arabs and Persians, which are as different as one can find among any two peoples in the world, at least within my experience. Shortly after our first meeting Ibrahim had looked me in the eye and declared: "You are good. In all the world there is no man better than you are. May God reward you for your kindness and your great heart. I shall stay with you to the end of my days, work for you and protect you."

I am sure that my relationships with Parviz, Abbas, and Murat were equally sound, particularly as this was our second season together, but I would never expect any of them to make such a declaration. Both Arabs and Persians conduct their personal relations with dignity, but with different channels of reserve. An Arab draws a magic circle around his womenfolk which he will not break, but he will talk about his religion as we do about the weather. A Persian is less reticent about his family, but considers his religion his private affair. Persians feel a hesitancy to discuss their intimate feelings; these are secret things that reveal themselves gradually in little ways, but are rarely if ever made the substance of an overt declaration like

Ibrahim's. Arab emotions rise to the stimulus directly, visibly and vocally, and there is no need to predict reactions: they are there before you know it. The difference is essentially the same as that in Europe between a Latin and a Nordic, using these words in their non-anthropological senses. I believe that these differences in ethnic personality are profound and ancient things; they are certainly important facts to realize if one is to work successfully in the Middle East.

As I viewed Ibrahim from day to day and chatted with him, these observations took form in my mind. It was not until near the end of the dig, however, that the Ibrahim affair became something more than a simple intercultural comparsion. One day he fell violently ill and had to be taken to town in the ambulance to visit the doctor. With illness the Persian language suddenly came to him, and he had no trouble expressing himself in this Indo-European medium. Despite the gravity of the affair, I came in for some heavy kidding. The dervishes rolled with laughter, until they got dirt on their beards.

Ibrahim was indeed an Arab, and my observations about his personality were correct, but he did not come from Kerbala. He came from Sarrakhs, an oasis located in the northeastern corner of Iran, partly in that country and partly inside the Soviet Union. He was a member of an Arab tribe that had settled there, in the midst of Turkomans and Baluchis, during one of the first centuries of Islam, before the time of William the Conqueror. Had I been any kind of linguist, I would have known from the start that his Arabic was too classical for Kerbala. His family lived in a tent just inside Iran. One day his mother sent him out to collect firewood and he wandered over the border. The Russians caught him and sent him to a slave-labor camp that was digging a big canal. Finally he escaped, but, terrified by his experience and afraid to stay home, he headed for Kerbala, which he had heard about vaguely, and where he thought that he might be far enough away from the Russians to live in safety. To his mind I looked like a Russian, and Lisa and the Duprees did not help much, for all three are blond. By the time of his sudden seizure, he had just about decided to come clean, in the belief that we were what we said we were, but fate revealed his secret prematurely.

During the long and archæologically unexciting period while we were excavating Trenches B and C simultaneously and finding nothing we had not expected to see, the Dameghan-Turujan feud broke open again after a few weeks of silent festering. Sayed Ali Akbar, who was Parviz's boastful sleeping-companion, and not a quiet man, taunted Murat continuously until tension had once more been built up to the danger point. The climax came when we were working in the painted-pottery level of Trench B, at a depth of about four meters, or a little over thirteen feet. We had come upon a pair of large stone bowls, beautifully carved. As they were very heavy, much conversation ensued as to how we should take them out. Finally Akbar, Parviz's strong but simple brother-in-law, carried them up the ladder on his shoulders, and for this feat he received much well-deserved acclaim.

There was also, in the trench, a much heavier stone that had to come out. As it was merely a piece of roof-fall, it did not matter whether it came out in one piece or many, but I did not want to have Parviz smash it with the sledge hammer for fear of shattering the Neolithic objects underneath. We could have broken it up with impunity after lining the bottom of the trench with brush and straw, with the stone on top of such a cushion, but that involved much work, and Akbar was certain that he could carry this third heavy object out as well as the first two.

Halfway up the ladder he paused, and the stone fell

off his shoulder, landing with an ominous thud on the precious floor. By his agonized expression I could see that Akbar was deeply humiliated, and hastened to tell him that it was not his fault. While I was doing this, Sayed Ali Akbar, the powerful hero, climbed down into the trench amid cries of *"Palawan! Palawan!"* ("Hero! Hero!")

Not only did he pick up the large stone with a flourish —during the previous week a professional strong man had been performing in Behshahr and we had all been to his performance—but he bounced up the ladder jauntily, carried the stone to the lip of the fan, and ran down it, heaving the stone onto the ground below. Without pausing he ran up the slope again, picking up on the way a gray donkey belonging to Medod, one of the dervishes. Now the donkey was known as Medod's jeep, a standard expedition joke. As the men outside the cave cried that Sayed Ali Akbar had picked up a jeep, those of us who were working in Trench B were dumfounded.

Somehow or other the joy and excitement caused by this feat suddenly turned to hatred and blows. Back at the lip of Trench B Sayed Ali Akbar began taunting Murat, who was working as pick man below. First Sayed Ali Akbar threw lumps of dirt on Murat's head, and then little stones, until in a sudden fury Murat threw his pick up at Sayed Ali Akbar, a distance of well over fifteen feet, and Sayed Ali Akbar caught it and threw it back, barely missing Murat's head.

At that moment I arrived on the scene and ordered Sayed Ali Akbar out of the cave. He refused to go, and stood there mocking me. Although he was as big as I and much stronger and at least twenty years younger, I did not lose a second, for this was a very critical moment. I reached out with my left hand and grabbed him by the nose. Too surprised to do anything, he let me lead him out of the cave and push him down the edge of the fan. "You are fired," I said, wiping my hands together.

Undergoing such a sudden shift of status from hero to a man who had just been fired was too much for Sayed Ali Akbar, and he stood there for some moments, trying to collect his thoughts. In a daze he plodded down the slope, until suddenly an idea came to him. Once more jaunty, he sauntered over to a beech tree just beyond the parking-area and climbed into a crotch twenty feet above the ground, where his face could be seen leering through a wreath of the shiny pale-green foliage of early spring.

From this perch our bird burst into song. It was soon clear that these were not ancient lays, nor ditties heard over the Tehran radio, but original compositions created on the spot by a poet of no mean magnitude. These compositions were directed against me, a natural target on account of my family name. For a half-hour I stood it, not wanting to be labeled a poor sport, but the work had come to a standstill and the men were looking at me as if expecting some action. I did not long disappoint them. Picking up an ax, I walked slowly down the fan to the foot of the tree and began to chop it down. In the eyes of the audience this was drama of the highest order. Above the din I could hear the normally quiet voice of Murat shouting with laughter. Before I had struck many blows our bird dropped through the outer branches on the far side and hied himself quickly away. That afternoon we could hear his derisive minstrelsy wafted faintly with the perfume of pomegranate blossoms from a hidden lair in the distance, but his silver throat had lost its magic. No one appeared to notice it, and the work went on. On the following Friday, Sayed Ali Akbar appeared in the hotel courtyard, very handsome in a well-tailored Western suit, accompanied by his lawyer. With an embarrassed smile he asked me to shake his hand, which I did. Then he begged me to take him back, saying that he was sorry that his fooling had gone too far.

But I could not do it. By that time we were engaged in very serious business and I dared not take a chance. I told him that he was a fine poet and had a splendid voice, but that his talents at the cave were wasted. He took this in good grace, and we parted friends. It was only after this that I learned that he was a landowner and, by local standards, a rich man. I was also told that he taken on the job only to participate in the excitement; he had not wanted to be left out of an activity in which the rest of the village men were having fun. Thus it had come about that he had spearpointed the last and most active round of the opposition of the locals to the men of Dameghan.

As Trench B sank deeper and deeper, a problem that had arisen in Belt Cave now grew to alarming proportions. Each day we received more and more visitors. Our activities were regularly reported in the Tehran newspapers and discussed in the radio news. The Shah even flew over the mouth of the cave in his private plane. One day two whole busloads of students from the University of Tehran arrived with their professors just to see our dig, and Louis and I did our best to show it to them. Although it was obviously becoming dangerous for much weight to be placed on the strip of original cave floor alongside the edge of the trench, it was not my place to forbid the students and their professors to go there. I could only warn them. We had already erected a fence of upright poles laced together with poplar branches that were supple with the sap of spring, and this fence stood a foot from the edge, but some of them leaned on it. Seeing it sway, Ahmad Tabrizi quickly snatched a billhook from the hands of a venerable and picturesque visitor from the Hazer Jerif country, and with the flat of the blade he pounded the tops of the upright sticks into the soft earth as hard as he was able.

This started a crack in the floor, which would have fallen in then and there, students and all, had not Abbas seen what was happening and stopped him just in time. Furthermore, as Ahmad had broken the billhook off at the haft, the old man from Hazer Jerif became justifiably angry. Luckily, a peddler, who visited the cave daily to sell candy and odds and ends, had just set down his basket of wares by the sieves, and I bought a new billhook blade from him. The substitution did not please the old man at all. His billhook blade had been old and highly polished, as well as razor-sharp. It had obviously been the object of years of tender loving care, never far from its owner's hands. Nothing could replace it. Louis Dupree took over my lecture to the students while I tried to pacify the old man. Meanwhile, the damage had been done to the floor, and the danger of an earthfall was greater than before.

On the 9th of April we had laid the floor of the early Neolithic deposit bare, and were standing on a surface of rubble. Whereas the upper layers had all sloped downward from the front of the cave toward its rear, the rubble surface sloped sidewise, from the eastern wall downward toward the western, at an angle of thirty degrees. Obviously the upper and lower deposits represented two entirely different cycles of deposition, with a considerable time gap in between. We decided, however, not to tap this luscious deposit until everything had been made shipshape and tidy.

A little while later Louis was in the pit cleaning up tag ends of Neolithic soil and I was upstairs directing the enlargement of a new excavation in front of Trench C, which would enable us to let in light and would give the bucket men plenty of walking-room between the new deposit and the sieves, when Louis made a discovery. In the top of the rubble he found two stone implements, made of cores, that looked very much like Lower Paleolithic tools; one looked like a hand ax, the other like a cleaver. He put these in his pockets without saying a word, and after a few minutes he climbed the ladder to where I was standing and showed them to me, still silent.

To say that I was surprised would be a masterpiece of understatement. I was astonished. All the talk we had had about Caspian sea levels went out the window. We might be in a deposit of the Lower or Middle Paleolithic culture, in the third or even the second interglacial period, something beyond our most extravagant dreams. This happened during the afternoon of the 9th. On the 10th we walked on air, cleaning the trenches as a steward polishes his galley on a millionaire's yacht, and this went on through the morning of the 11th. At noon we knocked off, planning to start digging the rubble after lunch, and returned to the hotel in the ambulance, piloted by the faithful Bizar, to whom some of our excitement had been transmitted.

Lunch was quickly over, and we arrived back at the cave before the return of the local men, who had gone to the village for their food. Climbing up the steep slope of the sifting-platform, we stood in the entrance to witness a scene of horror and devastation. The whole west side of the deposit had fallen in, covering our beloved rubble with soils of different colors. Three men were crouched trembling on the top of the floor that we had left at the rear of the cave. They were trapped. Louis and I seized the ladders, climbed down into the scene of destruction, and put the ladders up the other end, bringing the frightened men down.

They were townees who rode out with us in the morn-

ing and back again at night, and they were the only men
who ate their lunches in the cave. Earlier in the season
the Turujanites would not have tolerated their presence,
but by this time every man in Turujan who could lift a
shovel was on the payroll, except Sayed Ali Akbar, and
there was work in abundance. While two of the townees
had sat in the back of the cave, munching their bread,
the third had gone out front to get some firewood so that
they could make tea. As he walked toward his companions, his arms loaded, he felt the ground yield beneath his
feet, and in a panic he raced, as in a bad dream, dropping
the wood and vomiting on his shirtfront as he ran. Just as
he made the edge of the back platform the end of the
passageway disappeared in a cloud of dried bat dung.
This had happened a few minutes before our arrival.

By this time Parviz, Abbas, Murat, and the others had
arrived, having heard the sound of the ambulance's motor
and gears. Turning to Parviz, I said: "What wonderful
luck that no one was killed! If this had happened two
hours earlier or a half-hour later, some of us would be
dead."

"Not at all," said Parviz.

"Why not?" I asked sharply.

"Because two weeks ago I foresaw this, and paid one
hundred tomans [about twenty dollars free market rate]
to the endowment of an imamzadeh [shrine] up the road
a way, to make sure that no one would be killed."

I did not continue this discussion. It seemed unlikely
to me that Parviz had paid that much money out of his
own pocket for the divine protection of all of us. We had
heard persistent rumors that Parviz was taking a cut from
the men. If, in one way or another, they had shared in the
cost of the spiritual umbrella that had manifestly saved
our lives, I had no objection. Myself a capitalist, I wished
Parviz every success.

His patron saint, I soon discovered, had given us another break. The soil from the west side of the trench that had fallen in was almost sterile. In choosing the east or sunny side to dig, we had guessed correctly. People just had not sat in the shady half of the cave. The work of soil-removal thus became easier than we had expected. As the stratification had been ruined, this was a godsend. On the 14th we had a second slide, but it was a minor one and we had seen it coming. By the end of work on the 15th everything was shipshape again and ready for further work.

That evening Mr. Samadie, who had gone to Tehran for the purpose, brought down on the train a new member of our expedition, Bob Stevens, a professional photographer. Bob had been sent out by the University Museum to take pictures of archæology in action at our various digs in the Middle East, and he had already been to Turkey and Iraq. On the morning of the 16th he began shooting sequences with a movie camera, recording the work at the bucket line and sieves, the activities of our daily visitor the peddler, and whatever else was going on outside.

Hearing a commotion up there, I climbed out of the trench. Three textile workers were making a fuss, demanding to be allowed downstairs with us, making the usual Communist remarks. I soon had enough of this. First I ordered them off the premises. When they refused to leave, I tried to push them off, but they became very angry. Disappearing around the corner, they reappeared with sticks and rushed me.

Before they got near, Buzurg had dropped his shovel and grabbed a pick handle. This normally slow-moving man was over the platform in a split second and beating the invaders over the head. By the time Parviz had arrived to help, he had won the battle. The enemy was in noisy retreat down the fan. Parviz looked at Buzurg and then at me. Words were unnecessary. Now I knew why he had refused to let me fire Buzurg, and he knew that I knew.

"Damn it," said Bob Stevens, "you *would* do that while I was changing the film."

His disappointment was soon over, for inside the cave he found more than enough to film. Before any action had begun, the scene itself was well worth recording. Before the face had collapsed, our over-all trench had been a succession of orderly cubes, with floors at different levels, under a vaulted roof whose height in the center was twice the cave's breadth. Æsthetically it could have won the approval of Bulfinch or Wren. Now we found ourselves working at the bottom of a funnel. Our scene of activity had taken on the dramatic appearance of a surgical theater, its roofline broken by a circle of peering faces. Being at the bottom of an inverted cone also produced a weird acoustical effect in which, as on a stage, no confidences are possible. Everything Abbas said to me or I to Louis or vice versa boomed and reverberated toward the mouth of the cave, from which our words emerged as from a loudspeaker.

In this histrionic setting, tired and keyed up by weeks of frustrations and interruptions, I felt like an ancient prophet on the eve of a major revelation. The others, I could see, felt much the same. Louis, Abbas, Murat, Sayed Nosrallah, and I went to work on the rubble, which had now been bared for the third time, at a depth of twenty-five feet, in an area that we labeled Trench D. We found the same sequence of gravels and sands, with many flints and animal bones, that had turned up on the bottom of Trench A, but here we could see what we were getting, particularly as we were burning several pressure lamps at once to facilitate Bob Stevens's photography.

At three o'clock in the afternoon of the 16th I found a

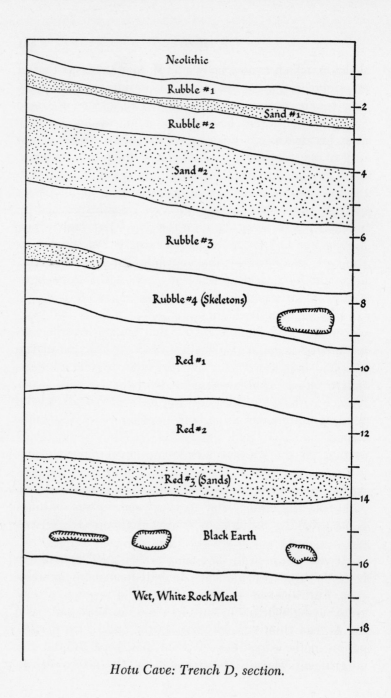

Hotu Cave: Trench D, section.

skeleton, which is now known as Hotu #1. It was that of an adult male, a big man with a long narrow nose and a very square, firm-chinned jaw, like a caricature of Uncle Sam. His bones had been gathered together some time after his death and poked unceremoniously against the wall of the cave in a bundle. Not all of him was there; most in evidence were his limbs and his face. Although the top and back of his skull were missing, other pieces of skull, which may or may not have been his, turned up about two feet away. Despite the disrespect with which his remains had been treated, he was just as human as you or I, and, as far as one can judge from bones alone, he could have appeared in any modern European or American gathering without exciting comment.

The incident with the Communist visitors had convinced Mr. Samadie and myself that our dig was becoming far too prominent a feature of the landscape of the Caspian shore for comfort. It had outgrown its administrative set-up. That evening in Behshahr we had a conference with two old friends, the chief of police and the head of the gendarmerie, both of whom had frequently visited the cave, and they agreed that a change was needed. As the site lay outside the city limits, it was a gendarmerie problem. On the morning of the 17th a gendarme rode out with us, and from that moment to the end of the dig either he or another like him was on duty, polite, friendly, and firm. Visitors caused us no more trouble.

It was just as well. The activities of April 17 were so feverish that we could have tolerated no more interference. Furthermore, at noon Mr. Samadie received a telegram saying that his mother had died in Gunabad, near the Afghan frontier, and that was the end of his participation in the expedition. With a gendarme present the government was still represented. In the afternoon we found the radius (lower armbone) of a second skeleton about two and a half feet below the level of #1, but we left this while Abbas and I concentrated on the removal of the first one. The next morning Louis, who had been carrying the trench downward in search of the bottom, reached the end of the stratified deposit at a depth of 12.5 meters, or forty-one feet.

Under it was a soft, sticky bed of white powdered limestone, a type of earth common in the bottoms of caves. So fluid was this underlying material that if we should dig it out of Trench D, more would flow in from the sides. Once its borders had been undermined, our precariously supported conical structure would collapse, smothering us like flies. Parviz, who had been watching from above, now begged Louis not to go any deeper, saying that his agreement with the imamzadeh did not cover this kind of foolhardiness, and that this time the walls would not only fall in but would bury us as well.

Faced with this opposition, Louis contented himself by shoving our crowbar down into the white stuff as far as it would go, which was seventy centimeters, making a total depth at that point of 13.3 meters, or forty-four feet. Along the northeastern face of Trench D the cave wall sloped inward, and we could see that Hotu was not a flat-bottomed cave like Belt, but a V-shaped solution cavity like the High Cave and Bisitun. To reach the bottom would involve digging with a spoon. We had a choice of two plans of action. Either we could stop work in Trench D, clean out the whole cave, except for the far end where a face had been preserved, and then excavate the gravels on a large scale, or we could confine our final activities to taking out the skeletons on which Abbas and I were working. There was no real choice. The men were too tired to go on much longer, they had planting to do, and we too were near exhaustion. So I paid off all but eight men, while Bob Stevens filmed the payment and handshaking, and we went back to the hotel to work on the bones.

On the 19th we came back to work with what we called in the field book a skeleton crew—just enough men to help us take out the skeletons. As far as we knew then, that was all the work that remained to be done, and it did not require a whole villageful of men plus added increments from town and country. But we were mistaken.

Skeleton #2, which had appeared the day before in the form of a radius in the forward face of Trench D, raised more problems than we had anticipated. As soon as Abbas and I had begun to work on it we discovered that it had two skulls.

"This is the *diva sefid* of Mazandaran," said Abbas, partly in jest and partly in wonder.

He referred to the so-called White Monster, a mythical two-headed dragon believed to have lived in that very region, slain by Rustem in Firdusi's immortal epic, the *Shahnameh*. Soon we found that we had to remove two skeletons, one running diagonally along the face on which we were working, and the other stretched out horizontally in the direction of the mouth of the cave. We could not take them out unless we first cut away at least two feet more of the front face, and to do this would bring us perilously close to the edge of the funnel, leaving no protecting lip or shelf of soil between us and the mouth of the cave forty feet above.

We had no choice. This cut had to be made. Nearly all the shovel men, bucket men, and sieve men had been paid off the night before. In the crisis Louis and I climbed up and down the ladder carrying pails of earth, and at one point I openly wept in frustration. Miraculously, our old workmen appeared from nowhere and took their accustomed stations, and the work went on as if yesterday's payoff had never happened. There were Mir Aksar, the water boy, puffing up the slope with two full buckets slopping on a shoulder pole; Medod, the donkey-owning dervish, in front of his sieve; and Anne Dupree's young assistant, Sayed Hashim, busily scrubbing flints with her at the basin. All of them were silent.

"Thank you all for coming back," I said, "but there is little money left."

The men looked at me in embarrassment, as if I had mentioned some indecent thing. Finally the luxuriant beard of Medod the dervish parted, and his lips could be seen as he prepared to speak.

"What is money anyhow?" he said.

As soon as I had seen what the removal of the skeletons involved, I had sent Bizar with the ambulance to search for acetone among the cities of the Caspian shore. Both the hotel proprietor and the pharmacist volunteered to go along, for they knew where to look for it. First they tried at Shahi, without success; then they went to Babol. None was to be found there either. Not waiting to return to Behshahr, the hotel proprietor thumbed a ride on a truck to Tehran, where he found it, and on Friday he returned with enough acetone for three complete skeletons. His quick and unselfish act enabled us to harden the skeletons with Alvar, and carry them unscathed to Tehran and America.

Meanwhile, on Friday morning, April 20, high drama was being acted out in Hotu. Abbas, who had agreed to work on Friday for the first time in either season, descended into the trench with me to remove the second and third skeletons. They were those of two women, one young and the other middle-aged, who had apparently been warming themselves over a small fire in the cave thousands of years ago when *crash!*—a rock fell from the roof, followed quickly by others, and the two women were felled. The face of the older one was ground into the hearth.

As soon as I had been able to make this reconstruction I discovered that the drama which had given us these women was about to repeat itself and remove them from our grasp. Abbas, barber that he really was, had shaved the earth from their bones as delicately as he would have shaved my cheeks, had I admitted to him that I knew he was a barber. I had just finished wrapping the skulls with cotton and bandages, like the heads of ladies in a hairdresser's shop, when we found the lethal stone. It was one of the rocks that had fallen from the roof. There it projected, threatening both skulls.

I told Abbas to stop undercutting, for fear it would fall.

"It goes in deep," he said.

"No, it doesn't," I replied. "Start taking it from above."

This he did. Before either of us could stop it, it began to fall, slowly at first and leaning forward. Abbas reached from above and I from below, but both pairs of hands failed to catch it and it crashed onto the skulls.

Maybe it was the exhaustion of oxygen by the pressure lamps, quadrupled for Bob Stevens's benefit. Maybe it was just the backlog of tension and fatigue. Whatever the reason, I felt the strength drain out of my hands and feet. Grasping the ladder, I crawled the forty feet to the top and lay gasping on my back.

A visitor remarked rudely that the boss was stealing a bit of shuteye, to which I am afraid that I made a much ruder reply, using a number of words that I had not learned from the missionaries. Before long Buzurg and Ahmad Tabrizi picked me up and carried me to the ambulance. Refusing to ride in so symbolic a vehicle, I sat up all the way in the jeep with Bizar at the wheel, was carried upstairs, and put to bed. At half past four Louis brought in the skulls, broken but not past reconstruction, and in the morning I was carried to the jeep so that I could ride to the cave and pay off the men.

That was my last view of Hotu, though I got a glimpse of the cliff face five days later when we passed it on our way to Tehran. The rest of the story would be routine except for one thing: the mistake I made in the Park Hotel in Tehran a few days later when I told Jim Bell and other journalists that I thought the skulls were of third-inter-glacial age. I was even foolish enough to repeat this esti-mate later to His Majesty the Shah in a private audience.

All that I can say in extenuation is that I actually be-lieved what I said. We had found what appeared to be Lower Paleolithic implements in the top of the rubble, and the swift pace of events had prevented us from going over them carefully in the meanwhile. Some of them were the coarse, crude, decadent type of implement made in many parts of the world during the Mesolithic; Hallam Movius had once excavated similar artifacts in the north of Ireland. Others bore on their surfaces the same kind of glossy brown patination one finds on flints that have been lying about on the surface of the desert for thousands of years. Some miserable Mesolithic character or characters could have picked them up on the ground outside and carried them into the cave to use as tool material. If the Piltdown hoax fooled the world, the Mesolithic hoax of Hotu fooled me.

It has taken us six years to begin to understand what we found in those few weeks at Hotu, and we now know that the importance of this cave is as great as if the skele-tons had been as old as we first thought. During these five years many distinguished persons in many institutions in several countries have worked over various aspects of our finds—the flint implements, the metal, the pottery, the animal bones, the fishbones, the bird bones, the mollusk shells, the soil samples, and the charcoal—and this work has not been completed. From the results already obtained by the friends who have been going over our finds from fish to pots, I have come to a firm conclusion: while digging is a very personal thing, analysis is one that takes many brains and twice as many hands, and the more work that is done by persons who have never seen the inside of Hotu, smelled the pomegranate blossoms in the springtime, or listened to Sayed Ali Akbar's taunting voice in the treetop, the better. Their task is an objective one and they will not be swayed by haunting memories.

Although no job in this field is ever completed, some can be done with more finality than others, and this is particularly true of Carbon-14 dating. Miss Elizabeth Ralph, who dated ten samples from five levels in Belt Cave, also processed twenty-two samples from seventeen levels in Hotu. One of these samples, the one from the hearth under skulls #2 and #3 in Hotu, she sent to Dr. J. Laurence Kulp at Columbia University for confirmation. Her date from this particular level was 9190 ± 590 B.P., and his was 9480 ± 250 B.P. The two dates are well within each other's ranges of probability. The skeletons were therefore about 9,335 years old, within a range of three or four hundred years, and the stones that killed the two women fell somewhere around 7400 B.C.

The twenty-two Carbon-14 dates that Miss Ralph obtained from Hotu arranged themselves naturally into eight groups, each of which corresponds to a different culture and is separated from the others in the face of the trenches by soil changes. Reading from top to bottom, these are: [1]

---

[1] Elizabeth K. Ralph, "University of Pennsylvania Radiocarbon Dates I, *Science*, Feb. 4, 1955, Vol. 121, No. 3136, pp. 149–51. In this original report, sample #P-35, Hotu Trench A Levels 39–41, from the software Neolithic, is dated at 4,730 ± 320 B.P., and #P-45, Hotu Trench B, 535–580 cm., from the painted-pottery culture, is dated at 6,515 ± 425 B.P. As these two dates are obviously impossible I am omitting them.

ISLAMIC	1,220 ± 230 B.P.	=	A.D. 730
PARTHIAN (?)	2,200 ± 280 B.P.	=	250 B.C.
EARLY IRON AGE			
(*12 samples*) from	2,685 ± 210 B.P.	=	735 B.C.
to	2,950 ± 230 B.P.	=	1000 B.C.
PAINTED POTTERY	4,830 ± 480 B.P.	=	2880 B.C.
SOFTWARE NEOLITHIC	6,385 ± 425 B.P.	=	4435 B.C.
SUB-NEOLITHIC	8070 ± 500 B.P.	=	6120 B.C.
VOLE-EATERS			
(*3 skeletons*)	9,190 ± 590 B.P.	=	7240 B.C.
(*2 samples*)	9,220 ± 570 B.P.	=	7270 B.C.
SEAL-HUNTERS	11,860 ± 840 B.P.	=	9910 B.C.

The Islamic date at the head of the list came from Trench C, from soil deposited outside the cave after its mouth had been sealed. As the topmost deposit inside was laid down sometime during the first five centuries B.C., the entrance must have been closed about or shortly after the time of Christ. The Parthian period, which this second date suggests, was an obscure stretch of history between the early and late Persian empires, neither of which is represented at Hotu. The third period in Hotu's history, covered by twelve overlapping dates from 735 B.C. to 1000 B.C. (with an outside range extending from 525 B.C. to 1230 B.C.), is the richest of all in soil depth and number of specimens. Its wealth of pottery and metal should throw light on the cultural connections between the eastern Caspian shore and its neighboring regions.

Before the Iron Age we find a clean gap of nearly two millennia, elsewhere occupied by the Bronze Age, which is totally lacking in our Caspian caves. Before that comes the painted-pottery date of 2880 B.C., with an outside range of 2400 B.C. to 3360 B.C.; this fits what we know of painted-pottery cultures in other parts of the Middle East. Our specimens include a few sherds of fine, thin, polished black ware, a de-luxe ceramic widely traded at that time.

Below the soil change at the base of the painted-pottery deposit we come at last to a Neolithic level like that of Belt Cave. Although fifteen hundred years earlier than the painted pottery, the soft, crumbly early Neolithic ware of Hotu was still a little later than the Belt pottery. Finer workmanship and better surface polish indicate progress.

In the rubbles, sands, and red and black soils of Trench D, Miss Ralph's figures block out four different occupations inside an otherwise confusing sequence of soil changes.[2] These dates, intimately interlocked with those from Belt Cave, reveal that both caves were dry enough to be inhabited about 10,000 B.C., well before the last ice age had ended in northern Europe. Exactly which flooding of the Caspian had filled them with water immediately before this we do not know. During the last ice age the sea rose twice, the second time to a level a few feet above the roofs of the two caves. Later, as the ice sheet was retreating in the north, it staged three minor rallies and each of these brought the Caspian up again, but how high we do not know. It is unlikely but not impossible that one or more of these oscillations could have flooded the caves between two periods of occupation. Quite probably one of them brought the edge of the sea to the beach just north of the road, where our seal-hunters could have clubbed their favorite prey to death within a few minutes' walk of their doors.

The sequence of dates and cultures in the two caves,

[2] Three preliminary reports on this cave were published before the Carbon-14 dates had been determined. They are: C. S. Coon: "Excavations in Hotu Cave, Iran: A Preliminary Report," *Proceedings of the American Philosophical Society*, Vol. 96, No. 3 (Philadelphia, 1952), pp. 231–49; Louis B. Dupree: "The Pleistocene Artifacts of Hotu Cave, Iran," ibid., pp. 250–7; and J. Lawrence Angel: "The Human Skeletal Remains from Hotu Cave, Iran," ibid., pp. 258–69.

from seal-hunting to Ramadhan-keeping, and the way the dates of the two series dovetail into one another, are illustrated on page 211. To me the most interesting part of this analysis is the separation of Trench D of Hotu into four cultural levels, represented by the four last items of the left column.

The top half of the section of Trench D (see the illustration on page 200) is occupied by four rubbles more or less separated from each other by layers of sand. How these were formed I do not know. Under the fourth rubble lies the level known as Red #1, which is a thin layer of reddish soil overlying black silt. Our experience in the High Cave of Tangier taught us that such a red-and-black combination can be a single unit with its top turned red through oxidation. Below it lay a similar combination, Red #2, and under that a sequence of red sand and fine black earth.

As the lowest of the red-black sequence had no charcoal, we could not date it, but its position makes it older than the 9910 ± 840 B.C. date of Red #2. From the point of European chronology even this established date could be called very late Upper Paleolithic, but it was technologically Mesolithic because the people who left the charcoal had already acquired the two precious possessions that are believed to distinguish the Mesolithic from earlier cultures: the bow and the dog. The Mesolithic was earlier on the Caspian shore than on the Baltic. From a climatic point of view this is easily understood.

Although Trench D was but a small hole and the bones and flints removed from it were too few to form a well-rounded fauna and industry for each culture, we nevertheless have enough specimens from all four to tell them apart, and to match them tentatively with the richer loot from Belt Cave. As for the fauna, 134 mammalian specimens have been identified from the dated layers. In the

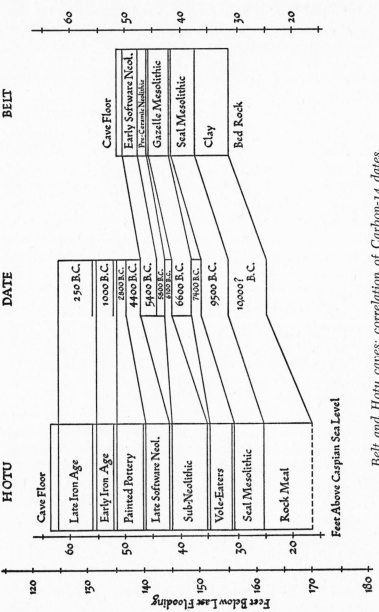

Belt and Hotu caves: correlation of Carbon-14 dates.

HOTU

Cave Floor

Late Iron Age

Early Iron Age

Painted Pottery

Late Software Neol.

Sub-Neolithic

Vole-Eaters

Seal Mesolithic

Rock Meal

Feet Above Caspian Sea Level

60

50

40

30

20

120

130

140

150

160

170

180

Feet Below Lake Flooding

DATE

250 B.C.

1000 B.C.

2800 B.C.

4400 B.C.

5400 B.C.

5800 B.C.

6100 B.C.

6600 B.C.

7400 B.C.

9500 B.C.

10,000? B.C.

BELT

Cave Floor

Early Software Neol.

Pre-Ceramic Neolithic

Gazelle Mesolithic

Seal Mesolithic

Clay

Bed Rock

60

50

40

30

20

A   B

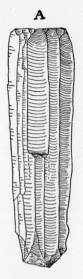

Neolithic blades from Belt and Hotu. Blade production reached its peak during the Neolithic, when cores as perfect as A, from Belt, and blades as regular and flawless as B, from Hotu, were run-of-the-mill products. Core A was probably discarded because a weak blow had detached a blade only halfway down the front. (One-half actual size.)

The Sub-Neolithic people who occupied Hotu about 6100 B.C. made anachronistically crude implements, often of coarse-grained local flint. Two views of a beaked or pointed flake with a retouched cutting-edge seen at the top left side of the right-hand view. (One-half actual size.)

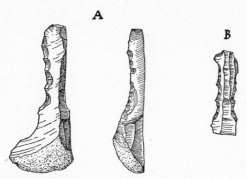

Characteristic of the Gazelle Mesolithic of Belt Cave are notched implements. A, shown in two views, is a piece of waste made in preparing a blade core. It was notched on both sides and may have been used as a saw. B is a fine blade notched on both sides. (One-half actual size.)

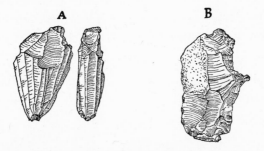

The Mesolithic vole-eaters of Hotu, so-called because of the large number of vole bones in their deposit, produced the microlithic blade core (A), shown in two views, and the notched trimming-flake (B), retouched in the form of a narrow beak or drill. (One-half actual size.)

second gravel we have 93 pieces, of which 71 are of domestic species—ox, sheep, pig, and dog. Of the rest, 18 are elk and 4 fox. The forest was there as it is today, and if the ox, sheep, and pig had not been domesticated, the people who lived there were very much interested in them. The fourth gravels, the ones that contained the skeletons, have

A   B   C

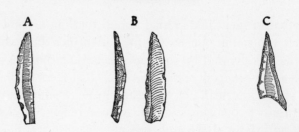

*Seal Mesolithic from Belt and Hotu. (A) Backed blade
from the Seal Mesolithic of Belt Cave. This small blade
was blunted by retouching so that one edge could be held
against the index finger while the other served as a knife.
(B) A closely similar blade from deep in the red soils of
Hotu. (C) From Belt Cave, a segment of blade especially retouched into a "geometric" form, and probably
used as a barb in a composite missile head. (One-half
actual size.)*

18 specimens: 1 ox, 1 pig, 3 sheep, and 12 small tunneling
animals known as *Ellobius*. Although they resemble moles
in habit, they are voles, digging with their front teeth instead of with their paws. As far as we could tell, these
little animals had been eaten, along with many small
birds, particularly thrush. The Hotu ladies, therefore, as
well as the man whose remains were found higher up,
were humble gatherers and collectors of birds and animals
too picayune to have interested the great hunters of earlier
times. In the Red #1 deposit all of 13 specimens found
were small rodents of this kind. In the Red #2 deposit of
10 specimens only 2 were voles, 2 were seals, 1 a dog, 3
gazelles, and 2 sheep, this time definitely wild. Down below in the lowest black we found the head of a humerus
of a wild ox, *Bos primigenius*, which some hunter had
broken. It is the biggest bone of its kind seen in the British
Museum, or it was in 1951.

Although many pieces of scrap material were found,
the number of actual implements recovered was smaller

than that of identified animal bones, totaling a scant 129. This is too small a series for final identification, particularly as it is divided by soil changes and Carbon-14 dates into a number of sub-series. But it is clear from an inspection of the flint artifacts that they group themselves naturally into two major divisions, those below the second sands and those above and from this level.

The flints from the upper division, numbering 73, are completely different from those of the Neolithic in either cave. Therefore we must assume that they were made by an entirely different group of people. As they killed animals belonging to species that were later—if not already —domesticated, their culture can be called Sub-Neolithic. Their implements consisted mainly of rough scraping-tools made on fragments of cores, but also included a few small blades and microlith cores. Our Sub-Neolithic cave-dwellers were also experimenting with clay, lumps of which turned up bearing cordage marks. We even found one piece that others have called a crude female figurine, and one or two odd conical pieces that could have been legs broken off similar effigies.

In the layers below the dividing-line the crude scrapers made on cores were absent, and the industry, in spite of the limited amount of material, shows much finer workmanship. The implements, numbering 53, are made on both blades and flakes, and include one very well made backed blade. Although both the fauna and the Carbon-14 dates indicate a time gap between the fourth gravels and Red #1, no such distinction can yet be made on the basis of implement types, largely because there are only 24 pieces from Red #1 on down.

We have no reason to believe that the people who lived in Hotu from its first occupation through Red #1 times were a different folk from the seal-hunters of Belt Cave, whose industry is so much more fully documented, or that they differed in basic tool-making tradition from the vole-eaters who followed them after a considerable time interval. The gazelle-hunters of Belt Cave could also have shared this tradition. But the Sub-Neolithic people of Hotu were birds of an entirely different feather, and the Neolithic inhabitants of both caves a third outfit. It is quite clear now that in early post-glacial times the Caspian shore was an important passageway for people moving between the eastern and western ends of this narrow corridor. In this respect the archæological finds confirmed our deductions based on geography.

The final report on Hotu has not yet been written, and I am not sure that it ever can be. Although enough of the Neolithic and Iron Age soils have been removed to give specialists in those periods a fair sample of cultural remains to work with, the underlying red and black soils and rubbles have not been adequately sampled. Someone must go back to dig out the rest of this deposit. As I found it by inadvertence and left most of the analysis to others, I can say in full modesty from my position on the sidelines that Hotu promises to be one of the great caves of the Middle East, just as the Caspian shore promises to be one of the world's great cave-digging regions. Future discoveries in Hotu and neighboring caves will undoubtedly bring many new facts to light, to fill other voids in the archæological picture. That the books are never closed on such a site and such a region is one of the charms of this work.

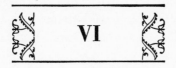

VI

KARA KAMAR: THE BLACK BELLY

As long as I can remember I have wanted to go to Afghanistan. In 1933 I raised the money from a private source for that purpose, but my superiors turned me down on the grounds that it was too dangerous. This was a mistake. No people I know are more kindly and hospitable or less likely to harm a stranger than the Afghans, who rank among the bravest and gentlest folk in the world.

In 1954 my chance came. Dr. Ahmad Ali Kohzad, Director of Antiquities of Afghanistan, had visited Philadelphia and been a guest on our Museum television show, *What in the World?* Froelich Rainey had driven the yellow jeep that we had used in Iran across the various mountains and deserts to Kabul. Two of our Museum staff had already dug at historic sites in the northern plain, and a house, two vehicles, and a cook were awaiting us in Kabul. After our experience at Hotu, I insisted on taking along a geologist. No more Mesolithic hoaxes for me. So I persuaded Dr. Henry W. Coulter, Jr., of the United States Geological Survey to take a leave of absence and join us.

Hank's first action was to prepare a geological map of Afghanistan based on all available sources. On this map he pinpointed the regions where the limestone formations were just right for caves that could have been inhabited by Pleistocene hunters. Thus, before we had our visas we knew exactly where we wanted to go. A band of outcrops of Jurassic and Cretaceous limestone skirts the foothills of the Hindu Kush Mountains on the border of the great inland plain drained by the Oxus, or Amu Darya, River. Somewhere along this band we could hardly help finding what we were looking for. Needless to say, from the standpoint of prehistoric archæology this whole area was virgin territory.

Our principal problem was simply to get there. Being a landlocked nation, Afghanistan is not easy to reach. Roads exist from Iran, but taking them involves first going to Iran and finding transportation; ours was already in Kabul. The other principal route was via Pakistan and over the Khyber Pass. Although historically interesting, this was the long way around, and expensive of time and money. Finally, my older son, Carl, Jr., a Foreign Service officer then in Damascus, discovered an air service from Jerusalem to Kabul. Having booked passage on this, we flew to Damascus two weeks early in order to make a reconnaissance of Syria and Jordan and a tourist exploration of Jerusalem.

Much to our chagrin, the air service from Jerusalem had been discontinued owing to a lawsuit, and we were forced to take the Pakistan route after all. We returned to Damascus to take the BOAC to Karachi, and then the train to Peshawar. Among other things I had to carry with me a set of tires for the yellow jeep, and this involved getting them out of Syrian customs and in again and then out once more; it also involved a hectic time in the customs sheds of Karachi. Although the air-conditioned express trains to Peshawar were booked solid for several weeks, we managed to get seats on a non-air-conditioned train that took two days and one night. This gave us a good chance to see the countryside. As we rolled over the vast Indus plain, with its magnificent trees and green fields, with high-wheeled oxcarts plodding along, just as depicted on the Bronze Age seals, we were grateful that our airline had let us down.

Peshawar is a city of ghosts. The huge and magnificent Dean's Hotel gives each patron a suite of rooms complete with fireplace and two baths. In the old Club, lofty and filled with leather chairs, the shades of colonels and their ladies could almost be seen, whirling and pirouetting about. A pair of giant Pathans at the bar served us drinks that would never pass their own lips, in the perfect subcontinental philosophy that one man's meat is another man's poison. Brother Rudyard with his black eyebrows and drooping mustache never stood nearer to anyone than he did to us that night. However, the spell was quickly broken. Before we went to bed the desk clerk asked me to sign a statement. Two Englishmen had complained that the hotel's brandy had been watered. Would I, as an American, state that it had not?

Next day I managed to collar two stock cars to drive us to Kabul, tires, baggage, and all. When they arrived at five in the morning of March 12, we discovered that the baggage compartments of both vehicles were filled with jerry cans. The drivers were taking enough gas for the round trip. Not only did the Afghan government forbid them to take return passengers, but they could buy no gas in Kabul except on the black market at great risk and cost. So we loaded most of the baggage into one car and rode in the other. By daylight we were already climbing Khyber Pass over a beautiful hard-topped road. Even more exciting than the well-known scenery was the succession of monuments and road signs, dramatically depicting, as we rolled along, centuries of history. It took little imagination to hear the bagpipes over the sound of the motor, or to see the red coats and brass buttons through half-closed eyelids in the pink and highly contrasting light of dawn.

At the Pakistani border post we were invited to sit on a porch and drink tea with the immigration and customs men, who recorded our credentials quickly and opened nothing. At the Afghan post we were waved on. Here we saw our first Afghan soldiers, Mongoloids in mustard-colored uniforms. These men were Hazara tribesmen from the high Hindu Kush, descendants of Genghiz Khan's soldiers marooned on a mountaintop for half a millennium. The first part of the road did not seem like a road at all; we followed optional tracks along a river bottom. When, however, we started to climb, we found ourselves on a real road. Although unpaved, it was a product of modern engineering science, and a stock car with extra springs could get through. It was beautifully graded in the gorges and up the flanks of the mountains. The highest altitude we crossed was sixty-nine hundred feet, according to Hank's altimeter. The scenery was incomparable: vast panoramas of mountains no camera could catch, snow-capped peaks, fine-quilted valleys green with terraced rice and wheat, the pale dust of almond blossoms, and the naked branches of walnut trees bent like the fingers of hundreds of witches. Above the tree line we met snow, and soon we could see it below as well as above us. Out onto the vast snow-covered plain we rode. Then we passed ducks floating on flooded fields, and Afghan gentlemen stalking them out of parked jeeps, with mufflers and shotguns. It was a wintry, even Muscovite, scene. Into the gray dusk of Kabul we rode over icy streets past the red-cheeked Mongoloid faces of more Hazara, and to the American Embassy.

Our cook's name was Shirindel, which means "Sweet-

heart." No one had told him that we were coming. As he
lived in a small outbuilding, the house was as cold as
Antarctica, with snowdrifts four feet deep in the front
yard. Eventually we got warm, fed, and bedded down.
During the next nine days we worked like fiends preparing to go north to the limestone country. Not only did
the usual maze of bureaucratic procedure face us, but
also materials were scarce. If we had not brought the jeep
tires from Damascus at fabulous cost, we could not have
driven the jeep, as the spare wheel of that vehicle was
missing. I sent a man to the bazaar and within two days
he produced one, but we soon discovered that it had been
stolen from the vehicle of a member of our Embassy's
staff. The coupling on the jeep's trailer had been broken,
and a new one had to be forged. The jeep station-wagon,
which had been brand-new the season before, needed a
thorough overhauling, and we had to find a baggage rack,
in itself a major undertaking, and have it screwed to the
roof.

Another problem was to ensure a supply of gasoline.
At that time it was in poor supply, owing to some trouble
about getting it up from Pakistan; all that was available
was Russian fuel, of low quality. We had to have gasoline
coupons, which had to be made out by hand. Some of
these said "for the city only," others "for the country
only," and still others "for town and country." One American I knew had run out of gas in Jalalabad in the middle
of the night, and found that all his coupons were marked
"for Kabul only"; he had been obliged to get the governor
out of bed in order to go on. Knowing this, we took care
not to imitate his error. However, as the clerk who made
out our coupons found the paper work fatiguing, he gave
us some fairly large figures. The smallest amount we could
get was twenty gallons.

As for foodstuffs, we had the disadvantage of being

second-class Americans. Not being employed by the government, we had no commissary privileges. While many items could be bought in the shops, these did not include pork products or alcohol. With nothing in the house to drink, we could not invite anyone back, and the only Americans I ever met in the Middle East who did not drink were missionaries and United States marines, two dedicated groups of people. Of the two, only the marines were represented in Kabul. As is usually the case, the more isolated and difficult the post, the kinder and more friendly the people; this was particularly true of all of our fellow countrymen in Kabul, from Ambassador Ward down.

We got off on the 22nd of March, ten days after leaving Peshawar, which is, I believe, a record for the course. Wholly aside from our eagerness to get to work, we had two deadlines to meet. One was the opening of Shibar Pass, which had been blocked for some weeks by snow. A string of trucks had just got through, and the drivers had told Shirindel, himself an old trucker, that we could make it in jeeps. The other was Ramadhan, here called Ramazan, which was slated to begin on May 3, provided the moon could be seen on the previous night. As the Afghans are second to no other Muslims in their strict observance of the month of fasting, May 2 was the last possible day of work. Falling in the middle of the best digging-time of the year, it gave us only five weeks to get north, find a cave, and dig it. As far as the government was concerned, we might have left a day or two earlier, had not the 21st been No Ruz, which is as important to the Afghans as to the Persians. To leave on the 20th would have been comparable to tearing a group of Americans from the bosoms of their families on Christmas Eve. It could have been done, but I would not have been able to look the men in the face, and they would not have thought much of me. On an expedition mutual esteem is the principal ingredient of success.

Our small group included, besides one Coulter and two Coons, Shirindel the cook, Alif Beg the bearer, Mohammed Nader Khan the inspector of the Antiquities Department of the Ministry of Education, and Mohammed Nader Saweri, a young man who had recently been graduated from a local secondary school and who spoke good English. So did Shirindel. My Persian was next to useless. What there was of it was the locally despised Tehrani form, full of Arabic words. In fact, I had a habit of creating Persian words from Arabic, which had worked in Iran. Afghan Farsi is reputed to be a much "purer" Aryan form. For example, in Iran if one wants to use the verb *to clean,* one says *tamiz kardan,* but in Afghanistan *tamiz* is replaced by *pur,* the same as our word *pure.* Not only is Tehrani Persian hard for these people to understand, but it is also considered affected and effeminate, two characteristics that I did not want to have attributed to me.

When I say that we got off, I am telling a little less than the truth. All of us got off except Mohammed Nader Saweri, who had not finished clearing with the authorities his permit to leave the city. Having discovered this at the last minute, I bade him stay behind, get his clearance, and follow us later by bus or truck. People would know where we were. They always do. From now until the end of this chapter I am going to refer to Mohammed Nader Saweri as *the interpreter* and to Mohammed Nader Khan (whose name also includes a Saweri if one wants to put it in) as *the inspector.* These terms, which accurately describe their functions, are used in lieu of nicknames, which Afghans of noble lineage do not like.

As we left the city after many delays, we bumped over what may be the worst road in the world open to urban vehicular traffic. It led us past a large and imposing cluster of buildings, the British Embassy compound, beyond which it improved. On the way we saw many men carrying wooden birdcages, each containing a single bird. These were fighting quail, a special breed with blue wings and bright-orange beaks, which the Afghans set loose in combat like gamecocks. They love to see animals fight. On No Ruz day in Kabul there had been a ram-butting contest and a fight between male camels, which arched their necks, salivated, and groaned at each other without inflicting much damage. The children even fight kites by gluing ground glass to the strings, launching the kites in the air, and then sawing at each other's strings.

The first part of our road lay over the Kabul valley flatland, a rich and lovely place covered with villages and farms, irrigated by countless brooks and ditches whose banks, as in Iran, are fringed with rows of closely spaced poplars, tight-limbed and erect, like double lines of soldiers standing at attention. As we paused for lunch we saw, high above us in the crystal-clear air, a flight of geese winging their way to Siberia. Before we could count them they had disappeared over the snow-capped wall of the Hindu Kush; there must have been at least three hundred, flying through the motionless upper air in one great V with two smaller V's inside it. Then another flight joined it and an intricate pattern of inverted V's took form, as if after years of practice. A mile high—two and a half above sea level—they could hardly be seen, heading from the Obi swamps to summer and to lay their eggs.

On this ride the tires on the jeep held up, for they were new; those on the station wagon went flat several times. Shirindel, who fixed them with Alif Beg's aid, told me that we should have brought new ones for that vehicle too. The trouble was that, in addition to deep ruts and sharp rocks, the road was full of horseshoe nails. As soon as a tire's tread is at all worn, in go the nails. The sides of the road are littered with scraps of dead tires; larger pieces are made into the soles of sandals and shoes. Many of the tires one sees on trucks have undergone major surgery, as cleverly stitched wounds along their sidewalls show.

In the middle of the afternoon we left the plain. Entering a narrow valley, the road began to climb. Now we were in shadow, and the air felt cold. Furthermore, the road was wet. Many of the ruts were so deep that our front-axle gear boxes stuck in the mud and our vehicles were supported in precarious balance, like a fat man lying on his belly on a piano stool. At such times we would get out and put our picks and shovels to good use. As the afternoon wore on and it was beginning to get dark, the valley narrowed to a canyon and the road to a shelf. On our left was a rising cliff and on our right a falling one. Here and there hollows had been carved from the rock to permit vehicles to pass, but with oversize trucks it was often a tight squeeze.

These trucks had been taken apart in a machine-shop yard outside the city, and stretched. Some were as much as ten feet longer than when they had left the factory. Also, they were overloaded. Many broke down; a common sight was a grounded truck beside the road, with a man sitting over a little fire cooking his supper; he might wait as long as two weeks until his partner brought the needed part back from the city. Normally a truck crew consists of a driver and a "cleaner," who jumps out when the truck is stopping and places a large wedge-shaped section of a log, fitted with a handle, under a wheel to keep it from rolling. When the truck starts he removes it and jumps back in again.

As luck would have it, we were limping and staggering along through this narrow morass in the middle of a procession of trucks, mutually incapable of passing or be-

ing passed. Hank was driving the jeep and I was following at the wheel of the station wagon when suddenly I
saw the jeep's trailer lunge to the left. We all stopped.
The trailer's left wheel had come off. If hearts really sink
at the sight of disaster, that is what mine did then. The
trailer, overloaded like everything else on that road, carried the bulk of our equipment and supplies, capped with
a gravel-sifting screen, and weighing at least a ton. The
bolts that held the wheel to the axle had been stripped
clean.

Before I could think of what to do next, others had
done that piece of thinking for me. The truck ahead of
us had backed up and its tailboard had been lowered.
The driver, employed by the Afghan Department of
Mines, was taking an empty vehicle back to his station
over the mountains. In almost no time at all a dozen large
and muscular men had appeared out of nowhere, some
with beards and others without; some wearing karakul
caps and others turbans. With Shirindel in command,
these men lifted the trailer, load and all, out of the mud
and put it on the body of the truck. I stood there, a mere
spectator, alongside an old man with a gaunt face, delicately arched nostrils, and a silky beard, who held the
reins of a camel. The two aquiline faces were posed together in profile as the man and his mount watched the
operation. "*Ali!*" the men shouted in rhythm, as they
heaved the trailer into the truck. Not only was the or-
ganization of this group effort flawless, the co-ordination
perfect, and the *esprit de corps* high, but when they finished they refused to take any money.

"In Afghanistan we help each other," they said, and
they certainly do.

By dark we reached Ghorband, a town built in the
folds of the mountain, and drove into the courtyard of a
chai khana, or teahouse, where we ate an excellent meal

and slept in comfortable beds—huge wooden frames laced with cords. The truck with our trailer aboard stood outside. In the morning the driver left long before we woke up, because his vehicle was slower than ours and he wanted to arrive at the first market town over the pass ahead of us.

We were off at 6:50 a.m. and over the Shibar Pass at 9:40, and the road was much better than that of the day before. The scenery was magnificent, but so is all scenery in Afghanistan. At the crest of the pass we met scores of men shoveling snow with one-piece wooden shovels; then moved on to a plateau covered with over a foot of snow, nearly eleven thousand feet in the air; then down a breath-taking gorge walled with pink granite, to Bulola. Here we found the truck and our trailer with the driver hard at work. He had found bolts and nuts that would fit, had drilled out the old bolts, and within a half-hour of our arrival the trailer was hooked to the jeep again, as good—or as bad—as ever. Bulola is a double row of shops flanking the road. I remember one man sitting cross-legged on a mat, polishing the gunstock of a rifle with delicacy and care; the stock was a flawless piece of rosewood intricately carved. Not since almost thirty years before, when I climbed about the peaks and vales of Morocco on a mule, had I seen anything like this, a fine, virile Middle Eastern culture, unselfconscious, and at work.

In the late afternoon we arrived at Do Ab ("Two Waters"), a way station built, as the name implies, at the convergence of two valleys. The community itself is a double row of modern buildings flanking the road, plus a government hotel built in the reign of King Amanullah (1919–29) in European style. Similar hotels are located throughout the country at places intended to be a day's ride apart, as they would be were the roads paved. Originally some, at least, were run by European managers.

English flush toilets, bathtubs, and hot-water heaters are all in place, but none work. Instead the servants bring oil tins of hot and cold water from the kitchen.

To my way of thinking, this showplace seemed bleak, cold, and dark, far less inviting than the Neolithic untidiness of the previous night's teahouse, which was as comfortable as an old shoe. Yet the inspector was very proud of it; he said half a dozen times how unhappy he had felt that "Modom" had been obliged to spend a night in so disgusting a spot as that teahouse when *this* fine hostel lay ahead. In it, as in many abrupt cultural contrasts, I found a dismal conflict of symbols which grated on my nerves like the sight of a crap game in a church. In it the Afghans seemed to lose their dignity, their most prized possession.

The next morning we were up shortly before dawn, and ready to leave soon after the valley had been flooded by daylight. The hotel looked less dreary now than the night before, partly because it was being filled up with people. As we moved out, the town officials, clerks, and elders moved in. What had been a government resthouse at night was now transformed into a town hall, social club, and general community center, with all of the salons and some of the bedrooms used as offices.

All that day Hank and I, at the wheels of our vehicles, looked at the rock formations along the roadside as much as we dared. From pink granite we went on to violet sandstone, and then to various shades of brown as the sandstone yielded to shale, but limestone we did not encounter until near evening. In the meanwhile we passed through marvelous country and saw some of the world's most interesting-looking people: moon-faced Hazaras, hawk-beaked and slit-eyed Turkomans, Tajiks and Uzbegs with snub noses and red cheeks like so many Finns or Irishmen, and tall, lean Pathans, any one of whom could pose as Hamlet alongside Walter Hampden and John Barrymore. The clothing they wore ran through the spectrum and a great range of styles, each of which would reveal to those who knew enough what tribe or race a man belonged to and his rank and occupation. As yet uncontaminated by the fear of not appearing "modern," they gladly posed for photographs.

Coming down the valley, we passed rolling country that looked like Montana, with wheat fields on the high slopes, then, near the bottom, an enormous terraced rice bowl. We passed collections of Turkoman domed portable houses known as *yurts,* some covered with felt alone, others with felt and straw mats, and still others with straw only; then black tents inhabited by nomadic shepherds called Sayad-i-Khayam, or "tented hunters," who, according to Shirindel, were "gypsies from Bombay, sah." Just before we reached the plain we saw little outcrops of limestone between other kinds of rock, but no caves.

The Oxus plain is Afghanistan's richest region, and its industrial center. Pul-i-Khumbri, through which we passed, is a city built around a huge cotton mill. Before sunset we reached Baghlan, the capital of the province of that name, where we were lodged in a fine modern building, the clubhouse connected with the local sugar mill. There we were entertained by the manager, Mr. Abdullah, who had spent two years studying the beet-sugar industry in Idaho and Colorado. In the morning he took us through his factory, a complete Skoda-made plant with a machine shop equipped with German machinery and operated by a German. Both coal and hydroelectric power are available in the neighborhood, and in use.

He explained how he ran a model farm to teach the local farmers how to grow sugar beets not only on their old farms, but on homesteaded lands formerly used for

grazing. We lunched with the governor, a most cultivated and charming man who, like Mr. Abdullah, spoke
perfect English and was interested in almost everything.
He discussed with Hank his scheme for restoring the old
bed of the Oxus River and watering millions of acres.
The only thing about his quarters which reminded us
that we were in central Asia was a two-yak-tail banner
standing in a corner in his sitting-room, the old Turko-
Mongol symbol of his office, as proudly displayed as
the skean dhu of a Scottish clan chieftain in London or
Canada. It is hard to express how pleasant it is to meet
men like these in the world's most remote places, doing
a marvelous job of guiding their people from the Middle
Ages to the atomic age without an intervening phase of
miserable semi-Westernization.

In the afternoon, stuffed with delicious food, we got
back to work; after all, we were searching for caves.
North and east of Baghlan the bedrock was limestone,
covered with topsoil and grass, much as in the Belt and
Hotu country, but without trees. Both Mr. Abdullah and
the governor had said that we were unlikely to find caves
there, and they were right. Nothing would have been
more agreeable than to excavate a site within commuting
distance of the Beet Factory Club, but in the morning
we moved on.

Our hosts at Baghlan had told us that we would find
caves at Haibak, and they were correct. The road from
Pul-i-Khumbri crosses a spur of the Hindu Kush on its
way to Tashkurgan, where it connects with the main
highway skirting the Oxus plain. On the way over this
shoulder we saw a number of limestone outcrops, and
examined one small rock shelter, but discovered nothing
worth excavating. In Haibak we arrived at 2:30 in the
afternoon, going immediately to the hotel, where we were
expected. Although built as part of the same program

as the Do Ab hostelry, this one had a different atmosphere. It had been lived in more, was not in such good repair, and the people in it were less self-conscious.

We were met by the mayor, a stocky, gray-haired man in a blue pinstripe suit with the jacket cut as a frock coat, and by the governor's deputy. Soldiers were called to guard our vehicles as we ate a splendid lunch of pilau, kebabs wrapped around lumps of fat, and a rarebit-like dish of cooked cheese which I had eaten before only in Albania. As soon as we were finished we drove out a side road with the mayor as guide. This road ran alongside a stream, which soon led us to a canyon of hard gray limestone through which we passed to a Tajik village. The whole setting reminded me of the Dordogne region in France, the world's Paleolithic center.

We saw many rock shelters, none of them very deep, and one man-made cave high in the canyon wall. As it was soon dark we decided to return in the morning to go farther up the valley. This we did, leaving the station wagon at the village and taking the jeep ten miles farther to a place where we were stopped by a huge rock in the middle of the road. This was actually the old truck road to Kabul, abandoned after the present one had been built; Shirindel remembered having driven over it. Walking beyond the rock, we found that the whole roadbed had fallen away.

Backtracking a mile or two, we came to a village of white houses perched on a rock, and were greeted by a half-dozen magnificent old men, blue-eyed and white-bearded, any one of whom could have been a prime minister. They were the village elders, and they gave us bread and tea. Across the canyon, some four hundred and fifty feet up, was a cave. As they pointed it out we could see its mouth. In it, they said, was a huge skeleton. From where we sat I could not see any way to get up, but they assured us that it was easily accessible. So we walked down the stream, crossed it on stepping-stones, and began to climb.

At first the path was smooth and the grade moderate, but by the time we had risen two hundred feet we were making a fair imitation of mountain goats. At a height of four hundred feet we came to a very perilous spot. Here the path was less than a foot wide. On the right the mountainside sloped up at an angle of forty-five degrees, and on the left was a sheer drop. We were walking above a concavity in the face of the cliff. As I looked over my left shoulder I could see the opposite wall of the canyon in finest detail, each crack in the rock, each tiny shrub trying desperately to grow in a verti-cal world. It was like looking through a microscope. I looked down and saw the white village as in an etching. I looked ahead and saw a blur. I could not see my feet. Feeling my way to a spot wide enough to hold me, I sat down slowly and with infinite care. My bones had turned to jelly.

The mayor, still immaculate in his pinstripe, had reached the cave, and Hank with him. Having been a mountain guide in his younger days, Hank was no more bothered by this path than was the mayor. The inspector, who was ahead of me, ran to tell Hank, who came back armed with a cigarette and a bar of chocolate which he had been carrying for just such an emergency. The cig-arette, the chocolate, and Hank's conversation restored me to a condition in which I was able to stand up and be walked down between him and the inspector. This was probably the most shameful moment of my life, or so I then felt. The inspector, who had annoyed me in a number of little ways, was behaving like a hero, and the fine mayor, who had greeted me like a top-flight V.I.P., was pretending not to notice my humiliation.

I do not know what is in that cave, but even if it contained a whole village of Neanderthal skeletons I could not dig it. Several days later I found that a pair of glasses I had had made so that I could see the front and rear sights of my rifle and the target at the same time might have saved me this degradation, for when I was wearing them I lost my fear of heights. Hank reported that although the cave had a dirt floor and there was flint lying about, it was also covered with huge blocks of fallen rock which would have to be removed before excavation could be attempted. Even if the path were widened and I got over my fear, it would be too difficult to move material and specimens up and down, and too dangerous for daily climbing.

In the afternoon we drove down the Tashkurgan road. First we saw a number of small caves in crumbly limestone of relatively recent deposition, and man-made tombs alongside them. Although there was flint on the ground, this was not a good area, because the caves had been formed in post-glacial times. Then, at 9.2 miles out of Haibak, we saw a magnificent cave across the valley, on the other side of a river, a little less than a mile away.

We drove to the riverbank, forded on foot, and scrambled up the opposite bank, then climbed a moderate slope to the cave. When we reached it, it looked quite different from its appearance from the road, as so often happens. It was the remains of a huge cave over one hundred feet deep and fifty wide, the roof of which had collapsed, so that only about twenty feet in the rear was still sheltered. The roof was of hard limestone, under which lay a softer, water-soluble stratum known as a *solution layer;* the progressive disappearance of the solution layer had at some critical point brought down the crust. There seemed to be about thirty feet of deposit inside, in which we decided to dig. And it was high time indeed, for only thirty-six days remained between us and Ramazan. The cave bore the same name as the village between it and the road—Kok Jar, which is "Blue Gulch" in Uzbeg Turkish.

The next day we drove to Mazar-i-Sharif, the capital of the province in which both Haibak and Kok Jar are situated, to get a permit to dig. On this drive we noted that the mountain in which Kok Jar is situated stands up alone as a solitary unit, geologically a different system from the others. In its back we saw other caves as the road curved around it. Still farther down the road we passed a village named Sar Kiar, behind which was a table-topped mountain about eight hundred feet higher than the road. The top four hundred feet of its height was cliff, the lower half *scree* (a steep slope strewn with rock). Right where the two elements met was a rock shelter, its roof blackened by fire. The outer lip of overhang was curved like a crescent moon, or like a huge mouth smiling. Noting its presence in our books, we called it "Smiling Boy," and drove on, for the road was long.

At Tashkurgan we emerged from the mountainous country onto the flat Oxus plain, here a desert. On it we could make up to thirty-five miles an hour. On the left we saw two big caves in the mountains, and on the right a row of white cliffs which, we were told, lay inside Soviet territory. On the ground alongside the road we saw a curious kind of flower, a coal-black jack-in-the-pulpit. Mazar-i-Sharif itself is a city built mainly along a single street of shops, off which branch covered bazaars and a fine blue-tiled mosque sacred to the Prophet's son-in-law, Ali. Although the majority of Afghans are Sunnis, this a Shi'a shrine. Our inspector, whose father was a notable Shi'a official in Kabul, took time out to make a quick visit for prayer.

At the far end of the town we came to the governor's house, flanked by a pair of giant sycamores in front of a large square. The governor, who spoke French, entertained us as lavishly as had his colleague at Baghlan. During the preliminary meeting I mentioned the fruits of his country—melons, grapes, and pomegranates. During the meal each of these appeared in turn, though all were out of season. In about two hours this competent and gracious gentleman had given us our permits, obtained medicine for the inspector, secured us some alcohol for our pressure lamps on a prescription, told us about his son at Cornell, and also about some excellent caves located in the next province to the west, Maimana. Furthermore, he was probably instrumental in our inspector's success in finding in the bazaar one brand-new tire for the station wagon, an almost incredible feat.

Back in Haibak we found that our interpreter had arrived on a truck. With him we moved out the next morning, March 29, to Kok Jar, carrying all our gear.

From March 29 through April 4 we excavated Kok Jar, working in three trenches. At first we found some flint, including one flake implement of Middle Paleolithic type, which was encouraging. As we went down, we found in all trenches a sequence of rubbles and clays, almost entirely sterile. At 10:20 a.m. on April 4 one of our bucket men, Abd el-Krim, emptying a bucket on the dump—for this soil was not worth screening—found a copper cartridge case coated with the yellow earth of level A-5, in which we were digging. A long argument followed, for some believed that it must have fallen in. At 11:20 we found a bone splinter, unstained and as elastic as if it had just come from a butcher shop, and at 11:45 the rim sherd of a modern glazed pottery jar.

I now asked the workmen and the villagers standing about to produce the oldest living inhabitant of the region, and a spry old man stepped out, stroking his long white beard. He said that he was sixty-five, but I think he was older. Upon questioning, he declared that forty years ago, when he was twenty-five, the level of the ground where we were standing had been as far below the present surface as the height of his nipples; he knew this from the exposed rock on the sides. In the area of Trench A the level had been just about where our present floor lay, at 3.80 meters or twelve feet eight inches, which was just right because the cartridge case was of a type manufactured at about that time. The sides of the gorge and the top of the rock had been forested then, but the villagers had cut down the trees for firewood and the goats had ruined the grass. With nothing to hold the soil in place, it had been washed down into the open cave every time that it rained. Swift floods had scoured deep channels, and slower ones had filled them and raised the level of the surface to its present height.

This was good enough for Hank and me. No geologist could have given a better account of the cycle of soil-erosion and gully-formation caused by deforestation, and I ordered the work to stop at once. Our inspector, however, disagreed. To back up his point of view he produced a rival graybeard, a man with round blue eyes and very delicate fingers who, he said, was a great poet. Declaiming with gestures and very conscious of his audience, the poet stated that the first graybeard's account was without foundation. He too had lived there forty years, and the landscape had not changed a particle.

Along with everyone else except the inspector, I believed the first witness. As our chances of finding an undisturbed deposit in this site seemed zero, we packed up and went away. The afternoon was spent in a frantic search for a new cave called Kara Kamar, or "Black Belly," reputed to exist on the other side of Kok Jar mountain, but we got the jeep bogged in mud and failed. In the evening we decided to take a close look at the rock shelter we had named Smiling Boy on our trip to Mazar-i-Sharif, and in the morning Hank, the interpreter, and I went to Kok Jar, picked up Khair Mohammed, Khan Shah, and two other workmen, and proceeded down the road to Sar Kiar.

Out of our time wasted at Kok Jar we had gained one advantage: we had found some excellent workmen and had trained two pick men. Khair Mohammed was a Tajik, short, blond, and wiry; he could have passed for a Yankee machinist in a small Connecticut town. Khan Shah, also a Tajik, was a bony, muscular man with a long nose and a sloping forehead who looked more like some kind of Turk, though, like the rest of the villagers at Kok Jar, he was supposed to be of Persian-speaking Aryan stock. In the short time we were there neither man became foreman, for there was no rivalry. Each had his own gang, working in separate trenches or at the two ends of a single long trench.

Although the Smiling Boy rock shelter looked good and we were growing desperate, it had several disadvantages. In the first place, it was over four hundred feet above the plain and at the time that we were interested in—the Pleistocene—it might have been hanging in mid-air without easy access, as the talus slope had been formed by rockfall from the entire face of the cliff, both below and above the shelter. In the second place, it was quite shallow, with no more than twelve feet of overhang, though originally it might have been wider. On the credit side was its location, a wonderful lookout for game, situated at the confluence of three valleys, visible for many miles, and within easy reach of water. Facing south, it got the sun nearly all the day.

We did not, however, settle for it at once, but con-

tinued our search for the elusive Kara Kamar behind the
Kok Jar mountain. Bogged again, we came out, returned
to Haibak, and went on a desperate ride to see an alleged
cave near Takt-i-Rustam ("Rustem's Seat"), which took
us over a path that soon petered to nothing on the back
of a limestone ridge. Returning from this wild-goose
chase, the inspector begged us to stop to see another ruin.

"Pleace, pleace, is history plyce!" he said.

The year before, he had begged one of my colleagues
to go there with him, using the same words, but they had
fallen on deaf ears. A "history place" could mean anything, but most likely a ruined mosque or other Islamic
structure. As we had nothing else to do except to go back
to the hotel, we gave in. The object of the inspector's
interest turned out to be a magnificent Buddhist *stupa*,
a solid limestone dome three hundred feet in circum-
ference and thirty high, with a square prayer house on
the top, all as highly polished and smooth as the chrome
trim on a new Chevrolet. It had been carved out of the
flank of a mountain, and the surrounding rock had not
been cut away; it was therefore hard to see and harder
to photograph. One approached it through a tunnel
that had been a natural cave; it was clear that this
cave had a deposit that might or might not have been
disturbed in the stupa-carving process. However, our
permit was for caves and not for historic monuments,
and it would be hard to separate stupa-digging from
cave-digging. At the foot of the mountain was a lamasery,
also carved from solid rock, consisting of a domed lotus
room with painted designs still visible, and a long series
of galleries in which the monks had lived.

We gave up. Smiling Boy it would be. We arrived
there at 8:30 a.m. on April 6, to find that twelve of our
own men from Kok Jar were already there and ready to
work, having walked about six miles. From the group of

locals standing by I selected four others, and promised to hire more as the work progressed.

"What is the name of this cave?" I asked one of the locals.

"Kara Kamar," he replied.

Turning to Khair Mohammed, who had been with us on our two previous attempts to find Kara Kamar, I asked him to explain this confusion.

"There are two Kara Kamars," he said. "I thought you wanted the other one."

He was right. With our field glasses we could just see the mouth of the other Kara Kamar for which we had been searching, a black slit in the green flank of another mountain across the valley from the mountain of Kok Jar. It looked fine, but it would have to wait for another season. The words *kara kamar* mean *black belly*. The rounded overhang of our cave's roof was thought to resemble a fat man's belly. It was black with the soot of countless fires.

Before laying out a trench we studied the inner wall of the shelter to decide which part of the deposit would be the deepest. The general configuration of the limestone indicated that the flow of water, which had produced the shelter in the first place, had followed a channel near the western end of the shelter, on the right facing out. As this should be the deepest part, we saved it for later treatment. After we had removed the inevitable goat dung we established a base line inside the shelter of the overhang and laid out Trench A at its eastern end, 3.70 meters (twelve feet three inches) wide and 8.85 meters (twenty-nine feet six inches) long.

The deposit in Trench A turned out to be a closely packed white dust, apparently identical with the powdered chalk that one cleans off blackboard erasers. It was completely lacking in moisture. Great clouds of it

billowed about, choking everyone. It had been produced
by the intense heat of countless fires and the polishing
action of the goat hoofs on limestone. This shelter, we
were told, had in olden times been a signal-fire station
from which messages were relayed up and down the valleys. In the chalk were a few potsherds of metal-age manufacture, a piece of charred goatflesh, several scraps of

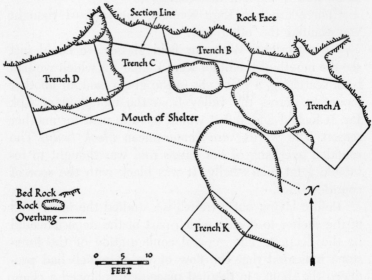

Kara Kamar: plan.

bone, and a number of heat-pocked flints which indicated
that something older might lie below.

From our perch on the side of the mountain we could
look down on the roofs of Sar Kiar, which is really two
villages. Along the road stands the larger and older one,
now partly in ruins. It is inhabited by Uzbegs, Turkish-
speaking farmers who are solid, heavily built men with
broad faces, only rarely Mongoloid. Many of the older
men did not speak Persian, and communicated with us
mainly by sign-language. Even among themselves they

have little to say, and this is a key to their temperament, which is dogged and phlegmatic.

The smaller and newer village is inhabited by Pathans, the aristocrats of Afghanistan, who speak Pushtu. These men had been brought north by the government some decades earlier, and had been given the Uzbeg village as a land grant. The reason for this move was clear enough. All of the other peoples of Mazar-i-Sharif province, particularly the Tajiks and Uzbegs, have kinfolk over

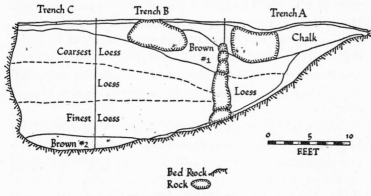

Kara Kamar: section.

the border, living in separate Soviet "republics" of their own. The kin of the Pathans live south of the mountains, and the Pathans are famed warriors, related to the ruling house. While the Uzbegs were eager to work in the cave, the Pathans came only as visitors.

As soon as we had found the first flint in Trench A, we put a gang of these Uzbegs to work building a path up the slope of the mountain from our jeep-parking area, to save us energy for the day's work once we got to the top, and to keep us from twisting ankles on the stone-strewn scree. On the second day we found brown cave earth underlying the chalk dust, and nothing in the brown earth. The floor was really the left side of a bowl.

It was lined by a layer of rubble—limestone flaked off the bedrock by temperature changes: heat, frost, or both.

We were ready to give up. Twenty-seven days to Ramazan. Sterile earth filling a bowl halfway up a cliff. Not a sign of a deposit. As a matter of fact, we had come across very few worked flints anywhere, and no trace of Neolithic, which usually reveals its presence by potsherds on the surface of mounds or in screes. Riding back with these somber thoughts, the inspector at least gave us a laugh. The station wagon had its daily flat tire. Hank, driving the jeep up to help, stalled it. When it was time to go on, the interpreter stepped forward to crank the jeep (as the self-starter had long since expired). The inspector remarked: "Estop, pleace, excooz me, estop! Mr. Serwar Khan cannot make the hindle! His hind is sick!"

Shirindel let out an irrepressible guffaw. We could not help joining him. It was a little mean of us. My Persian pronunciation was just as bad as the inspector's English or worse, but there are moments—and this was one of them. The interpreter had had a sore hand, but it was now all right; he cranked the jeep and we all went on, feeling somewhat relieved, as we wiped the tears from our cheeks. In tense moments on an archæological expedition, as in a submarine or an Antarctic cabin, a little joke is a wonderful thing.

Thursday, April 8, was a lovely day, and during it our worries were allayed. The brown cave earth was sterile only at its top; below the first twenty-centimeter level we found the bones of gazelle, fox, and birds, and also flint blades. Then we unearthed a microlith core, one of those tiny thimble-like pieces of flint from which Mesolithic man struck off his miniature blades, and we knew where we were. The material that we took out closely resembled the Seal Mesolithic of Belt Cave. Unless something was wrong, we were removing earth laid down nine to eleven thousand years ago, at the end of the last glaciation. From the work-schedule point of view this was wonderful news, for we could go straight on down to Paleolithic, if Paleolithic there were, without using up our precious days on the Iron and Bronze Ages, or even Neolithic.

At Hank's suggestion we started another trench, called K, in the open in front of the cave, to see how far forward the deposit went, for it was limited in the immediate front of the shelter by a huge rock that had fallen from the roof. At the same time we observed that among the thousands of white stones strewn over the scree were some pieces that had been retouched. Breaking open a piece that had not been worked, we found that it was flint; the calcareous coat that gave it its milky appearance was a product of weathering, just as in the case of the cleaver that Charlie Stearns and my son Carl, Jr., had found in the red soil over the High Cave seven years earlier. This discovery gave me a chance to employ more Uzbegs, who were asking politely for work. Once they had been shown what we wanted, they scattered over the tilted landscape, picking up white flints, and during the next few days I sorted tens of thousands of them, reducing their number to a few hundreds.

It is too early to say exactly what these flints are or mean. That they were washed down from a higher cave or from the top after the scree had been formed was clear. Some were very large, others small. Many were cores from which flakes had been struck in a generally haphazard manner. Both core and flake tools were represented, and the flake tools had been made without prepared platforms or retouched butts. As Hank pointed out, many of them would fit the palm of the hand very well, as if the toolmaker had intended to clasp them between fingers and palm without special use of his thumb. In any event, we now had two industries: a Mesolithic *in situ*, and a very crude chopper-and-flake culture of unknown age on the surface. If we found nothing else, we would not go home empty-handed.

During this third day we had trouble with rocks falling onto our work areas. A small one hit the sieve, and a round piece as big as a man's head tore through the rotten canvas of our cook tent. At first the Uzbegs said, or we thought they said, that wild animals were kicking them down from the flat top of the mountain, but we found it was the hoofs of goats which did it. From that moment on we posted a guard on the rim of the mountaintop to keep goats away, and the only thing that fell after that was a small, unidentifiable, grayish-green snake that broke its neck on the screen. We were told that its bite was deadly; we are always told that.

Two things were remarkable about our work at Kara Kamar: the length of time and the amount of effort it took to get there at all, and the smoothness with which the work proceeded once it had begun. Both Tajiks and Uzbegs were model workmen, and they got on well together. We had only one quarrel during the entire season, and that was a brief flurry between a simple-minded workman from Kok Jar who had just married a young girl, and the water boy, who teased him about it. The total casualty was one torn shirt.

More than in any other place I had worked in, I had a feeling of being close to nature. The vast expanse of mountains and valleys which we saw from the cave had been little altered by man, for it was grazing more than farming country. Every day a herd of over eighty horses was driven to pasture at the foot of our mountain, and one day we saw an antlered stag trot across the meadow, run up the side of a mountain to the west of us, and disappear around its flank. Besides the small snake that fell into the sieve we saw several five-foot puff adders and one cobra. Our only real danger, however, was from dogs. Both the Uzbegs and the Pathans kept them: huge, thick-set, heavy-coated dogs with broad heads and ears pruned by innumerable fights. Our Kok Jar water boy could not go to the Uzbeg village for fear of being torn to pieces, so he was put on the bucket line while an Uzbeg lad took his place. Every afternoon when the time came to leave Kara Kamar the dogs from the Pathan village attacked our vehicles. As I drove the jeep, whose door had long since been lost, my left leg was in danger. Once I cracked one of the dogs over the nose with the crank handle just as he was about to seize my ankle. We complained to the Pathans, but they could not restrain them. From then on we carried stones and shovel handles, and the best dog-swatters rode with me in the jeep.

Although I did not wish these dogs hard luck, I would have been happy if, somehow or other, one of them had been killed. One of their skulls would have made a valuable addition to my bone collection in Philadelphia, for, as far as I could see while they were snapping at me, they were identical with the Mesolithic specimens from Hotu. Mesolithic man had a valuable ally indeed.

We found no dog bones in Kara Kamar, but plenty of other animal remains, particularly after we had extended our digging-area along the surface of the sheltered floor in Trenches B and C. The combined trenches were now thirteen meters long, or forty-three feet. The brown earth containing Mesolithic implements went down two meters in Trench A, below which it gradually merged into a mixed soil, which turned into a fine yellow wind-blown soil known as *loess*. In Trench B the bottom of the brown soil sloped upward, and in Trench C it came almost to the surface; the brown soil here was only twenty centimeters thick. Luckily, the chalk dust was almost entirely confined to Trench A.

In Trenches B and C the brown earth was underlaid by an unmixed deposit of very fine loess. This continued down for four meters. It was easy to excavate, as it contained no stones and it had a wonderful consistency that kept it from crumbling. The side of the trench made a splendid face, on which we could see two minor soil changes. Above the first line of change the loess was the finest. Between the two lines the proportion of coarser grains in the soil increased, and below the lower line there were even more. These three loess deposits may have been laid down during one or more glacial advances of the last ice age, as part of the cold steppe formation discussed in Chapter One, or redeposited later. The usual geological interpretation is that these deposits represent the first, second, and third advances of that age. The animal bones found in the loess included many teeth and toe bones of horses—just what one would expect to find in such soil. The lower and middle loesses also contained several hearths, from which we collected good samples of charcoal.

One thing that puzzled us was the difference in the soils between Trench A and the other two trenches. Trench A was blocked off from Trench B by a nine-foot stone wall, made up of natural stones piled on top of one another. At least some of them must have been placed there as early as the first occupation of the cave in lower-loess times, for the soil around the foot of the wall was undisturbed. The question was: did these stones fall from the roof in such a fashion as to pile themselves up in this way, or did the people who brought horse bones into the cave build this wall for some purpose? In these trenches we found many other stones that had fallen from the roof at one time or another. The whole region is earthquake country; we even felt one minor earthquake during the night while we were sleeping in the hotel at Haibak. But could stones fall, one after another, each one just at a time when the level of the dirt floor had reached the top of the stone below it, so that they could be stacked in this position?

Whatever the answer, the wall had prevented the loess, which was blowing in from the direction of Trench B, from being deposited behind its shelter in as regular a manner as in front of it. For this reason we did not trust the stratification in the lower part of Trench A as much as that of the other trenches. This fact is of importance in the interpretation of the materials, and of the dates that we obtained later.

Under the lower loess in Trench C and in part of Trench B we came upon a second deposit of brown cave earth, very similar in appearance and texture to that above the loess. As the upper brown earth contained Mesolithic implements, it must have been laid down in post-glacial times when the climate was more or less the same as now. Therefore, the lower brown earth could well have been deposited in a warm interval of the last glacial period, if not, as seems more likely, in an interglacial. Unfortunately, there was only a small quantity of this soil. Being less than fifty centimeters thick, it overlay only the very bottom of the rock shelter, and we did not get more than five cubic meters of it (140 cubic feet) in all. But it contained both bone and flint.

Under the Mesolithic material we found three distinct cultural assemblages. Unfortunately, not one of them was represented by enough implements to give us a good sample. The Mesolithic itself contained only fifty-eight definitely used implements. In the upper loess and the upper part of the middle loess we found forty-three implements. Like the surface material that the Uzbegs had collected, these were of white flint. When broken, this flint was gray inside, which means that the white color was caused by its lying around exposed for a long period. The rate of deposition of the upper loess must have been slow.

All of these implements were flakes, or cores from which flakes had been struck. There were no disks, and no prepared cores of the kind found in Bisitun, though one flake showed a great deal of faceting. The principal implement type was a simple flake, retouched on a single edge. Although many experts of Paleolithic archæology have looked at these flakes, no one has assigned them to a previously described industry. All that one can say is that some of them look like the smaller and finer of the pieces collected on the surface. If the people who made them had fire—and it seems incredible that they did not in a climate as cold as that of Kara Kamar—either they did not use it in this cave, or its traces were somehow washed, blown, or otherwise carried away.

Immediately below this material, in the lower part of the middle loess and the entire stretch of the lower loess, we found a much more abundant flint industry, associated with the hearths from which we collected charcoal. Of this we saved eighty-two good pieces and threw away a large quantity of scrap. Of these eighty-two, thirty-two were all of one special kind of tool, a thick *end scraper* made on a blade or blade core by removing a series of small blades all around the working-edge, giving it a fluted appearance. These tools are also called *carinated steep scrapers* and *nosed scrapers*. They are characteristic of the Aurignacian phase of the Upper Paleolithic cultures of Palestine and France. Along with them we found the tiny blades that had been removed from them in the fluting process. Although they looked like microliths, there was no evidence that any of them had been used. The next most numerous implement was a simple blade. We found one drill, three bone awls, and not a single burin. This is an Upper Paleolithic blade culture, fifteen hundred miles east of the nearest site of the same general class—Ralph Solecki's Shanidar in Iraqi Kurdistan.[1] Either these people had a very limited toolkit, or they did not leave a good sample of their tools in this

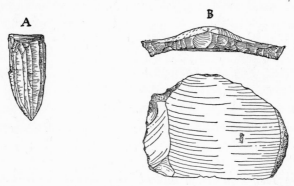

Kara Kamar: flints. (A) Microlith core from the Meso-lithic layer at the top of the deposit. (B) From the upper loess: a piece struck off the top of a prepared core to level the surface of its striking-platform. In the upper view, note the elaborate faceting on the edge, done to control the direction of the line of fracture. (One-half actual size.)

cave. In the brown soil at the bottom we found only nine implements, all white flakes, which could have come from the upper loess or from the slope outside.

This sequence was indeed a mystery—crude flakes, Upper Paleolithic blades, more crude flakes, Mesolithic blades. It looked as if two kinds of people, at the very least, had been involved in a series of alternate appearances and disappearances. First to use the cave were

[1] Ralph Solecki: "Shanidar Cave, a Paleolithic Site in Northern Iraq," Smithsonian Annual Report for 1954 (Washington, 1955), pp. 389-425.

hunters who made a crude-flake industry at a time when the climate was as warm as today. Then when it was colder they were replaced by an Upper Paleolithic blade-making group who built fires and knew how to make warm clothing. While it was still cold they in turn departed, and descendants of the first group, or others who had taken over their tool-making technique, came back

A   B

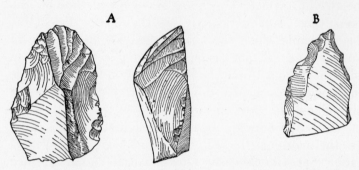

(A) *Two views of a typical steep scraper, one of the principal implements in the rich cultural deposit of the lower loess at Kara Kamar. Suited for working wood, bone, and other hard materials, this tool was fluted by the removal of a row of small blades around the working edge, by means of a punch. This procedure anticipated the microlithic technique in which the product sought was not the core but the small blades themselves. (B) A crudely retouched flake with its bulb end broken off, typical of the few rather formless pieces found in the brown earth at the bottom of the deposit. (One-half actual size.)*

again. Eventually they also departed, and after the glacial period Mesolithic men took over the cave.

Although the work of identifying the animals' bones has not yet been completed, it is possible to say that the principal animal hunted in Mesolithic times was a gazelle, along with some wild sheep, and that the wild sheep was also a favorite of the people in the earliest level. It is certain that domestic animals were not kept in the cave until after the floor had been completely deposited, because when they are kept in a cave their hoofs polish the surfaces of the rocks at the sides of the cave, as well as the rocks that have fallen and protrude through the floor. In Kara Kamar this hoof polish did not go an inch below the surface. The horse was hunted through the loess time, but particularly by the Upper Paleolithic blade people. Their successors killed a wider variety of species, and did not disdain the humble mole vole, an old friend from Hotu. Squirrels were eaten in Mesolithic and lower-brown-earth times, and tortoises more or less throughout the cave's occupation.

On Easter Sunday, April 18, we finished Kara Kamar. In the morning the BBC told us over our portable radio that Her Majesty Queen Elizabeth and Prince Philip would that very day attend the Anglican service six thousand feet up in the cool highlands of Ceylon. That was very fine indeed, but we doubted that even this splendid and royal young couple were any happier than the members of the University Museum expedition. We had left home on the 2nd of February and despite the facilities of modern air travel, it had taken until the 12th of March to reach Kabul. Kara Kamar had given us no human remains, but plenty of other problems.

With fourteen days left, the question was: another cave? Lisa was all for going to Maimana, which would have been fine had we had new tires for the station wagon. As it was, we changed one every twenty miles, and the tubes were now covered with overlapping patches. We voted against it, and ever since I have been wondering if we did right. However, we got back to Kabul late at night on the 21st. The jeep was a complete wreck. The trailer had bounced off, breaking both the hitch and the axle, and that was the end of it. We had been halted by a landslide that had required more than a hundred men to dig out; and the next day when we went for gas we found that our tickets had expired. Although we had not known it, they had been made out for a single month. It had been a splendid trip, but we had had enough, at least for the spring of 1954.

Nearly nine months later, on the 7th of December, Miss Elizabeth Ralph, the head of our radiocarbon laboratory, returned from Washington, where she had been running our charcoal samples in the laboratory of the United States Geological Survey, under the supervision of Dr. Hans E. Suess. She had gone there because all of the dates that she had found below the Mesolithic level were too old for her own equipment to count; Dr. Suess had installed a new set of apparatus which could go back much further. This is what they found: [2]

One sample from level #4 of Trench A, inside the upper brown soil, yielded a date of 10,580 ± 720 B.P., or 8630 ± 720 B.C. As this soil contained Mesolithic artifacts, this date places the Kara Kamar Mesolithic within the Hotu Mesolithic sequence, somewhere between the time of the seal-hunters and that of the two women who were killed by falling rock. Ralph Solecki's Mesolithic level in Shanidar Cave, northern Iraq, was dated by Dr. Suess at 12,000 ± 400 B.P., or 10,450 ± 400 B.C. It was apparently a very early Mesolithic phase comparable to the Seal Mesolithic of Belt and Hotu. These three sites, Shanidar, Belt-Hotu, and Kara Kamar, carry Mesolithic culture from the northwestern Zagros Mountains to the Caspian shore and on to the northern slopes of the Hindu Kush.

[2] C. S. Coon and E. K. Ralph: "Radiocarbon dates for Kara Kamar, Afghanistan, U. of Pa. II," *Science*, Vol. 122, No. 3176 (November 11, 1955), pp. 921–2.

All of the other samples from Kara Kamar gave dates over thirty-four thousand years old. These were five in number, all of them associated with the blade and steep-scraper culture of the lower loess. Solecki's "Aurignacian" level of Shanidar, which contained closely similar steep scrapers, was given the same date by Hans Suess. Unfortunately, the Mount Carmel caves of Palestine, which also contained these steep scrapers in an "Aurignacian" level, have not been dated because they were dug before the Carbon-14 method had been invented.

Moving far afield, we find the same kind of steep scrapers in the Aurignacian of western Europe. Although this particular cultural material remains to be dated, Hans Suess has obtained a date of 23,600 ± 800 B.P. and 24,000 ± 1,000 B.P. for two samples of a later Upper Paleolithic cultural assemblage excavated by Hallam Movius in the Abri Pataud, Les Éyzies, France.[3] This charcoal lay in a horizon known as Gravettian, immediately above the Aurignacian level, which could have been at least ten thousand years older and comparable in age to the corresponding materials from Kara Kamar and Shanidar.

The point of this French comparison is not that the cultures of Kara Kamar may or may not be related to the Aurignacian of the Dordogne country, but that since the glacial sequence in France has been worked out more or less satisfactorily, it may serve us as a basis for setting up a provisional local sequence. Movius's hearths are believed to have been formed shortly after the maximum of the second advance of the last ice sheet. A date more than ten thousand years earlier would carry us well back to the time of the second advance of this ice, or earlier. However, in central Asia the last ice age has

[3] Hans E. Suess: "U.S. Geological Survey Radiocarbon Dates II," *Science*, Vol. 121, No. 3145 (April 8, 1955), p. 488.

not been broken down into subperiods as in Europe. This analogy seems to suggest that the Kara Kamar blade culture dates from early in the time of the second advance of the last ice sheet.

Curiously enough, nothing comparable to the Kara Kamar blade tools has yet turned up in Soviet territory, on the other side of the Oxus, where much archæological material has been collected. The reason may be that the Russians have not dug enough caves to find it. They have published data on only one cave in that area, Teshik Tash in Uzbekistan, which contained the skeleton of a Neanderthal child, with characteristic flake tools. As it was dug before the days of Carbon-14 analysis, we do not know the age of its contents. However, one Neanderthal find *has* been dated. This is the jaw of Hawa Fteah, found in a cave in the kingdom of Libya in 1951. Hans Suess has given it a date of 34,000 ± 2,800 B.P This find has for the first time confirmed the contemporaneity of Neanderthal man with people who made Upper Paleolithic blades.

One mystery remains unsolved, and probably will continue unsolved for a long time. Who made the flake implements in the lower brown earth and upper loess of Kara Kamar? There is a lifetime of work in the caves of Afghanistan for a younger man.

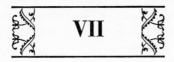

VII

THE WHITE PASS IN THE DESERT

Every time a cave is dug, one or more questions are answered, and an equal or greater number of problems is raised. The High Cave of Tangier told us that Neanderthal-like men who used flake tools lived on in the northwest corner of Africa well into the last thirty thousand years of the final ice age. By this time the Neanderthals north of the Pyrenees had disappeared. We had found out that the Strait of Gibraltar had been an almost insuperable barrier to human migrations during the Ice Age. In Bisitun, through one tooth and one armbone, we learned that people physically comparable to the High Cave dwellers, using a similar flake industry, had hunted in the Zagros Mountains, perhaps at the same time. The early Carbon-14 date of Kara Kamar—more than thirty-four thousand years ago, suggests that blade-using had already begun in the eastern part of the northern Eurasiatic zone early in the last ice age, and that the Upper Paleolithic way of life may be as old there as in France.

In Belt and Hotu we had been able to trace a complex sequence of goings and comings on the part of men of modern European racial type on the southern rim of the Caspian. The remains we had unearthed there disclosed new phases of the Mesolithic and early Neolithic cultures, with transitions leading from one to the other. These caves also suggested new ideas about the origin of European agricultural life, and furnished information about late Neolithic and Iron Age cultures which might be of interest to others.

Slowly, in spite of the many wide gaps that remained, our small but strategically placed discoveries were beginning to supplement the more extensive findings of other investigators. Now we began to see the dim outlines of a picture. Part of it showed what had happened during the last glacial period to different peoples and their cultures in the western and eastern outskirts of the land south of the climatic boundary of the mountains, from the Pyrenees to the Hindu Kush. We had not yet tackled the center of this zone because work had already been done in it and we were looking for virgin territory.

In seeking a point of origin, or even a corridor of entry, for the Upper Paleolithic cultures of Europe, on the assumption that they had not developed locally, we had succeeded only in narrowing the field by a process of elimination. Morocco was eliminated. The mountains of Iran were apparently eliminated, and in Afghanistan we had worked north of the mountains in Upper Paleolithic territory proper. The only place in the whole Middle East where a sequence of flakes and blades had been found was the rim of mountains and fertile land around the Arabian desert, in Palestine, Lebanon, Syria, and Iraq. In a dozen caves from these Arab countries, stratified deposits had yielded what seemed to be different parts of an orderly sequence from a Middle Paleolithic flake culture, with burins and a few blades, to an Upper Paleolithic blade culture comparable to those known in Europe.

In one site only, Shanidar in northern Iraq, had Car-

bon-14 dates been obtained. These placed the whole sequence of Middle to Upper Paleolithic cultures beyond
the range of the testing instruments, or older than thirty-
four thousand years. This merely showed that the transition from a Middle to an Upper Paleolithic culture could
have been as old in the Middle East as in Europe. But
we really do not know when, let alone where, such a
transition took place. Dating the sites in Palestine and
Lebanon had depended on the establishment of a succession of wet and dry periods, which was done largely
by studying the alternation of deer versus gazelle bones
in the successive levels, on the theory that when deer
bones are most frequent there is more forest, and when
gazelle bones predominate, the grass and desert cover
predominates. However, both animals were present at all
periods, and this sequence has not been supported by
later evidence. Further attempts to date the sites near the
shore on the basis of former Mediterranean sea levels, as
our 1947 Tangier expedition had tried to do at the other
end of the Mediterranean, had not met with unqualified
success.

In the winter of 1954–5 I was faced with the alternative of going back to Afghanistan to dig more caves and
see what else I could find to elucidate the strange sequence of Kara Kamar, or working somewhere in the
Arab lands, where a fragmentary transition from Middle
to Upper Paleolithic cultures appeared to have been
found, but where many problems remained. It seemed to
me that although archæologists had dug all around the
fertile rim of the desert, not one of them had excavated
a stratified site in the desert, which might have a separate and complementary history.

Although it is hard to imagine, now that the Middle
Eastern mountains are mostly barren outcrops of limestone, the desert and its rim were once very different

places. Before men felled its forests, the mountains were covered with trees, including the famous cedars of Lebanon, and on its inner rim the forest reached down to a grassland within which lay the desert. Before the arrival of domestic camels and goats, the desert itself contained scrub vegetation, as well as water in springs and holes. It was much like our own American desert, with Asiatic equivalents of sagebrush, piñon and tumbleweed.

In trying to visualize the environment of Ice Age man in the Middle East we must forget the present scene of man-made devastation and picture in our minds three environmental realms. Two of these, the forested mountains and the open plain, were distinct, while the third, between them, was transitional. One would not expect forest and open plain to have harbored the same animals or the same people. In moist periods such as the pluvials, when the ice sheets of the north had driven the storm-bearing westerly winds southward, the plain would be far richer in game than the forest. In dry periods, corresponding to interglacials, the plain would be true desert and the forest a better place for hunters. In the intermediate warm intervals, like the time when the Upper Paleolithic people were first seen in Europe, the climate would be about the same as it is today, and the landscape the same but for the activities of goats and camels.

Although one must expect to find that people moved back and forth between forest and desert as rainfall varied during the fluctuations of the last ice age, nevertheless the forests and the deserts were inhabited by two different kinds of animals, each adapted to its own environmental conditions. In the same way, the human requirements of living and hunting on these two kinds of terrain must have tended to produce different kinds of people by the process of natural selection. Heat and water economy impose different stresses on the organism, and hunting vast herds of hoofed beasts in an open expanse where one can see long distances takes a set of natural abilities different from those required for sudden encounters with single animals in forest glades. Skeletons of partly Neanderthal people had already been found in Palestine and Lebanon, both forest country. In the desert we might hope to find men of a different kind.

Several persons, including Dr. Henry Field, had picked up surface artifacts at various places on the desert, and I did the same in odd moments during my trip to Saudi Arabia in 1952 as a guest of Aramco, as well as in 1954 while awaiting transportation to Afghanistan. Both of us had collected flake implements of a rather indeterminate nature at a number of exposed places, but the best site of this kind which I saw was at a place called Tel es-Suwaish, exactly on the border between Jordan and Saudi Arabia, a half-mile east of the Tapline road. Here an acient island in a long-vanished lake may have served as a perfect blind for Paleolithic duck-hunters, who had left their worn-out tools behind them.

These tools had been buried, and then uncovered, by the wind. The desert sun had heated them as hot as the copper pennies a blacksmith tosses out his door to fool unwary children, and the desert night had chilled them. Wind and sun, heat and cold had burnished and polished them to a rich glossy brown, until they looked like petrified taffy. Henry Coulter, Lisa, and I had come out from Amman in a rented Pontiac, and we picked up nearly a bushel of them in a little over an hour. All were on the surface; a hasty scratching with an entrenching-tool failed to reveal others within easy reach.

Whatever they were to be called and whoever had made them, they had been left there at a time when the desert was not only in full flower—before the time of goats and camels—but also when there had been enough

rainfall to make a lake. That must have been a long time
ago. When gathered, the flints did not look very impressive, but when finally sorted they fell naturally into three
groups. The majority were flakes made by the single-
prepared-core technique also employed at Tangier and
Bisitun, though they were smaller than the flakes from
those two sites, and less finely made. There were no
points at all among them, and no specialized finished
implements. It is possible that this was a factory and not
a habitation site, and that the hunters worked on their
implements while waiting for thirsty animals and water-
fowl, and then took their implements home with them.
What we found may have been merely the scrap from
the tool-making, together with a lot of worn-out tools.

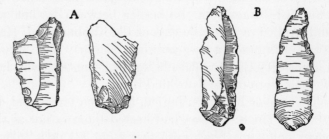

*Tel es-Suwaish: Several hundred flints, highly polished
and deeply patinated by the sun, were found on the
eroded surface of this open-air site in the Arabian desert.
The series forms a cultural unit of which broad flakes
(A) and coarse blades (B) are characteristic. These are
shown in two views. (One-half actual size.)*

The second group consists of small flakes with the
butts broken off, and roughly retouched around the
edges. Implements similar to these have been found
at Kharga Oasis in the eastern desert of Egypt. Our specimens, and the Egyptian ones as well, were also made
from prepared cores. It is possible that in this site they

were simply implements of the first group which had got
lost instead of being carried home. They could also have
belonged to a later stage of the same culture. The third
group was easily distinguished from the first two because
it was unpatinated, and therefore probably more recent
than they. It consisted of small flakes and cores, without a
single finished implement.

In Palestine, flint implements similar to the first group
had been found in two caves: in Mugharet Umm Qatafa,
by René Neuville and Moshé Stekelis, and in the Tabun,
one of the Mount Carmel grottoes, by Dorothy Garrod
and her associates. In both caves these flakes overlay
hand axes of a late type which were attributed, rightly
or wrongly, to the latter part of the third interglacial
period. This would make the hand axes nearly one hundred thousand years old. Judging by their similarity to the
flakes that overlay the hand axes, our flakes from Tel es-
Suwaish were probably somewhat younger.

While over a dozen sites had been excavated along
the once forested rim of the desert, only one had been
dug in the desert itself: that of Wadi Dhobai, in Jordan,
excavated by John d'A. Waechter in 1937. As his site
was probably later than Tel es-Suwaish, he found no flints
of this type. Yet the surface of the desert was covered with
these flakes, which could be picked up literally by the millions. If we could find them in a stratified level inside a
desert cave, we might be able to determine their age, or,
at least, see what animals the men who made them had
hunted.

Near a place called Turaif, which is the northernmost
pumping station on Tapline inside Saudi Arabia, first
Henry Field and then I had also collected blade implements that included a high proportion of burins. Waechter had also found these *in situ* at Wadi Dhobai. As
there was no other industry present, he could not date

them in reference to anything else. The presence of arrow-heads with them suggested, however, that they might be as late as the Neolithic. On the other hand, the particular ones that we had found in Turaif could have been earlier. In any case, it would be good to find such blades in a many-layered desert-cave deposit where the exact relationship of this typically Upper Paleolithic implement to other cultures could be determined.

Our search for desert caves passed through several phases. In 1954, while Henry Coulter, Lisa, and I were staying with my son Carl, Jr., and his wife, Janet, in Damascus, we made a trip to a site called Kherbet al-Umbashi, southeast of that city in the lava-block country. This is the most sinister type of desert. The face of the earth is strewn with immense black boulders, pock-marked and shiny. In summer they absorb the heat of the sun like stove lids, and in winter they chill off like ice cubes. Hardly a spear of grass grows between them, and few animals have found ways of adapting themselves to life in this hideous waste. This did not seem like a Paleolithic hunting-ground; but the lava might be recent, and we were told that it covered caves.

Our host on this trip was a wealthy landowner of Kurdish descent, Mr. Husain Ibish, who had been on several hunting trips to Africa, and who lived in a desert castle. In his blue jeep, in which he led the party, he carried not only two retainers whose guns bristled outside the curtains, but also several hampers full of fine foods and wines. He even had ham, which he would not eat, for his Christian guests.

Kherbet al-Umbashi was a great heap of animal bones bent and cracked by heat. During some kind of volcanic eruption a blister in the surface of the earth had burst open beneath them, and then lava had flowed upward out of the blister, toasting them and twisting them into

grotesque shapes. That is one explanation. Another is
that villagers who lived near by threw thousands of animals into the blister hole in sacrifice, to persuade the eruption to stop. If this was the case, their sacrifices were in
vain, for the lava flowed and slobbered over the entire
region.

Mr. Ibish was in the process of having tons of these
bones removed to his oasis farm for fertilizer. As he had
found a number of flints and other artifacts among the
bones, he wanted to know what it was that he was destroying. The bones were mostly those of domestic animals. The flints, the pieces of polished stone, and especially the pottery were identified as being of early Bronze
Age type, and this material was dated by Carbon-14 analysis, from samples sent in before I saw the site, at the
beginning of the third millennium B.C. Caves there were,
and we explored several of them carefully, but they
were in lava and not in ancient limestone. We regretfully
decided that this was not our site, despite the anticipated
pleasure of having Husain Ibish for a host.

Somewhat over seventy, with an eye as keen as a
hawk's, this old man was known to be one of the world's
best shots. At one point on our journey we flushed a
flight of bustards. Mr. Ibish, my son, and several others
were out in a flash, and three birds came down. It was
my private opinion that Mr. Ibish had shot them all,
though out of courtesy he refused to claim them. When
his retainers fetched them in and they were still fluttering around, I picked one up to give it the *hallala,* the
traditional merciful cutting of the throat which renders
any animal fit for consumption by the faithful and also
—which is what I had more in mind—shortens its suffer-
ing.

"No," Mr. Ibish bade me firmly but with complete
courtesy. Removing the bird from my hand and from the

reach of my knife, he handed it to one of his men. "It is a wild thing," he explained, "and must be permitted to die in a state of freedom."

His man opened a small artery in the neck of each bird and released it to flap its wings into eternity, as each one did, slowly and in utter dignity. When the birds were finally motionless Mr. Ibish's man picked them up off the stony ground and handed them to his master, who presented them to my son and to the other diplomats of the party.

This and other excursions taken in 1954 convinced us that the best way to find our target was to consult maps, as we had done in Afghanistan. Although Henry Coulter could not again take time off to come with us, he found the appropriate geological map of Syria and pinpointed on it the best limestone in the desert. This was a ridge, or series of ridges, of nummulitic limestone, a type of stone composed mostly of the shells of a variety of tiny marine animals which lived during the Eocene period, over fifty million years ago. The ridge stands just north of the ancient ruins of the city of Palmyra and its modern oasis town of eight thousand people, Tadmor. I should have known this without a map because I had just finished reviewing Julian Huxley's *From an Antique Land,* which contains some beautiful color pictures of the tombs and colonnades of Palmyra, all built of good solid pink limestone. This stone could not have been hauled from quarries very far away.

During the winter of 1954–5 I carried on a correspondence with the director of the Syrian Department of Antiquities, Dr. Selim Abd el-Haqq, who gave me permission to search for and excavate caves in the desert. Lisa and I arrived in Damascus on the 22nd of February, where we were met at the airport by my son Carl, Jr., my daughter-in-law, Janet, and several grandchildren. Having a home to go to was a wonderful thing, and it was also pleasant to see my old Syrian friends.

By the 5th of March we were ready to go, permits and all, for during the previous two weeks the paper work had been completed. According to the Syrian law, an expedition was supposed to consist of a minimum of five persons: a director, an assistant director, an architect, an epigrapher (decipherer of ancient inscriptions), and a photographer. We were two. I had been through this in correspondence earlier. Lisa holds a degree in landscape architecture and has drawn plans and sections of all the caves I have worked in. As Paleolithic man neither built structures nor carved inscriptions on them, there was no need for a proper building architect or for an epigrapher; and as I had with me a battery of cameras, from a Hasselblad on down, with a boxful of lenses and attachments, as well as a stroboscopic flash set, I felt even better prepared than usual to do my own photography. Under the circumstances Dr. Abd el-Haqq waived the personnel requirements.

The next hurdle was the question of whether I was to do a *sondage* or a *fouille*. These two words, inherited from the French regime, have no proper Arabic equivalents. In English they mean a *test pit* and an *excavation*. In the regular city-site archæology, which was all the Syrians knew about, the archæologist gets a permit for a sondage, and then goes about his site sinking pits to see whether the place is worth digging or not. If he decides to risk a full-scale dig, he goes back or sends back word and gets a permit for a fouille. In city-site archæology one employs hundreds of workmen, who move dirt about by the ton in little iron carts on narrow-gauge tracks. Such a dig may take several seasons. In cave archæology the total amount of soil excavated in a single site may not equal that removed in a city-site sondage.

Furthermore, everyone knows where city sites are, not only because of the columns and building blocks standing or lying around, but also because they have been mentioned in world literature. There usually is no question of discovery. With caves the biggest problem is to find them.

Quite obviously the sondage-fouille dichotomy was not applicable to our particular case, but somehow our situation had to be squeezed into the existing legal framework. Which of these two words was to be used was of vast importance to me, for in the case of a sondage the government keeps all finds, while in that of a fouille an equal division is made, with the government holding the right to "unique objects." While the unique-objects clause, designed to prevent the loss of national treasures, could be, and in some countries has been, abused, it seemed hardly likely that scraps of flint, with the like of which the surface of the desert is covered, could be considered national treasures. Therefore when Dr. Abd el-Haqq handed me my permit, written in Arabic and signed and sealed, and told me that it was for a fouille, I left his office feeling very satisfied. Undoubtedly I would be allowed to take home whatever I might find, and send half back after it had been studied. I had never had trouble with officials in any country I had worked in, and saw no reason to expect any in Syria, where I was well known and had many friends.

March 5 was a beautiful day, cold and crisp and clear; the air was like sparkling water. Carl, Jr., whipped the station wagon through the scrambled city traffic and out onto the tarred road that leads north to Homs, Hama, Aleppo, and eventually to Turkey. It was high time to start, for in 1955 Ramadhan was due to begin on April 22. Past village after village we rode, past groves of walnut trees, just coming into leaf, past olives, apricots, and pomegranates, all in flower. The snow of Mount Lebanon gleamed to our left in the morning sun, and the vast flatness of the desert rolled out to the right to an indefinite horizon, proving, if anyone doubted it, that the world is round. Like my boyhood hero George Borrow, I felt that it was indeed wonderful to be alive.

At Qutaifa we turned right off the paved road and bumped over a roadbed that had been filled with crushed stone in preparation for paving. Here and there it was possible to drive over the smooth surface of the plain alongside, but in most places cultivation prevented this. We went through two desert towns, Jairud and Qariatain, behind each of which ran a limestone ridge, and in each ridge, high up at the top of the scree and under an outcrop, were caves. However, Palmyra was a long way off and there was no time to stop, as we wanted to arrive there before dark. Night driving in the desert is not recommended unless one is versed in celestial navigation.

Beyond Qariatain the formal road ended and we were free to ride on the desert, with a choice of several tracks. An Irish geologist, Dr. David Burdon, who works for UNESCO in Syria, searching everywhere for water, told me that in his trips all over the desert his chief enemy is not sand, but mud. That is why every desert route consists of a number of alternate tracks, and if all are too sticky the driver may create another.

On the 5th of March the desert was in flower. Tiny blades of grass had pushed their spearpoints up nearly everywhere, and the channels over which the recent rains had drained off were bright green. Flowers of many kinds were blooming, and casting a rich medley of perfumes into the air. It was hard to keep the women in the car, so busy were they botanizing. This annual conversion of the desert from monochrome to polychrome also interested vast herds of camels, which were busy keeping the verdure down as fast as it could pop up. The black tents of Bedawin dotted the landscape. From some of them rushed fierce shepherd dogs, their ears and tails docked from many a canine war. I was glad that I was not in a jeep, as in Afghanistan, and that my left leg was safe.

We lunched at Qasr al-Hair, an Umayyad hunting-lodge partly removed to Damascus by the Department of Antiquities. Leading off to the right from it is the track to the farm of the Amir Sha'alan, paramount sheik of the Ruwalla, a noble tribe made famous by T. E. Lawrence. To the left, far to the north, we could see the gleaming silver rotundity of an immense oil tank at T-4, a pumping station on the Iraq Petroleum Company's pipeline to the Mediterranean. Just when the sun was half hidden behind the mountains of Lebanon we came to the rim of the Palmyra depression and saw silhouetted along it a row of tall, square-topped structures, the outermost of the Palmyrean tombs, all in deep red. Then to the left rose the gleaming cliff of Jebel Tar en-Nouaisser, a mesa-like mountain from whose face much of the pink limestone of the ancient city had been cut. Another dip and we rode between rows of Corinthian columns to the mustard-colored stucco of the Hotel Queen Zenobia.

A half-dozen Arab gentlemen, mostly in robes and bearded, rose from chairs on the veranda and greeted us. Among them were the owner of the hotel, a large, broad-faced, blue-eyed man who spoke to me in classical Arabic, pronouncing each letter slowly and distinctly, so that it was impossible not to understand him; an old man with a face like one's great-grandfather from New Hampshire, who was the sheikh of the land immediately around Palmyra; and Ali, the manager of the hotel, who talked French, and who became my firm friend and, I hope, still is. Before very long we were greeted in English by an officer in a well-pressed uniform, stocky, brown-eyed, and with a big mustache. This was Amin Qudsi, the security officer, whose duty it was to inspect our passports. With him we went to the town, where we met Ubaid Tahir, the chief of the local Antiquities office, who had been designated by Dr. Abd el-Haqq as our inspector. A short, thick-set man with the broad hands of the oasis-dweller, he looked more like a Turk than an Arab. On the tip of his nose and over one cheekbone I noticed a pair of blue dots about a quarter of an inch in diameter. Later I discovered that all the Tadmor people of the older generation bear these distinguishing tattoo marks. With him we agreed to go cave-hunting in the morning.

We were up at six thirty and ready to go off in a rented pickup truck, but we soon discovered that this was impossible. The previous evening a young man who spoke English had sat at our table, uninvited, and asked me a series of personal and leading questions, fixing upon me a baleful and unblinking stare with his apparently pupil-less black eyes. This basilisk had finally demanded my papers, whereupon I had asked him for his own credentials. When he failed to produce any, I told him that in official matters I would deal only with persons in official positions, and that, besides, I had already cleared everything with Amin Qudsi.

Now it seemed that he had been working secretly all the while for a Captain Othman, commanding officer of the desert patrol, who had said that we could not go more than five kilometers outside the town. This limited range was, of course, useless. When we went to see Captain Othman we were told that he had left for Damascus. Then we went to see a Captain Mahmud, in charge of the garrison, who said that it was none of his business. Finally we tracked down a lieutenant with medical insignia who was Captain Othman's deputy. He said that we should telephone Colonel Shawqat in Homs, to obtain permission to go more than five kilometers outside; when we asked the favor of using his telephone, which was the only one that connected with Homs, he said that it did not work and that we should use Amin Qudsi's. At Qudsi's office we learned that *his* phone connected only with the lieutenant's.

Faced with this runaround, we returned to the lieutenant's office, where I politely asked him his name. He refused to tell me. Then he said that we should drive to Homs, where Colonel Shawqat would be in his office until two p.m., and that he would give us a guide. The guide turned out to be a fat Damascene artisan who had less knowledge of the desert tracks than ourselves and merely wanted a ride to the tarred highway so that he could go home. At this point I returned to Amin Qudsi's office, and he gave me a genuine guide, a Bedawi with tattooed hands who really did know the way.

With these two ill-matched passengers in the back seat we left in the direction of T-4, in the belief that if we could not make Homs by two o'clock we could at least phone Colonel Shawqat from the office of the pumping station, where Mr. Murdoch, the manager, had been told by his Damascus office to expect us. We found the pumping station apparently in a state of siege, surrounded by a high barbed-wire fence and guarded by a small garrison of Syrian soldiers at the gate. Failing to obtain their permission to communicate with the British oilmen inside in time to do us any good, we kept on for Homs over a road like the Qutaifa-Qariatain stretch, on which we could make good time at the cost of our spines and tires. During the last half-hour we drove through a pouring rain, and found Homs soaking and dripping.

We made it at one thirty, and were taken immediately to Colonel Shawqat's office. This gentleman in-

formed us that he had authority to let us circulate within
ten kilometers of the town, instead of five, and he telephoned the lieutenant in Tadmor so to instruct him. This
time the telephone worked perfectly.

The next morning we really did look for caves, with
Ubaid Tahir seeing to it that we did not exceed the ten-
kilometer limit. This was a little hard for him to do, as
our speedometer was marked in miles. In a flattish valley
to the northeast we found a series of rock shelters, a bit
small but good enough if nothing else should turn up,
and a deep cave called Mugharet Ash-Shahira, or "Ocher
Cave." The Bedawin go to it to obtain lumps of ocher.
The Ocher Cave's mouth is nothing but a hole in the
ground, and inside it you stumble over a pile of fallen
rocks for about twenty feet until you come to a deep
tunnel. Therefore it is not the kind of cave which can
be easily excavated, though there may well be something
of interest in its innermost recesses, where the ocher
comes from.

After lunch Amin Qudsi told me that Captain Othman (who had miraculously returned from Damascus)
insisted on our taking a soldier with us, which meant
that there would be no room for our wives. Lisa and Janet
stayed in Palmyra to look at the ruins. The soldier turned
out to be a fine young man from Qariatain who unsuccess-
fully tried to persuade us to dig the caves in back of his
home. We explored the flanks of the Jebel Tar en-Nouaisser and found the remains of several beautiful caves,
all of which had been ruined by the ancient quarrymen.
Over the whole face of the scree and on the ground below, we picked up dozens of flint implements. At least
two known cultures were represented: an Upper Paleolithic blade culture with end-of-blade scrapers, burins,
and steep scrapers; and a Middle Paleolithic culture resembling the handiwork of Neanderthal man, which in-

cluded spear points and side scrapers, both made on large flakes. These implements had quite obviously been washed out of their stratified earthy beds after the quarrymen, employed by the vainglorious *nouveaux riches* of old Palmyra, had torn the roofs from their caves. We were in, for there must be other such caves that had not been quarried—provided, of course, that we could avoid being strangled by the all-enveloping web of local and national bureaucracy.

The ancient civilization of Palmyra was an ephemeral thing, like that of Nevada ghost towns, which it resembled in physical setting and (in my opinion) in taste. In imperial Roman times a group of local desert-dwellers, known as Nabateans, grew rich on the caravan trade that passed through their oasis on the way from Mesopotamia to Damascus and the seaports of the Phœnician coast. Seeking the most ostentatious manner to spend their money, they built temples and a forum and then began thinking about ancestors, which they had to have in order to get space in the imperial social register. So they constructed tombs, some underground and others reaching to the sky in lofty if narrow towers. Knowing nothing of architecture or sculpture, they imported artists, architects, and skilled workmen, probably many of them Greeks, just as we imported Italians to build the lake-front palaces of Chicago. Yet the Palmyreans knew what sort of things they wanted.

Many visitors whose knowledge of architecture and whose æsthetic taste in such matters are far ahead of mine have found these ruins beautiful, and I will not, if I can help it, discourage any potential tourists from visiting Palmyra to the profit of Ubaid Tahir, his sons, and the Syrian Directorate of Antiquities. Except for the long row of columns of the forum, and the view of the medieval Arab castle through an archway, I found them

unappetizing, particularly the tombs. Perhaps it was because the quarrymen who brought the stone to Palmyra
had ruined some of the world's most important Paleolithic caves, or perhaps it was because I passed between
them day after day in the midst of some crisis with the
bureaucracy or the workmen; anyhow, they are not my
cup of tea. The æsthetes and the tourists can have them.

At some point in the early centuries of the Christian
era the river of sweet water that had flowed out of a
hillside, creating this garden in a desert, turned warm
and sulfurous, as it has remained ever since. Palmyra
was abandoned, to be reoccupied centuries later by
Arabs from various places, men whose digestive tracts
could be trained to endure this chemical. Soft-gutted
strangers like ourselves must bring drinking-water out of
Damascus in jerry cans and other containers.

On the evening of our dash to Homs and back, Carl,
Jr., and I were invited to tea at the office of the *kaimakam,* or mayor. Amin Qudsi went along with us. Among
those present was also the local judge. The mayor, a very
friendly person, showed me a letter that he had received
from the mayor of Palmyra, Nebraska, telling him what
the weather was like out there. Enclosed were a few
snapshots of that community, including one of a garage
and another of a graveyard in which the tombstone of a
family named Duffield was visible.

"Please explain this to me," asked the kaimakam.
"Why did this man send me this letter and these pictures?"

"Out of friendship," I replied.

To the kaimakam my answer was completely unsatis-
factory. There must be, the expression on his face said,
some angle to it, some request that the mayor of Palmyra,
Nebraska, would make now that he had got his foot in
the door. As I obviously was not going to tell him what

this was, it was equally obviously some kind of very subtle Israeli plot, which out of courtesy he would pretend to ignore.

At that time the Arab-Israeli conflict was already at fever heat, and it was currently believed that everyone who had anything to do with the Israelis by even the most remote chain of guilt by unwitting or involuntary association was on their side and against the Arabs. Knowing this, I was not surprised when the judge, who himself could have passed for a handsome Sephardic Jew, confronted me bitterly with the question: "Why do you Americans support the Jews?"

Having heard this at least once a day since arriving in Syria, I had prepared a set of answers. But as the question was of the "When did you stop beating your wife?" category, nothing that I might say could be satisfactory.

The judge then asked me another question, speaking Damascene Arabic rapidly. As I was still thinking about the former question, I did not catch the words. Amin Qudsi, trying to be helpful, translated it as follows: "Do you believe that men are descended from donkeys?"

"No," I replied, "I do not believe that men are descended from donkeys."

In Arabic the words for *donkey* and *monkey* are *himar* and *qird,* which bear no resemblance to each other. The close resemblance between their English equivalents had thrown Amin off balance, and here I was on the verge of another Colonel Blackie incident. Fortunately, the judge chose this moment to take his departure, leaving me feeling about as bright as either of the two animals mentioned.

It took me three days in Damascus to get things rearranged. Dr. Abd el-Haqq seemed disturbed that the army had not honored his request that we be given permission to circulate and work in the desert, and he re-

peated it over the telephone in my presence. Not daring
to risk a repetition of the delays we had encountered at
Palmyra, I went to check with Colonel Adnan Malki, the
head of the Syrian Army G-3, a huge, handsome man
with boundless energy and a booming but pleasant voice.
Having received me with courtesy and friendship, he told
me that Dr. Abd el-Haqq had not notified the army at
all the first time, but that on the second occasion he had
really done so, and the order had already gone out to the
desert. Captain Othman, the colonel said, had been acting strictly on his standing orders, and would give me
no trouble in the future. This I found to be correct.

In the meanwhile, I searched Damascus in vain for
the vehicle I wanted, a Dodge power wagon. Instead I
settled for a beaten-up old British World War II Chevrolet weapons-carrier that had high clearance, four-
wheeled power, and a lid in the cab roof for anti-aircraft
gunnery. Although slow, bumpy, and awkward, this tar-
nished juggernaut could go where pickups were left behind. Because we had not yet located an unspoiled cave
to dig in, I needed something to explore mountain wadies
with, and this vehicle could do it. As the Armenian con-
tractor from whom I rented it had been using it for hauling dirt, he let me have it only with considerable disapproval. It was not elegant enough for the father of a
diplomat to be seen in. Indeed, Amin Qudsi, who had
come to Damascus with us in the station wagon, post-
poned his return to Palmyra once he had heard its description.

At sun-up the weapons-carrier arrived at my son's
door, driven by a short, chunky, and extremely weather-
beaten Armenian named Garabed, who appeared to be
about my own age, though he was ten years younger.
He soon loaded all our gear, including the gravel screens,
into the body of the truck. The cab contained only two

seats—separate bucket arrangements for the driver and the anti-aircraft Bren-gunner. Garabed and Lisa occupied these seats while I rode the load in the rear, under the open sky.

Halfway to Qutaifa it began to rain, and when we got onto the dirt road to Qariatain the rain turned to hailstones the size of peas. All three of us got wet, particularly me, before the downpour let up a bit. While driving along we noticed, lying on the road, three blankets, a man's jacket, and a pair of metal scales of the type held at arm's length by Blind Justice. Being an honorable member of the driving fraternity cognizant of some kind of code of the road, Garabed was loath to pick up these objects, but I made him stop and retrieve the blankets, which I sorely needed. Just before we reached Qasr al-Hair the sky turned a deep purple-black, like the lips of a Senegalese Negro, and this time the hailstones were the size of marbles. In the midst of it all, the motor stopped and Garabed got out in defiance of the weather. The distributor wires were wet. He dried them and we went on.

In my frigid and sodden perch I nursed a small flask of Zahlawi arak, which I had bought at a roadside shop on the way back from Beirut some time before and had saved for such an emergency. At five o'clock we drew into the courtyard of the Hotel Queen Zenobia, to be greeted by Ali, the usual dignitaries, and my very old friend Leslie Carver, a high official of the United Nations in Palestine, along with his wife and stepson.

"You turn up in the strangest places," said Leslie. "Come in and have some Scotch."

I needed no second invitation.

The next morning we went cave-hunting in the weapons-carrier, taking with us a Negro soldier named Abdallah and a man named Saleh who had attached himself to Garabed from the moment of our arrival. Saleh was a big chap, nearly six feet in height, heavy-boned and powerful. A big head covered with light-brown hair was partly concealed by an open-faced Balaklava stocking cap, the brim of which he wore pulled down under his chin. His face was broad, his nose was snubbed, his eyes were blue; in a few years he would make an excellent Santa Claus. In a private version of the English language as commonly spoken by British soldiers when ladies are not present, he greeted me enthusiastically and swore undying fealty to my person and obedience to my tiniest wish. He had served in His Majesty's forces during World War II, he said, and had been a good soldier. He was most gallant in taking my arm to help me into the weapsons-carrier, and insisted on carrying my cameras.

Ubaid Tahir expressed some doubt about the idea of employing Saleh, on the grounds that he had hired him in the past at the city-site excavations and that all had not gone too well. Even his stony heart softened, however, and Saleh came along. Saleh was a native of a place called Salamia, near the mountains, and Salamia is full of the Agha Khan's followers, Ismailis, a locally unpopular sect to which Saleh stoutly denied that he belonged. He had a wife, several children, and no landed property on which to grow food. He was not only an outsider who looked and spoke differently from the rest of the inhabitants of Tadmor; he was also desperately poor, and seized upon every opportunity to earn a little money. Amin Qudsi provided him with free cigarettes, and everyone did their best to help him, but he had recently been obliged to sell his wife's wedding ring in order to buy bread for their children. Whether or not he was to work for me was almost literally a matter of life or death; Ubaid Tahir knew this, and that was why he reluctantly gave in.

Of course I did not know all these things on the morning of Sunday, March 13, when we set out in Garabed's chariot in search of one good cave to dig. But I smelled something in the air as far as Saleh was concerned, and I had learned early in my career that wherever I happen to be working, the locals know much more about their own business than I shall ever find out. Except in special circumstances involving some outside consideration beyond their knowledge or range of competence, I always trust their judgment above my own. Enough trouble arises from natural and unavoidable causes without my creating it. At that time the Arab-Israeli situation permeated all human relations with its poison, casting every outsider, including Saleh and myself, under suspicion. Although neither Ubaid, Saleh, nor I had done anything to produce it, it hung over our heads like a black cloud, and all of us were well advised to be on our best mutual behavior.

To all outward appearances, this cloud was soon forgotten as we crossed the northwestern rim of the depression and began climbing in the remains of the old Aleppo road, now fallen into virtual decay and rarely traveled by motor vehicles. We left the quarried face of Jebel Tar en-Nouaisser on the right, and crossed a field of flint which glittered like sequins after the rain. This field was composed of row after row of solid sheets of taffy-colored flint laid down between layers of some other stone that had subsequently rotted away. Tilted by earth movements to a forty-five-degree angle, these sheets had been broken away a few inches above the level of the ground, and the fragments covered the earth between the ridges. No Paleolithic man could have dreamed of a more abundant source of fine-grained tool material, which came in any size he might wish.

A few hundred yards beyond this flint field we topped

a rise and saw a vast panorama ahead. To the right of the Aleppo road stood a row of mountains, all formed after the fashion of Jebel Tar en-Nouiasser, and to the left a plain seven miles wide, as flat as the bed of a lake—which indeed it once had been. Beyond the plain rose the stony shoulders of Jebel Abiodh, the "White Mountain," creased by several wadies, and it was to the westernmost and deepest of them that Ubaid directed Garabed. This wadi is called Wadi ez-Zkak, or the "Vale of Shops," and as the name itself implied the presence of caves, my hopes rose as we approached it.

Never have I seen more skillful driving than Garabed's that day. He guided the weapons-carrier over washes and banks that nothing on wheels had any right to cross. In my opinion he could not have done as well in a half-track or tank, owing to the height of the water-rounded stones he had to straddle. Up the Vale of Shops we climbed for over five miles, and on the way we passed about twenty trees of an unknown species, spreading like beeches, with hard-looking bark, varnished leaves, and lush red blossoms.

"When I was a boy this wadi was full of them," said Ubaid, "but the Bedawin have cut all the rest down. These are too hard for their axes."

A few shallow and empty rock shelters we saw, but not one with a floor and not a single cave; nothing worth excavating. Finally we came to a fork, high up, where a family of Bedawin had pitched a tent. Near it were a cistern in which water from the mountainside had been collected, and the site of an old windmill that Dr. Daniel Schlumberger, a French archæologist who heads the French Mission in Kabul, had once excavated. At this place there were caves, two of them, but they were man-made. We crawled back down the valley. As we were about to set wheels on the plain, I saw a cave miles away near the top of another mountain of limestone. The sun, setting just south of the so-called Hama Gap in the mountains, the opening through which float the clouds that water the Syrian desert, was darting its rays into the mouth of a cavern that at any other time of day might not have been visible at so great a distance.

We crossed the plain, and worked our way around a field of barley which the townsmen of Tadmor had come out hopefully to plant during the rain, and up a narrow gully, and there it was, fifty feet long by twenty wide, with a good dirt floor and a tunnel running into the mountain at the higher end. Although it faced northwest, it commanded a fine view over the plain, which once must have teemed with game. Its name was Taniat al-Baidha, the "white pass," because it was located near a saddle of the mountain. This was our cave. We had fifty-two days before Ramadhan to dig it.

That evening when we were all assembled in the hotel I asked Ubaid if I did not have to report our discovery to Dr. Abd el-Haqq before digging. He looked at my permit for a long time, as did everyone else in the room who could read official Arabic. This language, which is only vaguely intermediate between classical and colloquial, is even harder to understand than the instructions on an income-tax blank. After much head-scratching and glasses-polishing, the consensus was that the paper was valid for a fouille at any cave in the neighborhood. It was all right to go ahead and dig the next day. To this interpretation Ubaid Tahir officially agreed, to my intense relief.

The next morning we laid out an area that we called Trench A in the higher portion of the deposit, and proceeded downward. Ubaid had told me that the two best pick men were a youth named Mohammed and a man in his thirties called Ibrahim. A third man, Saleh (not

to be confused with Saleh the ex-British soldier), served
as foreman. Even on the first day I suspected that Mohammed, Saleh the foreman, and Ubaid were all related
to one another. Before many days had passed I knew that
Mohammed was Ubaid's son and Saleh the foreman his
brother. However, it served no purpose for me to let on

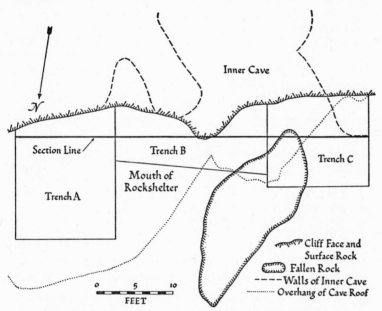

*The Cave of the White Pass: plan. The inner cave, dis-
covered in excavation, is indicated at the top of the drawing.*

that I knew, and finally the relationship became too obvious to warrant further concealment.

These two received the highest pay. As matters worked
out, Mohammed was not very skillful, much to his father's
disgust, but Saleh the foreman was a jewel of a man. He
was able to keep order without raising his voice. He also
performed feats of carpentry and masonry that saved

me many a dollar. Ibrahim was competent also, but lacking in imagination. After Mohammed's clumsiness with the pick had been amply demonstrated, he was replaced by an elfish little old chap named Abu Hasan who was one of my best pick men anywhere, the equal of Abbas and Murat in Belt and Hotu, and this is high tribute indeed.

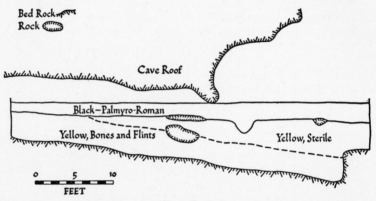

The Cave of the White Pass: section.

Our Trench A was a four-meter square. Level #1 consisted of a thin layer of gray ash overlying a grayish-brown cave earth. In the grayish-brown earth we turned up a copper trigger-guard and an iron arrowhead, three pieces of glass, and sixty-eight wheel-made gray pot-sherds. The animal bones were all of domestic species, particularly sheep, goat, and camel, and none were fossilized. I gave Ubaid and his brother Saleh a lesson in bone-identification, to which they were very attentive.

The camel has four very distinctive bones, the cannon bones, corresponding to the third and fourth metacarpals and metatarsals in man—that is, the third and fourth long bones in the palm of the hand and arch of the foot. As with all animals with cloven hoofs, these two are fused. Every cannon bone of a cloven-hoofed animal is divided at its lower or foot end and terminates in a pair of ridged disks, on whose smooth and rounded

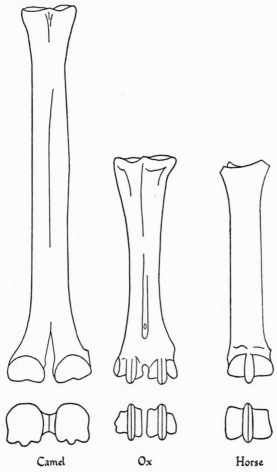

Camel   Ox   Horse

Camels, oxen, and horses: the front cannon bone. The camel's cannon bone is easy to distinguish because it forks at the lower end like a Y. The ox's looks like an oversize goat bone. The horse's cannon bone has a single condyle to match its single toe. (One-fourth actual size.)

surfaces the toe bones move as the animal walks. In the case of horned animals, the sheep, goat, ox, and gazelle, these two disks are parallel to each other because the animal's hoofs are narrow. In the case of the camel, which has broad foot pads to support his great weight on the desert sand, the two disks are not parallel, but are set at an angle of about thirty degrees to each other, to accommodate the pads. Once this distinction has been learned, it is never possible to mistake camel remains for those of other animals. Even in the American branch of the camel family, including the llama, alpaca, vicuña, and guanaco, this tell-tale Y shape in the cannon bones is present.

As I explained these things to Ubaid and Saleh to the best of my ability, the other Saleh, the British soldier, who was lifting buckets of earth out of the trench and handing them to the bucket-carriers, strained his ears to listen, fascinated by this bit of alfresco instruction. As a result he smacked his head on the roof of the cave several times, drawing blood. Each time this happened the other men roared with laughter, and Ubaid shook his head pseudo-reproachfully, muttering: "Salamia, Salamia!" (the name of Saleh's native village). This was when I found out that the poor man was an outsider in the tight Tadmorite social system. Others hurt their heads and hands as well, but no one laughed. The xenophobia of Turujan was recurring in a desert setting.

At noon there began a ritual that was to be repeated unaltered for the rest of our stay in the Palmyra region. Ubaid, Lisa, and I sat on chairs at a table set with plates, knives, forks, and spoons. We ate European-style food, no matter how unappetizing, which came partly from the hotel, partly from Ubaid's household, and partly out of cans. Our luncheon conversation was entirely in French, though during the work hours in the trench Ubaid and

I often forgot ourselves and talked Arabic together. Mo-hammed waited on his father and on us, like a clumsy but devoted butler. The rest of the Tadmorites, with Saleh the foreman in the place of honor, knelt in a circle, eating purely local foodstuffs—better, in many instances, than what we were getting—with their hands, in traditional Arab fashion. Meanwhile, Garabed sauntered down the valley to where he had parked his weapons-carrier, gath-ered enough brush for a small fire, found a sheltered nook, produced out of his pockets some pieces of wire, a cut of mutton, and a jackknife, and proceeded to cook himself some delicious-looking shish kebabs, which he ate in solitary grandeur.

From time to time one variation would occur in this pattern. When a workman—usually Saleh the British sol-dier—fell out of favor, he took his food over to the weap-ons-carrier, sat in it or in its shade, and ate alone. But this was a very shameful thing that cast a hush over the Tad-morite circle, and was never allowed to happen two days in succession, at least with the same man.

After luncheon Ubaid would excuse himself very for-mally, take off his shoes, and pray. Then either Saleh the foreman or Abu Hasan would start the praying in the other lunch area, and all of the older and some of the younger men would follow them. Lunching and praying yielded a clear picture of the precise social peck-order of these people. So cut and dried was their system of dealing with one another, so entirely formalized their whole pattern of living, that each man's behavior was al-most completely predictable. Subtlety in dealing with them became unnecessary and even wasted, except in the case of Garabed. Being more like ourselves, he was less predictable and more responsive.

Ubaid assured me that the pottery in the grayish-brown cave earth was of Palmyrean manufacture, and therefore of Roman date. As he had been working on the city-site ever since he was a boy, he knew as much about this stuff as any man living, and perhaps more. He also assured me that nothing earlier had ever been found in the oasis, and this was encouraging, for it rendered unlikely the discovery of vast layers of Iron Age and Neolithic material underneath, as at Hotu. So when, just after lunch, we ran into an entirely new yellow soil, packed with bones that gave out a fossil ring when struck, I was not surprised, but I was very pleased.

These were primarily the bones of several kinds of horse-like creatures, including probably asses and half-asses (*Hemippus*), with some gazelle and pig. Although we had found some pieces of flint in the very bottom of the grayish-brown layer, mixed with Palmyrean sherds, it was evident that these had chafed off the top of the yellow layer. Down below there were none at all. On the second day of digging we hit bottom in Trench A, at 1.60 meters (five feet four inches) on the uphill side, and 1.90 meters (six feet four inches) on the downhill face, only four meters away. Thus, while the top of the yellow deposit, like that of the grayish-brown above it, was level, the floor of the shelter sloped at an angle of about thirteen degrees, the very angle of the fracture line of the limestone of which the mountain was composed. As one moved away from the crest of the mountain the yellow soil grew thicker.

We now laid out Trench B to follow this slope. As we dug below the Palmyrean layer, which had a constant depth of about sixty-five centimeters (two feet three inches), we found that the yellow layer soon became sterile on the top as we moved valleyward. Trench C, which carried our total area of excavation some fifteen meters (fifty feet) to the end of the sheltered area, confirmed this. What we had was a deposit of yellow soil, originally about two and a half meters deep. The bottom meter had been laid down at the angle of the floor during a period of human occupation. During the time it took for the top meter and a half to accumulate, it was unoccupied.

In Palmyrean times, about and after the time of Christ, city people had come out to the desert to pasture their animals, and had found the cave to be a convenient shelter. They had leveled off the floor, and the flints that occurred in the top part of the bone-bearing deposit at the high end of the cave were strewn over the entire upper surface of the yellow layer. Many fires and the humus produced by the rotting of mats and brush beds had given the upper gray-brown soil its organic component and therefore its brown color.

Needless to say, I did not arrive at this reconstruction all at once, but only after much thought and a considerable absence from Syria. Whatever period the yellow soil represented, the desert was wetter than it is today, or it could not have supported the animals whose bones lay in it. Besides the two or three members of the horse-ass family, we had two species of gazelle: the ordinary Arabian gazelle found there today, and a large animal very much like the goitered gazelle of Belt Cave. We also found several pieces of a large horn core, triangular in section, which most closely resembled the horn core of the water buffalo, an animal not before reported in wild form in the Arabian desert. Even more exciting was finding bones of a wild camel, as fully fossilized as those of the gazelles or other wild animals. As we had plenty of domestic camel bones in the Palmyrean-Roman deposit up above to compare them with, there could be no mistake in identification. Another common animal in this yellow soil was the wild sheep, which could have been *Ovis aries*, a reputed ancestor of the domestic sheep.

The desert could have been wetter without a great

difference in climate, because before the hills and mountains had been deforested there could have been running streams even with the present rainfall. Even today the Tadmorites grow a crop of barley at the foot of the mountain in which the White Pass is situated. The rain blowing in over the Hama Gap, which had wet us so thoroughly on our first journey in the weapons-carrier, could have been absorbed into the soil instead of washing it away, had the forest cover been permitted to remain. To account for this varied lot of animals required not so much a change of climate as a difference in treatment of the land.

Like the material from the desert site of Tel es-Suwaish, the flints excavated in the Cave of the White Pass form a nondescript assemblage of broad flakes (A) and coarse blades (B). In both types the bulb ends were removed, and the flints retouched on several or all edges and either or both sides. (One-half actual size.)

In the Cave of the White Pass we found exactly 650 pieces of flint, most of which we threw away as unused scrap. 31 cores had been produced by the method of turning the piece from end to end to find a good place to strike; 11 other cores had been used as side scrapers. 12 implements were patently flakes, 15 might by a generous stretch of the imagination be called blades, and 24 were intermediate pieces, flakes of a generally flat and rectangular nature. Although this assemblage was not numerous enough to be given a name, its general character showed an apparent kinship with the second group of material which we had collected the year before on the desert at Tel es-Suwaish; also with the millions of similar pieces strewn all over the Arabian desert, from Saudi Arabia to northern Syria.

It was the first time that this special Middle Eastern industry had been found in a geological horizon, and with a fauna, which, luckily, was a very rich one. And it was only the second time, to my knowledge, that the bones of wild camels had been found in the Arabian desert in a fossil state.[1] This discovery has a direct bearing on the origin of the domestic camel, which has been very much a mystery. Unfortunately, the yellow earth of this cave contained not a single scrap of charcoal or other evidence of fire. After our return from Syria we hoped that we might use either hyena droppings or snail shells for Carbon-14 analysis, but we did not have enough for this purpose. It would have taken about a bushel of droppings or 2.2 pounds of snail shells, and we did not have that much of either.

As we finished our work in the Cave of the White Pass, we were both pleased and disappointed: pleased with the flints and animal bones, and disappointed that we not only lacked dating-material but also had found no other layers under the Roman deposit except the yellow soil. This deposit could be tied to nothing at all, for no other people had chosen to inhabit the cave between the time of the yellow-earth folk and the Palmyreans. That was the bitter truth. What we needed was something else to go with it—in other words, another cave.

[1] Neuville found them earlier in the Judæan desert of Palestine. See René Neuville: "Le Paléolithique et le Mésolithique du Désert de Judée," *Archives de l'Institut de Paléontologie Humaine*, Mém. 24, 1951, p. 214.

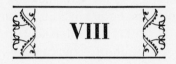

JERF AJLA: THE HEIFER'S OUTWASH

On Wednesday, March 23, we finished our work in Taniat al-Baidha—the Cave of the White Pass—and on the way back to Palmyra we looked at a new cave which Ubaid had found that morning. This cave was called Jerf Ajla, a name hard to translate. *Ajla* means *heifer*—that is easy. But *Jerf*, which comes from a root meaning *to wash away*, has a number of meanings. In this case it probably refers to a long fan of gravel and rubble, formed like an iceless glacier, which had been swept down through a gully between Jebel Mqeita'a and Jebel Marbet el-Hasan, two foothills of the massif of Jebel Abiodh. This outwash, if so it may be called, emerges from its confining walls from north to south and, once out on the edge of the plain, bends to the right and west-ward, bordering and blocking the mouths of a half-dozen caves. Only one of these was high enough above the surface of the outwash, open enough, and big enough to warrant the risk of excavation.

From the standpoint of location and exposure this was a far better site than the Cave of the White Pass. Although of lower altitude than the first cave, it was still high enough above the plain for the purposes of early hunters. Before the outwash had been deposited in front of it by soil-erosion it must have stood a good fifty feet above the land surface, and it still commanded a view of many miles over the ancient lake bottom. We could, in fact, see the dust trails of vehicles coming from Damascus a full hour before they arrived, which meant that a

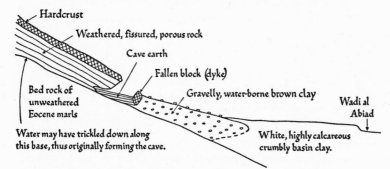

The Cave of the Heifer's Outwash was formed by water trickling through a tilted deposit of soft, porous, and fissured Eocene limestone, overlying unweathered marls of the same period, and capped by a layer of harder material (hardcrust) which formed the roof. In front of the cave stands a bed of white calcareous clay, laid down when the plain was a lake, and later cut through by a seasonally dry, seasonally torrential stream, the Wadi al-Abiad. From time to time as the underlying rock dissolved away, blocks of hardcrust fell off the overhang, forming a dike in front of the cave. This dike held in the cave earth containing flint and bones, and kept out the gravelly brown clay of the outwash flowing from a near-by fissure. It was for this outwash that the cave was named. (After W. J. van Liere.)

Pleistocene hunter could see a herd of horses as far away as a long day's walking distance and plan his stampede or ambush well in advance. In addition it had a southern exposure and received the full warmth of the winter sun slanting under the roof, which stood twenty feet above the present floor. Before the existing deposit had been formed, the roof had been even higher. Even today the roof overhang left twenty feet of shelter, and before

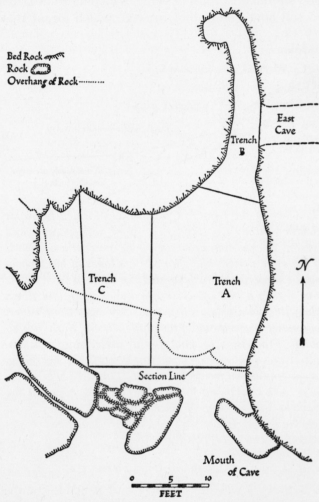

The Cave of the Heifer's Outwash: plan. The inner cave to the east of the main passage, discovered in excavation, is indicated at the upper right.

the rocks that bordered the deposit had fallen, it had reached out at least thirty. In the ancient brook now buried under the outwash there had undoubtedly been water in the days when this cave was inhabited by hunters.

Having moved the gear over to the new cave, we left Mohammed and Ibrahim to sleep there, and were out bright and early to start work. We laid out Trench A, which was six meters by four, not counting a tail that ran into an inner cranny resembling that of Bisitun, and spent the entire day working on a single twenty-centimeter layer. Although containing very little bone, this layer yielded over eight thousand pieces of flint, each one of which had to be washed and examined. In each case I had to make a judgment as to whether or not it was worth saving. Eight thousand judgments in one day is a lot of work.

In this layer two soils were encountered. The top was a peaty black material obviously formed of rotten goat, sheep, and cow manure, and in it most of the flints were coarse blade-trimming flakes hacked and nicked into crude scrapers or saws. These could well be the emergency tools of Bedawin, who are known to use flint for cutting meat, shearing sheep, and other simple technical operations when the proper metal tools are not at hand. Luckily, these coarse pieces were few and the soil containing them thin. In fact, in some places the underlying rich brown cave soil rose through it to the surface.

Once the scrap had been tossed out, the rest of the pieces numbered about four hundred. They included classic Upper Paleolithic blade tools such as end-of-blade scrapers for cleaning skins and steep channeled scrapers of the type found at Kara Kamar, and Middle Paleolithic-style points made on flakes, of the type found at Bisitun, suitable for hafting on spear shafts. There were burins of at least two types, made on both flakes and blades, one bone awl, and a small number of microliths. The industry seemed to be Middle Paleolithic, Upper Paleolithic, and Mesolithic, all at once, and in a single, apparently homogenous soil.

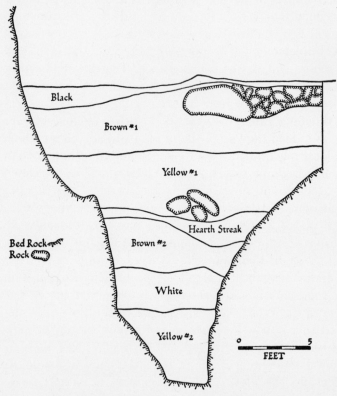

The Cave of the Heifer's Outwash: Section.

It is unlikely that this wide range of archæological types could have been manufactured at once by a single people, because in other stratified sites in the Middle East, particularly in Palestine and Lebanon, the two principal industries here, the flake culture and the blade culture, are always found in separate strata with several intermediate cultures deposited in layers between them. How the mixture took place, however, is difficult to see. Furthermore, the bones that came out with the flints all seemed to be equally fossilized. What might have happened is this: As we might expect in a desert, the periods of occupation were intermittent, and at the same time the soil was deposited at a slow rate and remained very soft. Implements got trodden into the soil, which showed no subsequent signs of disturbance. This is not the most satisfactory explanation in the world, but at the moment it seems to be the most likely one.

Whatever else they were, most of the implements were big, as indeed they might be in view of the sizes in which the local pieces of raw flint came. They were bigger than the hundreds of similar implements which were strewn over the ground outside the row of caves. These smaller implements outside must have been washed out of other, more poorly sheltered deposits, gutted by the outwash or exposed by roof-fall from shallower shelters and caves.

In view of their unusual diversity I would have liked to study these most interesting implements carefully on the spot, but Ubaid's activities prevented this. At the Cave of the White Pass he had, about the third day, decided that it was his duty to write numbers on objects, and once when we had unearthed a small and uninteresting Palmyrean pot he licked his pencil and dug its point into the clay surface, inscribing it with a crude number eleven. I did not mind this much because I did not want the pot, but I objected in general principle to defacing an object. Later he tried to write on the White Pass flints, but, finding their surfaces too glossy, he was reduced to pasting bits of gummed paper on them and writing on those. At night he took them home to register them in two books, recording under each item its length and breadth in centimeters as well as its number and a description.

This procedure was his interpretation of one of the many regulations of the archæological code, which requires that the inspector shall measure, number, and register all objects found. It was intended to apply to large objects such as vases, statues, and the capitals of columns, or to such small assemblages as strings of beads; the writer or writers of the rule book had surely never envisioned this procedure as a part of the processing of tens of thousands of flints.

In a patched conical tent that he had rented at my expense, he sat with his brother Saleh, his son Mohammed, and two other workmen, measuring, labeling, and numbering flints, and inscribing the information so derived in his books. This left me shorthanded at the trench, and without a foreman. Garabed, in the meantime, had found a daytime role for himself: washing the flints in a huge basin, with water brought all the way from town in fifty-gallon drums. As soon as Garabed had finished washing a score or so of flints and laid them out to dry, Mohammed would appear and demand a new batch to number and measure in the tent, and I would tell him he had to wait.

Finally I went to the tent and told Ubaid that if he insisted on keeping his brother inside doing clerical work I would dock his pay and find a new foreman. That brought Saleh out into the open, where he remained from that day on, and where he, like the rest of the men, was much happier. In his place appeared a procession of young clerks from the town, but for the rest of that season's work Ubaid spent most of his time in the tent, scribbling and droning. He told me that he was obliged to copy all this data into another set of books when he got home, and that this kept him up most of every night.

Palmyra. Columns in the Agora.
Photo taken with a Minox camera.

Palmyra. Classical ruins at sunset. Photo taken with a Minox camera.

PLATE XXIV

Palmyra. A field of raw flint shining in the early morning after a rain.

PLATE XXV

The Cave of the White Pass in the desert, seen through a telephoto lens from across the wadi. The entrance of the cave is obscured by the fan of sifted earth deposited in front of it in the process of excavation.

PLATE XXVI

The Cave of the White Pass, seen from inside before excavation. As the roof of this cave
is very low, many heads were hit on it. Note the camel's cannon bone in the foreground.

The Cave of the White Pass, Trench A, Level #1. Photographs like this were taken at
each level of every trench, the average level being 20 centimeters deep.

PLATE XXVII

The Cave of the Heifer's Outwash. The cave was formed by water seeping through a layer of porous limestone. The rocks in the foreground are pieces of the hard upper crust which fell as the roof was progressively undermined by erosion. To the left of the cave mouth is the round tent in which the inspector, Ubaid Tahir, and his men measured and numbered each flint.

Ibrahim and Abu Hasan excavating flints in the rich Upper Brown earth.

PLATE XXVIII

Saleh the foreman builds a bridge of stones and plaster over the entrance to the inner cave. On the left is Saleh the British soldier.

Collecting charcoal for Carbon-14 analysis.

PLATE XXIX

The Cave of the Heifer's Outwash. Measuring the
depth of a level in Trench A with a meter tape.

PLATE XXX

The Cave of the Heifer's Outwash. Amin Qudsi, government security officer, stands on the right, Ubaid Tahir, the
government inspector, on the left. The burlap structure at
the left is my shaded "office," rented to me by Ubaid Tahir.

PLATE XXXI

So literal-minded was this man that I believe he would have slit his own throat if he had found orders to do so in the regulations of the Antiquities Department. I tried to persuade him that his procedure was not required by law. I even wrote a letter and sent a telegram to Dr. Abd el-Haqq, begging him to tell Ubaid that it was unnecessary, but, as far as I know, my requests went unheeded.

As we dug layer after layer and as I hastily sorted thousand after thousand of flints, someone had to count the scrap pieces that we discarded. At first I had Mohammed do this, but I soon devised a trick to keep up the spirits of the team and take the minds of the workmen off their quarrels, which were incessant. The trick was to have one man do the counting, and let the others guess the number. The one who came nearest would be given a pound (around thirty cents), and he would count the next batch. At the very beginning Mohammed and a youth named Mohammed Awwal began playing a back-and-forth game in which the one who had just finished counting secretly told the other the number, and so on ad infinitum. But I caught Mohammed telling Awwal on the second round. From then on, Saleh the foreman did the counting, wrote the number on a slip of paper, and showed it to me before the guessing began.

As far as I could detect, Saleh carried out this service, which he greatly enjoyed, in complete honesty, even in the Western sense, to the end of the dig. Yet I have a suspicion that some subtle kind of rigging still went on, though the mechanism remains a mystery. My suspicion is based on statistics alone. Every time a workman felt depressed or unusually unhappy, then by some miracle he won the pool. And the poor men won more frequently than their richer neighbors, who hardly won at all, though all participated. Maybe Saleh did nothing but look like a Sphinx bursting with a secret, and then open his mouth in a mellifluous laugh at the denouement. Maybe the richer men deliberately guessed wide of the mark. I do not know. But if they did rig it in some way, it must have been because it seemed far more sensible to them to use my newly invented sport as a means of keeping the poor men happy than to stick to the rules of a silly game. Both they and I got our money's worth out of it.

Owing to the menace of the numbers racket that went on in the tent, I invented another device, not to please them but to preserve my own sanity. This was a game called "school." When faced with hundreds of unprocessed pieces of flint, I hauled every man out of the trench, off the bucket line, and away from the screens, and sat them down on straw mats on the area destined to be Trench C. There I put them all to work cleaning the flints of a given stratigraphic level with old toothbrushes, chewed sticks, carpet needles, and anything else that came to hand. Then I showed them how to sort the cleaned flints, lecturing on the different kinds of implements and their uses. Some caught on very quickly, while others merely went through the motions. Although this could serve only as a rough preliminary sorting, I gained a little time.

The first day at the Heifer's Outwash was so trying that the Coon family failed to rise at the usual time, which was around five thirty, the next morning. Because it was Friday we thought we had some part of a day off, but no. Without knocking, Ubaid Tahir burst into our bedroom while we were still in bed and, without excusing himself, announced that he had to get off his biweekly report to Dr. Abd el-Haqq, and that I had to write a biweekly report too. This was news to me.

At eight fifteen we went out to the Cave of the White Pass to finish drafting the plan and section, and returned

at 12:30 p.m. On the way out we passed the carcass of
a sheep which had died, and which shepherds had flayed.
One big bird sat beside it, too gorged to move. On the
way back we saw that ten more birds had joined it. The
first one, in an attempt to take off in flight, skimmed the
ground for a few feet, beating the flints with the tips of
its wings. It gave up, waiting awhile longer for the digestive process to set it free.

In the afternoon we were visited by a delegation
headed by Amin Qudsi and the kaimakam, who announced that Ubaid Tahir was perpetrating a family
racket, that our pay scale was much too high, that Saleh
the foreman in particular was getting too much money,
and that paydays were so infrequent that men had to
borrow. I refused to dock anybody, and I stood up for
Saleh, but I did agree on their last point. Every time I
had suggested to Ubaid that I pay the men, he had said:
"No, at the end of the work."

As my visitors pointed out, these men were poor and
needed the money. Some of them really had been forced
to borrow in the town against their payday. From whom
they were borrowing I did not inquire. So I informed
Ubaid, who had been forced to listen to this exposé and
whose face was the color of fresh liver, that tomorrow
would be payday and that from now on the men would
be paid every Thursday afternoon. In the presence of
these officials he was forced to agree.

The next morning when we rode out over the desert
to work we saw twenty-three birds sitting in the neighborhood of the dead sheep, but the sheep itself had disappeared. In the afternoon, on the way back, we found
only bare ground, for all the birds had lightened their
loads and flown away. Then it suddenly came to me why
we find so few remains of fossil man outside of caves. In
the days before burial had been invented, when people

left their dead exposed, the ancestors of these very birds had done their traditional work, eating all they could and carrying the bones away to their nests in crannies in the cliffs to feed their young. The place to look is in the crannies, and that is one of the types of deposit from which Chinese medicine-hunters have retrieved the teeth of fossil man-like creatures.

That noon the atmosphere in the first-class luncheon area was a trifle thick, but all the amenities were preserved, including some French conversation on general topics. That night we paid off the men, under Amin Qudsi's supervision, and my son, daughter-in-law, and two grandsons arrived with supplies and mail. The next day was a day of excitement caused by a snake. Luckily, my grandsons had left before this event occurred. A five-foot adder, locally believed to kill in thirty seconds after the bite, crawled out from under a rock beneath which Mohammed and Ibrahim, the night watchmen, hid some of their cooking-utensils; it slithered between the legs of the men on the bucket line and wriggled diagonally in front of the horrified sieve men to a new haven under a larger rock. Garabed now left his washbasin and ran to his weapons-carrier, from which he returned with a can of gasoline. A human flame-thrower, he poured the liquid under the rock and tossed a match in. The rock shook, and the snake was presumably cremated.

Ubaid and I looked at each other. We had each lost the best parts of two eyebrows and one mustache. This gave us something very much in common, and we both laughed. In fact, we laughed so loud and uproariously that work in the cave halted. But only for a moment. Quickly recovering his decorum, Ubaid ordered the men back to work.

During this period I could say without exaggeration that, like the hero in the television serial, I led three lives.

One life was composed of my relationship with official Palmyra, greeting the hotel-owner and his friends; reading tourists' passports to advise various officials on the political status of visitors and on their probity; and keeping several British visitors, who had left their passports in Damascus, out of jail. A second was conversing with the hundreds of tourists who came to see the ruins, like a couple from Norristown, Pennsylvania, just five miles from my home, and three handsome old ladies from Germantown, who were on a Mediterranean cruise. I even lectured to a visiting medical association.

The tourist season had opened during the last week of March, and nearly every night the hotel was full. No two expeditions could have been more unlike than the previous year's journey to northern Afghanistan, where Americans are as scarce as Andaman Islanders in Grand Central Station, and this one. Had our cave been located in that station, we could hardly have met more people we knew. Janet's grandmother had visited Palmyra on horseback three quarters of a century before, and the annual tourist crop has ballooned ever since.

One evening a large and shrill-voiced spinster from a northeastern state found herself without a room reservation. When she was put in a room with two other ladies she had hysterics and strode about the town vainly looking for another hotel, which of course did not exist. She ended up spending the night in Qudsi's house, and to get rid of her, he sent her to Homs in a taxi the next morning at his own expense. Over this incident I lost much face among the workmen. Every time that Saleh the British soldier blew his top, which he was doing with increasing frequency, the workmen compared him to the funny American lady, whom they said he should marry, and shook their heads in disapproval.

The third life, the one I had come there to lead, was

so absorbing that I would have much preferred to sleep
out in a tent with Mohammed and Ibrahim, had Captain
Othman let me. Each day as we dug downward, layer
after layer, something new and fascinating turned up. In
Trench A, beneath the usual excremental frosting of black
compost we found that the rich brown soil went down
1.30 meters, or about four feet four inches.

In this brown soil of Trench A we found 35,312 pieces
of flint. Of these I saved 2,007 for later consideration as
possible implements. Ultimately, in the Damascus Museum, I reduced the total count from all trenches in this
soil to 1,131 implements, of which 57 per cent were made
on blades, 35 per cent on flakes and flake blades, and
4 per cent on blade-trimmings. Most of the cores were
disks from which flakes had been removed on alternate
sides. Most of the flake implements were points made
from prepared cores, obviously to serve as spearheads.
Like the equally fine specimens from Bisitun, they had
an optimum butt diameter, in this case 9.50 millimeters,
or three eighths of an inch. The blade implements were
blades used as knives, end-of-blade scrapers for cleaning skins, steep scrapers, notched scrapers, and burins,
in that order of frequency.

What we had here was a mixture of at least two industries, both of great delicacy of workmanship. One employed a Middle and the other an Upper Paleolithic
technique. The two peoples who made these implements
could work both wood and bone, kill animals with spears,
and clean their hides. One bone awl, typical of the later
industry, bore witness to its makers' ability to sew skins.

As the quantity of implements was greatest near the
top of the deposit, I had the impression that the more
advanced types of blade tools were concentrated there
and petered out as we dug downward through the five
levels into which we had divided that soil. Actually, it

did turn out that the blade implements of Upper Paleolithic type, particularly the notched scrapers, end-of-blade
scrapers, steep scrapers, and burins really were more numerous near the top, both absolutely and proportionately, but some of them were found all the way through.
Flake implements, particularly points and side scrapers,
increased proportionately as we went downward.

Under the brown soil we came across a yellow deposit of coarser material, but this was far from homogenous, as it contained numerous thin *lenses* (discontinuous layers) of brown, and even of white, earth. In this
yellow soil the special Upper Paleolithic blade tools of
the upper brown soon became very scarce. The yellow
soil went down to 2.25 meters, or seven feet six inches. In
it only a fifth as many implements were found as in the
brown soil, with flake tools rising to 61 per cent and
blade tools descending to 31 per cent. The other 8 per cent
were core disks. Side scrapers, points, and blades used
as knives accounted for 90 per cent of all implements,
and only four burins, or 2 per cent of the whole, were
found. No progression in any tool type from top to bottom appeared in this soil.

Under it we came upon a black streak caused by the
burning of many fires in a series of hearths which seemed
to cover the whole cave floor, but they contained little
useful charcoal. This streak varied in depth from three
to fifteen centimeters (six to twenty inches), and was un-
derlain by a second brown soil which we called Brown
#2. Averaging about one meter (3 feet four inches) thick,
this took us down to a depth of 3.80 meters, or twelve
feet eight inches. At this point Trench A was about half
the width it had been in the Brown #1 level, owing to
the inward slope of the cave wall. Before removing the
soil of Yellow #1 we had blocked off the inner crevice
from the area of Trench A, saving it for later treatment.

Its stratigraphy was obscure and we did not wish to mix up our levels in Trench A as we went down.

Brown #2 had more than twice as many implements as the yellow soil above it, despite its smaller cubic content. The ratio of blades, 29 per cent, was virtually the same as in the yellow, but the proportion of disk cores doubled from 8 per cent to 15 per cent, and 2 per cent of all implements were made on blade-trimming flakes. It is possible that the two brown layers originally contained the same industry of flakes and blades, and that later people trampled their own implements into the top of the upper brown layer. The industry of Brown #2, rather than showing mixture, indicated a state of transition from a flake to a blade culture.

Side scrapers made on flakes were the dominant tools of Brown #2, followed by used blades, while points came in a poor third. In Brown #1, points had been the most numerous tool. We found fifteen burins in Brown # 2, the greatest number in any level below Brown #1— 3 per cent of the whole, as compared to 7 per cent in Brown #1 and 2 per cent in Yellow #1.

Under Brown #2 was a deposit of powdery white material which reached to a depth of four meters, or thirteen feet four inches. This was two and a half times the body length of most of our workmen. While not very deep compared to Hotu, it was still quite a way down, and much ladder work had to be done. Saleh the foreman rigged a pulley at the mouth of the trench for hauling buckets. This was the first time I had had to use such a rig since Tangier.

This white powder was almost completely lacking in flint, bone, or other material, but at the very bottom of it, in front and on the cave-wall side, we found a pocket of brown earth in a very limited area. In this pocket was contained nearly all the flint of this level. This amounted to twenty-seven pieces, of which eighteen were blades and one was a burin.

As we looked at the section running down the long side of the trench to its mouth, we could see that the lines of separation between the different soils ran in a single direction, which was inward and upward, just the way the wind blew the powdery dust from the valley into the cranny. We could also see that the brown soils did not extend as far inward as the yellow and white ones. This suggested that the brown soils had been formed by human occupation as well as by wind action, while the lighter-colored ones owed more to the handiwork of the wind. However, when we got to the bottom of the white deposit we found a second yellow soil underneath it, and the line between white and yellow was as level as if it had been laid out by a carpenter. Some force more closely dependent on gravity than the wind had made this floor.

That force could only be water, and water meant, if not a wetter period than at present, at least one with a more constant flow. The soil was so fine and so evenly laid that the water which leveled it could not have flowed in from the wadi outside, for that would have brought in coarser material. The only other possibility is that the water flowed from a small spring within the cave itself. This could have been possible, when the rock overhead was covered with soil and vegetation, without a very great increase in rainfall.

At this point our trench was only two feet wide, and I put Abu Hasan in the front of it and Ibrahim in the rear. Before he had been digging in this yellow material very long Abu Hasan handed me some pieces of dark amber-colored flint, which I saw went together. In fact, they were pieces of a hand ax that he had broken with his pick. We managed to retrieve all of them, and I glued them together. It was a beautiful hand ax, finely made, in the best workmanship of the later Lower Paleolithic tradition.

What a sequence we now had! What a cave! Hand axes like these, to my knowledge at that time, had been

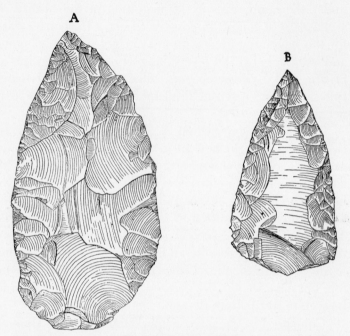

The lower and middle levels of the Heifer's Outwash deposit contained a progressive sequence of Middle Paleolithic core and flake implements related to those found beyond the desert rim on the coast of Palestine and Lebanon and in the mountains of Iraq. (A) An exquisite thin hand ax from the bottom yellow soil. (B) Weapon point made on a prepared flake. (One-half actual size.)

found in the earliest stage of the Middle Paleolithic prepared-core flake industry in France, North Africa, Palestine, and elsewhere in Syria, but in Palestine and the other Syrian sites they were rare. With this discovery we now had a succession of levels which carried the Middle Paleolithic from its beginning to its end, finishing with an intrusion of Upper Paleolithic blade tools. To cap it all, Abu Hasan called me to his side. He had found charcoal under the hand ax. For the first time in the history of archæology it might be possible to get a Carbon-14 date for the beginning of this industry. I got out my cameras and strobe light and everything else to photograph it *in situ*, and every scrap was collected in tinfoil as carefully as if the Queen of England had dropped her pearl necklace in a gutter.

The yellow soil carried us down to 6.10 meters, or twenty feet four inches. In it we recovered 5 fine hand axes, 5 cleavers, 3 small hand axes, 6 used disk cores, 75 flake scrapers, 20 points, and 15 used blades. Here we had the elements, in capsule, of the flint industries found above, in addition to the hand axes and cleavers. The soil change between this Yellow #2 and the white material above represented a time gap, the only clear one in the whole sequence below the black material at the top, but nevertheless the germs of the later cultures could be seen in this bottom deposit.

Compared to the Cave of the White Pass, the Heifer's Outwash was poor in bone. Not a scrap that belonged to a human skeleton appeared, and the majority of what we did find was horse and gazelle, both of which appeared throughout. In the brown soils, lenses, and pockets the horse seemed to predominate, and in the yellows and whites the gazelle. In the bottom yellow the same wild sheep that we had found in the Cave of the White Pass also appeared. It was impossible for me to identify all the bones, but it would be easy enough later under laboratory conditions, with not only the help of my own staff and the collections from the earlier caves, but also the co-operation of trained zoologists in various institutions.

What I called horse bones in the field could easily turn out later in the laboratory to be the wild ass, or the so-called half-ass, *hemippus*, an animal that became extinct within the present century. At any rate, no major climatic change could be established on the basis of my spot identifications, or through later ones to be made in America.

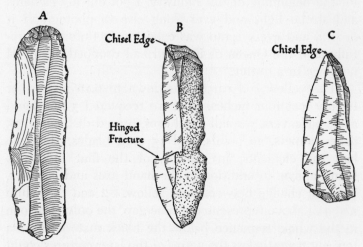

Throughout the middle soils in the Heifer's Outwash deposit, blades are found alongside flakes, and blades are in the majority in the top brown soil. Among the commonest blade types are A, fleshers or end-of-blade scrapers used for cleaning hides. B is a burin or chisel, made by removing a small piece from the left side. The scar so produced ends in a characteristic hinged fracture. C is an angle burin. (One-half actual size.)

If the Bedawin were to leave the desert for twenty years, it could probably come to support many of the animals I was able to identify.

Once Trench A had been finished, we turned to Trench B, the inner crevice, which turned out to have a couple of minor chambers. In order to get to it and move the soil out conveniently, it was necessary to build a bridge over its mouth. Saleh the foreman supervised this work, mixing plaster that he had brought from town, and fitting each stone into place as the men handed them to him. The finished product, which cost me less than fourteen dollars, could have graced the gateway to a churchyard garden. It pleased Saleh very much to have the chance to show his skill as a master mason.

In Trench B we found mostly the upper yellow and white earth, for neither the brown sequences nor the lower yellow reached it. The implements were mostly flake tools. The Upper Paleolithic people probably did not go into the back of the cave very often, but squatted in the entrance. On the other hand, the few Mesolithic pieces were almost all found in the narrow rear cavity. Trench C was the western flank of the outer deposit, which reached down only to the white earth; the Yellow #2 soil, which contained the hand axes, lay wholly inside Trench A territory. In Trench C we were able to separate the top deposit with its crude trimming-flake tools from the upper brown, and in the yellow we kept the implements found in brown lenses separate also. Luckily, Carl Jr. was with me most of the time we were digging Trench C, and he and Janet were a great help. Nothing that we found in Trench C altered our sequence determined in Trench A.

On the day we found the first hand axes, our workmen were unusually well dressed, as if in anticipation of this discovery. The reason was, however, that we expected the arrival of the *Time-Life* correspondent from Beirut, and Ubaid had decreed that everyone should be decked out in his finest so that foreigners would not get the idea that Syrian workmen were shabby. As Saleh the British soldier and Abu Hasan had no clean and untorn clothing, Ubaid said that they must keep out of the pictures, or none could be taken. Faced with that ultimatum, I bought each of these men a new blue-denim coverall and a new headcloth and headband. The correspondent arrived after many delays and difficulties, and the pictures were taken.

But that was not the end of our picture trouble. Ever since the second day at Taniat al-Baidha we had been accompanied to the caves by a teen-aged soldier named Mohammed Freah. Before he was drafted he had been one of Ubaid's workmen, and his brother was one of our bucket boys. Now he was doing his military service in his home town, which gave him a chance to lord it over his contemporaries, and to be officious with that suspicious foreign character, myself.

He too was anti-photographic. Although he spent most of his time asleep in the tent or under a vehicle, he woke up at odd moments to show his authority. One day we were visited by a handsome Bedawi flock-owner, dressed in a beautiful new set of robes of many colors, and I took a picture of him in Ektachrome with my Hasselblad. Later, when Mohammed Freah happened to wake up, the Bedawi told him with a bit of pride that he had just had his picture taken, and in color.

Leaping to his feet, Mohammed Freah placed the man under arrest and announced to all of us that he was taking his prisoner back to the garrison that afternoon after work. I told Mohammed Freah that it was I who had suggested the picture and had also taken it; therefore, it was I who should be locked up and not the poor Bedawi, who had his flocks to tend to. But the soldier scorned this idea and went back to sleep. When he finally awoke, the prisoner was far away, by what means I was careful to have no idea.

Our principal source of trouble was, as Ubaid had predicted, Saleh the British soldier. On several occasions he had broken into uncontrollable screaming over some real or fancied insult or injury at the hands of the other men. One afternoon when we were getting out of the vehicles an old man whom we had picked up in a barley field on the way back brushed or otherwise inadvertently touched Saleh, and Saleh made a great outcry. Now, the old man was the town's *muezzin*, a holy person. Abd er-Rezzak, our most loquacious workman, quickly flew to his rescue, and in the fracas tore Saleh's shirt. Saleh then nursed his grievance for a couple of hours, and after we had sat down to dinner he stalked into the hotel and stood by my chair screaming in a high-pitched voice for about half an hour. No one would put him out.

Early one afternoon about a week before the end of the dig Saleh gave signs of another oncoming attack, and Ubaid and I took steps to minimize the disturbance. First I gave Saleh an aspirin and told him to lie in the shade of a vehicle, but he would not stay there. Then we set him to work at a sieve where he would come into the least possible contact with the other men, but this made little difference. The fit came on. In the beginning he had complained of a headache, but now his grievance was that the sun was too bright, as indeed it may have seemed to him because the pupils of his blue eyes were widely dilated. Ubaid and I, he cried, were responsible because we had told him to sit in the sun.

As I tried to ignore him and Ubaid to calm him, his voice grew in loudness and pitch, his eyes bulged from their sockets, and flecks of froth began to appear at the corners of his mouth. Turning to Ubaid and me, he cried out in the tones of an ancient prophet: "The Jews are better than you are!!"

This was too much for Ubaid, who jumped up and down in anger, clenching and unclenching his fists. Mo-hammed Freah woke up, leaped out of the tent, and began smashing Saleh's face with the butt of his rifle. Now the froth welled out of his mouth like warm champagne from a shaken bottle and, mingling with the freshly drawn blood, fell lightly, in the form of pink foam, on his new blue collar.

By the time I had succeeded in stopping this butchery, Saleh's face was in bad shape, but I could not find that any bones were broken, and his eyes were intact. I sent him back to town at once in a truck and saw him no more until the day of our departure, when he confronted me, mute and patched with bandages, in front of the hotel, his eyes pleading. This incident was also the end of Mohammed Freah, who was replaced by an amiable Bedawi soldier who spent his time visiting the tents of neighboring tribesmen and bringing gypsy dancers to entertain us. But this was a bit too late. Even if he had brought Salome, Sheherezade, and all the dancing girls out of the *Thousand and One Nights*, their combined talent and charm would not have been enough to erase from my memory the grim numbering of flints in the tent and the pink froth on Saleh's lapel. The Heifer's Outwash will probably turn out to be our most important cave, but it was not our happiest one.

On Saturday, April 16, we returned to Damascus, four Coons in the family station wagon, and Ubaid and Garabed in a truck with the collections. According to the laws of the Antiquities Department, these had to be delivered directly to the doors of the Museum, under the guard of its official representative. On Monday the 18th I was able to see Dr. Abd el-Haqq, who explained that he was off for Paris that very day and would not return for nearly two weeks. In the meantime, it was my job to lay out the finds and divide them into two parts.

I was glad to have this opportunity to sort the flints and find out what we really had, because the processing routine in the tent had limited my acquaintance with them. They looked handsome spread out in rows and categories on the tables, and my fellow workers, who had dealt previously with pottery and statuary, admired them as much as I did. One day we were visited by a very famous man in the Arab world, Major H. St. John Philby, a British Muslim who had lived most of his life in Saudi Arabia. Philby's knowledge of the Arabs is equaled only by their deep respect for him. On the morning of his visit the basement of the Museum was washed and dusted, and everything was put in apple-pie order. No earthly king could have been received with greater veneration. After his visit my stock in the workroom went up several hundred per cent.

In the upper offices of the building, however my stock fell near the bottom of the scale on the afternoon of April 22. My genial protector Colonel Malki, who had straightened out my army permit in five minutes on my last visit to Damascus, attended an international soccer game that afternoon. A sergeant standing behind him shot him twice point-blank through the head, and then shot himself. It was a tense time, anyhow, because that very night the religious officials saw the moon, and cannon announced the beginning of the holy month of Ramadhan. For some reason that it is not my business to seek to understand, the volatile elements in Damascus chose to blame Colonel Malki's assassination on us Americans. This seemed unwarranted to me not only because we do not ordinarily assassinate people but also because I had never heard him spoken of except as a friend. Although I was among the most minor sufferers, in Colonel Malki I lost a badly needed champion in the interdepartmental struggle that all foreigners dealing with the government have to face.

On May 1 we left for a brief vacation in Cyprus. I

had done all I could in the Museum until Dr. Abd el-Haqq should return on the 8th. On the 9th he received me and promptly informed me that I had broken the law on several counts. I had gone out without an architect, epigrapher, or photographer. I had dug a fouille when my permit was for a sondage. I had not notified him where I planned to dig. As it was a sondage, I could have none of the specimens.

For the next few days I busied myself photographing the flints and some of the bones. Then I went home to Pennsylvania, wrote a preliminary report on the basis of my field notes and what I had written down in the Damascus Museum, mailed a few letters, and waited. On February 12, 1956, I received a cable stating that I could have on a year's loan the animal bones and some sixty flints that I had selected. The Carbon-14 samples would also be sent, the whole lot under a ten-thousand-dollar insurance bond. Two weeks later they arrived by air freight, and the process of identification began. The flints have been seen by Hallam Movius, Bruce Howe, John Waechter, and Ralph Solecki, all of whom had valuable comments to make. The bones are being cleaned and alvared, and some of them have already traveled to the Museum of Comparative Zoology at Harvard, where Barbara Lawrence Schevill, the Curator of Mammals, has inspected them. Dexter Perkins, Jr., Jane Goodale, and Theresa Howard Carter, who worked on my bones from previous caves, are engaged in identifying the present lot. Our principal problem at the moment is to separate the wild-ass bones from those of the half-ass, but this task need not hold up our conclusion that throughout the time of occupation of the Heifer's Outwash, the climate was, with minor variations, much as it is at present.

Although we do not yet know the exact boundaries of this time span, we have a valid date for one point inside it. After our Carbon-14 samples arrived in Philadelphia our government announced its intention of testing H-bombs in the South Pacific from April to June 1956. The fallout was believed likely to make Carbon-14 research precarious in the path of the westerly winds that blow off the Pacific Ocean and across North America. One Carbon-14 station in the world was, however, impervious to this fallout, for it is situated southwest of the testing-grounds. That is the New Zealand government's station at Lower Hutt, near Auckland. Early in April, Elizabeth Ralph, the head of our University of Pennsylvania Carbon-14 laboratory, sent samples from our Syrian collection to Dr. G. J. Fergusson, the head of the New Zealand station.

On June 5, 1956, a radiogram from Dr. Fergusson informed us that a large sample from Trench A, layer #8, taken from near the bottom of the upper yellow soil of the Cave of the Heifer's Outwash, was 43,000 $\pm$ 2,000 years old. As of June 1956 this is the oldest Carbon-14 date yet found at a site once occupied by human beings.

A single Carbon-14 date is always a precarious thing; when we have obtained a sequence of dates, we will be on firmer ground. Still, this date is technically impeccable, and it fits the circumstances in which it was found.

Tentatively, it means that the Middle Paleolithic prepared-flake culture of Palestine, Lebanon, Syria, and Iraq, with its gradual evolution of blades and burins, had reached a high point of development forty-three thousand years ago. The famous caves of Mount Carmel in Palestine were dug before Carbon-14 dating had been invented, and so was another site, Ksar Aqil, in Lebanon. John Waechter, who is working on the Ksar Aqil material, finds that the three sites, Mount Carmel, Ksar Aqil, and the Heifer's Outwash, together form an unbroken sequence from hand-ax times to the Mesolithic. Implements precisely like those from A-8 of our cave can be found at corresponding levels of the other sites. Therefore, Dr. Fergusson's figure gives us a peg on which to hang the whole Middle Eastern sequence by cross-dating. At present it looks as if the A-8 date belongs in the time of the first advance of the last ice, which means that the material in the lower yellow soil at the bottom of our cave should be of third-interglacial age.

Although no charcoal was found in the Cave of the White Pass, we have not given up hope of dating the deposit. Samples of the bones from the yellow soil are being sent to London, along with samples of bones of different layers in the Heifer's Outwash. Dr. Kenneth Oakley of the British Museum will determine the fluorine content of these samples, in the hope of tying the White Pass bones into the Heifer's Outwash series. This is a reasonable procedure, because the two caves are near each other, the geology of the two regions is identical, and the rate of fluorine-deposition should be the same for both. When he succeeds, we may be able to see whether the White Pass deposit is older or younger than forty-three thousand years. Then we will have some notion of the age of the desert culture of the whole Arabian peninsula.

Archæology proceeds step by step, with cumulative results. Our work in the desert caves of Palmyra in 1955 has meaning principally as it helps to solve problems uncovered elsewhere in the Arab countries of the Middle East. I hope that others will carry it further.

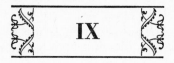

IX

THE MEN IN OUR CAVES

F ROM THE SEVEN CAVES with which this book is concerned we removed over one hundred and fifty thousand
pieces of flint and enough animal and bird bones to make,
if reassembled, a flock of sheep, a herd of cattle, a sty of
pigs, a stable of horses, a flight of geese, a pride of lions,
and a small rookery of seals. We also found the bones of
about fifteen human beings, some represented by single
teeth, isolated jaws, pieces of wrist bone, and other un-
satisfactory fragments; only six or seven specimens were
complete enough for solid laboratory study. From four of
the caves we also removed about a peck of charcoal, in-
valuable for telling dates, and from all of them we took
soil samples for geological study. Only in two did we
make any considerable collection of pottery.

The finds from these seven caves are, of course, only
seven drops in the bucket of prehistoric archæology,
which, during the last century, other excavators have filled
almost to the brim. If these caves have any unusual
interest it may be partly because they are situated in
countries that are either little visited or very much in the
news. Our efforts to get to these countries, the routines
we had to follow in them to find and dig caves, and what
we had to do to get the specimens home for study took

much more time and effort than the actual work of excavation.

The physical or political remoteness of all but the first cave further enhanced their importance, because few other prehistoric sites had been dug very near any one of them. All were in archæological terra incognita. Finding something new in each place only whetted our appetites for more, because each discovery stated a new problem rather than solved old ones. The only exceptions may have been our two last caves: the White Pass in the Desert and the Heifer's Outwash. What we found in them may help to explain the sequences found in the caves that others had dug in the Fertile Crescent around the desert.

The contents of our seven caves and one open-air station which I have described in the order of their discovery fall naturally into three major groups: the Middle Paleolithic flake industries, the Upper Paleolithic blade industries, and the post-Pleistocene Mesolithic and Neolithic cultures. Together they cover the greater part of the one-hundred-thousand-year period during which caves in Europe and the Middle East were occupied: from the third interglacial, through the height of the last glacial advance, and into the present geological era.

Middle Paleolithic flake industries were found in the High Cave of Tangier, in Bisitun, in the two desert caves near Palmyra, and in the open-air surface site of Tel es-Suwaish on the Saudi-Jordanian border. Only the High Cave and Bisitun contained Ice Age human remains. The Bisitun fragments were probably Neanderthal, but the maxilla and teeth from the High Cave may not have belonged to people of that race. According to L. Cabot Briggs, the Tangier specimens were examples of a local breed more primitive than Neanderthal in details of tooth structure.[1] These High Cave dwellers also developed a local flint industry that does not occur in proved Neanderthal sites. They made flake implements beautifully worked on both sides, as well as tanged points. Comparable flaking was done in parts of Africa south of the Sahara. The Tangier animal bones also include many African species now confined to the tropical realm. Whatever the relationship of the Tangier industry may turn out to be, its peculiarity suggests that Neanderthal man himself never reached the Atlantic along the southern shore of the Mediterranean.

Moving over to the cave of the Heifer's Outwash, in the middle of the Syrian desert, we found a long series of previously known Middle Paleolithic flake industries that followed one another without interruption. Other excavators had unearthed them in Palestine, Lebanon, and Iraq, but their sequences were incomplete. Similar implements can be picked up on the desert only in a few places where cave roofs have collapsed and the soils underneath eroded. This was no desert culture, but an extension of a mountain-and-forest culture into hilly and well-watered parts of the desert. Now that we have a Carbon-14 date for part of the sequence, we can begin to tie the whole of it into its geological and chronological framework, which is the first step in finding out how the Middle Eastern sequence is related to that of Europe.

The open-air site of Tel es-Suwaish contained flints unrelated to this sequence but belonging to a type found all over the desert from Syria to Saudi Arabia. These are flakes with broken striking-platforms, retouched on all edges. Apparently the desert was a refuge with a flake

[1] L. Cabot Briggs: *The Stone Age Races of Northwest Africa* (American School of Prehistoric Research, Research Bulletin #18, Cambridge, Mass., 1955).

culture all its own. In the western desert of Egypt a similar industry has been found. Local people can develop the same kinds of tools in different refuge areas to meet the same needs and conditions.

Although the few implements that we found in the Cave of the White Pass are still unrelated to anything so far found in stratified sites, they look like the flints from Tel es-Suwaish and the whole desert complex. While the Heifer Cave, five miles away, belongs to the mountains and forests, the White Pass goes with the desert. This difference points up the marginal position of the Palmyra region, which once formed the borderland between the two environmental realms, though today everything around it is desert.

Despite its lack of Pleistocene stratification, the Cave of the White Pass is our only undisturbed and uneroded desert-culture site in the whole Arabian peninsula, and its yellow soil was full of animal bones. From them we can reconstruct in some detail the animal population of the northern desert during the period, whenever it was, in which the enigmatic flints found with the bones were made. Three different species of the horse tribe ran rampant. Wild sheep climbed the ridges, and gazelles nibbled fresh grass on the plain. Instead of monopolizing the pasture as they do today under Bedawin protection, camels, as wild animals, competed for food on equal terms with others grazers, and this competition no doubt prevented them from ruining the landscape.

From the list of animal species alone we cannot tell which was older, the cultural sequence from the Heifer's Outwash or the single desert culture found in the White Pass, because the bones of the same animals were found in both caves. Soil studies and fluorine analysis of bones from these neighboring sites may give us a tentative answer, but before we can place the desert culture definitely in its proper time scale someone will have to do more digging in the desert. As it belongs to six different countries, all of which have different sets of regulations about archæology, this should be possible in one place if not another. The men who lived in desert caves during the Pleistocene could hardly have known that their territory would some day be partitioned, and they probably lived in all six areas, without passports.

The cave at Bisitun, small, rich, and accessible, produced from its crannies a Middle Paleolithic flake industry similar in broad outline to those of Palestine, Syria, and northern Iraq, but much more limited in the number and variety of implement types. It also had a higher proportion of blades than any of these others—that is, of blades made on prepared cores, probably in most cases without the use of the punch. This may mean that the industry of Bisitun was more highly developed than the others simply because it was later, or it may mean that Bisitun was an isolated drinking-place in which local people invented local variants of a widespread tool-making tradition at the same time that other techniques were being invented elsewhere. Without Carbon-14 and other objective tests, we cannot say. Anyhow, there was no Upper Paleolithic at Bisitun. Upper Paleolithic men would have camped in such a well-watered bivouac had they been anywhere in the neighborhood. Their conspicuous absence from this garden spot may in itself be significant, particularly if future excavations in the neighborhood, as in Mr. Watson's cave, confirm it.

The flakes at the bottom of Kara Kamar and those above the blades in the loess deposit of that cave have drawn a complete blank, as no flint expert to whom I have shown them is willing to say anything about them. At the present state of our knowledge of central Asian archæology they are only a source of embarrassment, and will so remain until someone else finds something like them. I am told that they are too few to constitute an industry. Flint experts like to work with hundreds of implements that they can sort out and study on a statistical

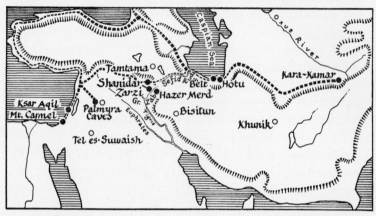

Possible Stone Age Migration Routes in the Middle East. During Upper Paleolithic and Mesolithic times, similar blade tools were made on both sides of the east-west mountain barrier in western Asia. Some of the implements found to the south, at Mount Carmel, Ksar Aquil, the Heifer's Outwash, Hazer Merd, Zarzi, and Shanidar, match others from the north, excavated at Belt, Hotu, and Kara Kamar. Blade-using hunters may have crossed the highlands over a route still in use: up the Great Zab and down the valley of the Sefid Rud to the Caspian shore. Or they may have walked around Turkey and over the low Transcaspian Trough.

basis, rather than with a dozen or so ill-defined pieces that may not be a representative sample.

Our only Upper Paleolithic blade industry, located in a proper stratum of its own without embarrassing neighbors, is that of Kara Kamar. This too, like the stuff below it, is a meager bag, hardly a statistician's delight, but it is all we have from a vast territory. It clearly belongs in the same archæological universe as the Upper Paleolithic of Palestine, Syria, and Iraq, but it has a much smaller number of specialized tools, many more crude pieces, and no burins. The key tool in this site is the fluted steep scraper. Individual steep scrapers from Kara Kamar could not be distinguished from others found in Iraq, Syria, and Palestine. It is hard to believe that a cultural connection between northern Afghanistan and the Palestine-Syrian area, involving the manufacture of this tool, did not exist in late Pleistocene time.

We cannot as readily tie Kara Kamar up with Europe. The Carbon-14 date of older than thirty-four thousand years which Dr. Suess and Miss Ralph have given its Upper Paleolithic culture makes it certainly contemporary with the greater part of the blade industries of western Europe, but it does not tell us which of the two, the central Asiatic or the European, began first, or what was the relationship, if any, between either and the series from Palestine and Syria.

The blade industry that we found so highly concentrated in the top brown soil of the Cave of the Heifer's Outwash is—excepting a few Mesolithic-looking pieces that came mostly from the inner chamber—a standard Upper Paleolithic toolkit, with burins, steep scrapers, end-of-blade scrapers, and other blade tools of the kind already found both in Palestine and in the Kurdish Mountains of northern Iraq. The steep scrapers themselves link it to Palestine on the one hand and to Kurdistan and Kara Kamar on the other. Similar blade tools are found on the surface in front of broken-down caves in the mountains north and west of Palmyra, and it should be possible to find them somewhere *in situ*. Then we can see whether the association of flakes and blades in a single soil is a chronic situation on the desert, or just a Heifer Cave peculiarity.

In Belt Cave we found the first Mesolithic industry to come out of Iran, associated with a fluctuating fauna. Sea and forest animals alternating with grassland types reflected the rapid climatic changes that took place on the Caspian shore with the final retreat of the glacial ice-cap in the north, and the lowering of the inland sea level. Luckily, our Carbon-14 dates for this sequence are in order. The only site in the Middle East with which this Mesolithic material can be compared in detail is Ralph Solecki's cave of Shanidar in Iraqi Kurdistan. His Mesolithic is very similar to that of Belt Cave, and the dates are approximately the same. Had we dug other caves along the Caspian shore above the glacial high-water mark, we might have found Upper Paleolithic material to fill in part of the gap between Shanidar and Kara Kamar, as well as to show us what the Belt Cave Mesolithic might have evolved from. This is another badly needed project.

Aside from three splendid skeletons, Hotu Cave gave us little Mesolithic material. That is not the fault of the cave, for a good sample of the flints and animal bones is surely still there. Whoever digs the rubble again will have to clean out the remaining Neolithic and metal-age soil from the back and sides of the cave. Another cave-in may end in a loss of life, dramatically foreshadowed by the positions of the skeletons we excavated. But Hotu should be re-excavated.

Taking what we have for what it is worth, both the implements and the animal bones from the lowest deposits of Hotu could have come from the Seal Mesolithic of Belt, which was of the same Carbon-14 date. Scanty as their contents were, the top Hotu rubbles produced something that so far is unique: an assemblage of very coarsely made flint implements accompanied by the bones of animals that were either already fully domestic or in process of domestication. The date of this culture, which we called Sub-Neolithic, lies between those of the truly Mesolithic and the Neolithic industries of Belt Cave. As its flint industry was totally different from those which preceded or followed it, we assume that it was made by a group of animal-tamers who came, stayed a few decades or centuries, and went away. The eastern Caspian shore of Iran was not a refuge area like Bisitun, but a super-highway. Unfortunately, our Mesolithic material from Kara Kamar is quite meager, but what there is of it fits in with Belt Cave, both in implement types and in date.

Whatever these connections may mean in detail, collectively they indicate that by the time the ice sheet had begun its final retreat in the north, people living on the fringes of the northern Eurasiatic realm, in Iraq, Iran, and Afghanistan, had already become Mesolithic hunters, using bows and arrows and dogs, and working wood with chisels made of antler. Forests, lakes, and streams offered them a rich bag of fish, wildfowl, and game. This way of life was carried into Europe as the forests moved northward, and lasted there until after the arrival of Neolithic farmers around 3000 B.C.

In the northern fringes of the Middle East, the Mesolithic and Neolithic cultures were older than in countries farther north, beyond the mountain barrier, because in the south the climate ameliorated earlier. Our Neolithic discoveries were limited to two regions, Tangier and Belt-Hotu. The Tangier Neolithic was distant from the point of Neolithic origins, and late. It could not have begun much before 3500 B.C., and it lasted until Roman times.

When the place of origin of the Neolithic is found,

it will probably turn out to be no more than a few hundred miles from Belt and Hotu. These caves still have the oldest Carbon-14 dates for the Neolithic, though older ones will no doubt be found elsewhere. Because of the presence of the Sub-Neolithic deposit in Hotu we must postulate that the Belt Neolithic people had come into that well-favored countryside from somewhere else, not long after 6000 B.C. At first they had no pottery, but they soon began to make it, a soft, poorly fired ware, painted red with ocher and burnished by rubbing with pebbles. This pottery is still unique, and its position in the history of pottery-making is therefore unknown. The Belt Neolithic people cannot have invented it on the spot, because no developmental stages are seen. By 3000 B.C. they had learned to make another kind of pottery which is much easier to trace. This was a thin-walled variety, mostly cups and bowls, painted in black designs on a red surface. Similar vessels have been found on the Iranian plateau and in Mesopotamian mounds, from about the same date.

After the Neolithic, our lake-shore caves were vacant until early Iron Age people used them as a dump for the broken necks, legs, and bodies of a kind of wheel-made pottery related to wares found in Turkey in sites dated at around 1000 B.C. After the people who threw this trash into Hotu had gone, the caves lay empty through the whole brilliant Achæmenian period—the flowering-time of the Persian Empire—only to be reoccupied intermittently until a few centuries after the time of Christ. Then the mouth of the cave was sealed by earth sliding in from the plateau above.

In spite of the hundreds of thousands of flints and potsherds we found in our seven caves and related sites, we came upon human bones in four caves only: the High Cave, Bisitun, Belt, and Hotu. Their scarcity makes them precious, and shows that man's handiwork is bulkier than his body. Also, the more man's body resembles that of other animals, the more meager and undifferentiated his product.

Tangier and Bisitun, being Middle Paleolithic sites, gave us stray bits of Neanderthal or men like him; Belt and Hotu gave us enough skeletons from both Mesolithic and Neolithic cultures to know that men of modern European type lived on the Caspian shore in early post-glacial times. They belonged to the same race as the Upper Paleolithic hunters of Europe. They were Nordic. Their continuity with the modern races of Europe and with living Iranians and Tajiks is apparent. Our cave-digging in the Middle East has not given us clear scientific evidence of the details of the evolution of modern European man, nor of his relationship with Neanderthal, but it has helped piece out the general picture. Further discoveries in Europe and revaluations of old ones have now given this picture a much sharper focus than it had when I started.

In Europe, we still do not know whether human beings lived through the cold of either the first or the second glacial period, but recent evidence from France and Germany indicates that they probably did weather the third one. In one place near Leipzig, hunters killed mammoths passing over a narrow game trail between the edges of the Scandinavian and Alpine ice sheets, and their tools have been found in subsequently deposited gravels. These tools include both flakes and blades and a few specialized forms.[2]

While they may have lacked the tailored clothing that their Upper Paleolithic successors could have worn,

[2] Rudolf Grahmann: "The Lower Paleolithic Site of Markkleeberg, etc.," edited by H. L. Movius, Jr., *Transactions of the American Philosophical Society*, N. S., Vol. 45, Part 6 (Philadelphia, 1955), pp. 509–687.

the Europeans who killed mammoths in a corridor between ice sheets must have found ways to keep warm, and must also have been very rugged. Natural selection must have molded them into a form capable of survival under the most rigorous conditions. Unfortunately, we have very few bones of the men who lived in the north before the middle of the third interglacial, and no clear evidence whether one or several races were involved. The entire lot consists of one chinless jawbone of first-interglacial age (Heidelberg); fragments of a single faceless braincase from the second interglacial (Swanscombe); a nearly complete skull lacking its lower jaw, from what is said to have been a warm interval in the third glacial period (Steinheim); two skulls from a German cave of the third interglacial (Ehringsdorf); two more from a French cave of the same period (Fontéchevade); a chinless jaw of the same period from another French cave (Montmaurin); and fragments of nearly a score of skulls, faces, and limb bones from a Croatian cave (Krapina), likewise third-interglacial.

The people whose remains these are had brains of modern size and shape. Steinheim and the Krapina population also had faces as large as living Australian aborigines. Some of the Krapina jaws had chins; Montmaurin had none. The Fontéchevade skulls could have had smaller faces, judging by the shape of the foreheads, which are nearly fully preserved. If these bones represent one population, it was an archaic European one in which, by third-interglacial times, small faces of modern type may have begun to replace the older, larger ones, which represent a stage of evolution through which any racial stock could pass, and most have.

In the Middle East even fewer remains of equal age have been discovered. Two lower jawbones from Palikao, in Algeria, go back probably to first-interglacial time, and they are chinless like Heidelberg. An equally primitive fossil jaw was blasted from a sandstone quarry near Rabat in Morocco in 1924, but its age cannot be determined. In Palestine it is possible that some of the skeletons from the Mount Carmel caves, Mugharet es-Skhul and Mugharet et-Tabun, are of late third-interglacial date, here more appropriately called *interpluvial* (between rainy periods), and that the same is true of a skull from the cave of Mugharet el-Zuttiyeh near the Sea of Galilee. Like the skulls from Ehringsdorf and Krapina, they show close kinship to modern European man, as well as some features shared with that very famous if extinct kind of human being, the centenary of whose first discovery in Germany was celebrated there in 1956 —Neanderthal man.

In Europe as well as the Middle East, Neanderthal man made his first appearance toward the very end of third-interglacial time, when the permanent snow line on the Alps and the mountains of Scandinavia was creeping downward and storms off the Atlantic were growing in violence: the fourth ice age was on its way. Something happened then to the population of Europe, something that we do not yet fully understand. A new people moved into well-favored hunting-grounds and squatted in places that have since made names for themselves as vacation spots, such as Gibraltar, Tangier, the principality of Monaco, the Dordogne valley in southern France, the hills around Rome, the Crimea, and the well-watered coasts of Lebanon and Palestine. Why the newcomers were allowed to usurp these lush locations from their predecessors, and where the earlier tenants went, are two of the many Neanderthal mysteries.

Like most of the known Europeans who had preceded them, the Neanderthals had large faces and prominent brow ridges, and on account of this over-all similarity much confusion has arisen among anthropologists as to which particular fossil skull is Neanderthal and which is not. If we remember that big faces and big brow ridges are only the hallmarks of a particular evolutionary stage common to mankind, there is no reason to confuse the two kinds of skulls, any more than living Chinese and Negroes should be confused because both have low-bridged noses. The Neanderthal skulls were large, low, and broad, with a flattening on the rear portion of the vault; the position of the articulating surfaces known as *condyles* which balance the skull on the top of the vertebral column was far to the rear, compared to modern skulls, and the head was held a little forward. The face itself was long, pointed, and muzzle-like, and the nose both long and broad. Although it protruded greatly because of the general shape of the face, the nose did not spring from the cheeks at a right angle, as many of our noses do, but its sides blended into the facial structure with little transition, as an essential part of a major architectural scheme, rather than as a conspicuously separate organ.

Even more than the skull itself, the bones of the trunk and limbs show distinctive features that separate Neanderthal from other European peoples of either earlier or later age. His trunk was long, his arms and legs short, and his lower arm and calf particularly short. His feet were short and broad, as some of his footprints, found in a cave in Italy, show clearly. His hands were also broad and stubby, and in certain dimensions his finger bones were broader than those of living people. In cross-section his limb bones may be seen to be very thick-walled and heavy, with small marrow cavities. The limb bones of the third-interglacial cave-dwellers of Krapina in Croatia were, by contrast, thinner-walled and more spaciously hollowed, like those of modern men.

Archæologists have tried to relate the flint tools of Neanderthal men to those of other people living before and after them, and possibly alongside them. This is difficult for two reasons. Many of the sites of third-interglacial age originally attributed to Neanderthal on the basis of tools alone may have been occupied by other people. Both the non-Neanderthals and the Neanderthals happened to be passing through the same general evolutionary stage of tool-making, and it is hard to tell which techniques were held in common and which ones were borrowed. The tools definitely associated with Neanderthal skeletons are mostly flakes, including points and side scrapers, and many of them were struck from disks. Whether or not Neanderthal men were related to the Europeans who had preceded them cannot be told from flints alone.

The oldest and best-known theory about Neanderthal man is that he was descended from the men who lived before him in Europe and was the immediate ancestor of those who followed him. While the first part of this hypothesis has its adherents, few professionals believe the second. Neanderthal man had too many anatomical peculiarities, wholly apart from primitive evolutionary traits, to have evolved alone into modern European man.

A second theory is that Neanderthal men evolved from their European predecessors, but in a separate direction from the ancestors of modern European man. Neanderthal men went so far in their own line as to become a new species, which became extinct as they were replaced by other men—of modern type—who had evolved from the same general ancestors. This theory is upheld by one of the greatest living paleontologists.[3] It has the advantage of greater biological simplicity than

[3] Sir Wilfrid E. LeGros Clark: *The Fossil Evidence for Human Evolution* (Chicago, 1955), pp. 62–3.

the first, and does not wholly violate the evidence of the flints.

A third hypothesis, published by J. E. Welker in 1954,[4] proposes that Neanderthal man was an invader from the Far Eastern climatic realm who, like Attila and Genghiz Khan in later times, breached the spine of Asia through the Zungarian Gates to wander into the vast and strange domain of grassy plains, wide lakes, swamps, and green forests stretching from the Altai Mountains of central Asia to the Atlantic. China is an almost unexplored archæological realm. Yet the skeletons of the early cave-dwellers of Chou Kou Tien can be compared to the later Neanderthal race on two particular counts.

The Chou Kou Tien people's limb bones are thick-walled and thin-channeled like Neanderthal's. Their faces also have puffed-out cheekbones, from which the nasal skeleton emerges in a nearly continuous plane. As far as our evidence indicates, these features are unlike those of the Europeans who preceded or followed Neanderthal. However, in the Far East this same relationship of nose to cheeks still obtains among living Mongoloids, and it has been carried over the Bering Strait on the faces of American Indians.

This is just a theory, not a proved reconstruction. Where the Neanderthals of Europe and the Middle East came from is still a mystery, but it is one capable of solution. Where they went is easier to explain, for they appear to have been absorbed into the populations of Spain, Italy, the Middle Eastern states, and possibly North Africa, sometime during the middle of the last glacial period.

After the Neanderthals had had their day, fully modern European peoples moved into the caves of southern

---

[4] J. E. Welker: "Neanderthal Man and Homo Sapiens," *American Anthropologist*, Vol. 56, No. 6 (1954), pp. 1003–25.

France during the first warm interval of the last glacial period, carrying with them an elaborate toolkit of specialized blades, including burins. It is a dogma of archæology that this flint assemblage bore little relationship in either form or style of manufacture to that of their Neanderthal predecessors, and that it was as superior to it as a carpenter's whole toolbox is to a hatchet. Where these people came from, from whom they were descended, and how they acquired these excellent blade tools are questions with which we opened our whole study of flints, ice ages, and fossil men. We still cannot answer them.

It would help greatly if we had a good series of human skeletons from the very beginning of the Upper Paleolithic; but only one skull, found in the cave of Combe Capelle in southwestern France in 1909, can certainly be assigned to it. In the later phases of the Upper Paleolithic, covering the second advance of the last ice sheet, the second warm interval, and the third advance, over a hundred skulls have been found, and from them the characteristics of the Upper Paleolithic population of Europe have been determined. Living duplicates of these people could be found in many European countries today.

They could not have been descended from Neanderthals, either in Europe or elsewhere. There were two alternatives: Either they were descended from the older, pre-Neanderthal peoples of Europe, like Fontéchevade and Krapina, and had been living in some still-to-be-discovered area during the Neanderthal interlude, only to return to their ancestors' hunting-grounds once most of the Neanderthals had disappeared. Or else they were strangers from another geographical realm who had evolved physically and developed their distinctive blade culture elsewhere, and then come north after the first peak of the fourth ice sheet.

Both explanations remain theoretically possible. While much work has been done on the Paleolithic in Europe, most of it was completed long ago, before modern methods of excavation and flint-analysis had been invented. Before we can accept the old and oft-repeated theory that the Upper Paleolithic flint industry of western Europe bore no relationship to the preceding cultures, we must await the final reports of those specialists, French, American, British, and other, who have begun to restudy the flints from the oldest Upper Paleolithic sites, which are comparatively few, and to dig new sites of the same age, using modern techniques. These specialists will also, we trust, restudy the older flint assemblages left behind by third-interglacial men whose bones have long been mislabeled Neanderthal, and re-evaluate those from open-air sites dated at the time of the first advance of the last ice sheet.

Paleolithic excavations in Europe have been concentrated in small areas, particularly in regions of abundant limestone, and therefore caves. Many larger areas in which people must have lived and chipped tools at various times can never be dug because their sites were bulldozed out long ago by the ponderous marches of the ice sheets. Nevertheless, enough evidence remains to tell us eventually whether or not the complex blade culture of Europe evolved on the spot. Local biological evolution was certainly possible, because the genetic shift from a large to a small face and from a chinless to a chin-bearing jaw is standard evolutionary procedure through which more than one race has passed on more than one continent.

When I began working in caves, more or less by accident, the European field was well populated by professional archæologists, while the Middle East was wide open. If Upper Paleolithic man had really invaded Europe, as most people believed, then there was room for a part-time digger like myself to do primary cave-exploration in the Middle East and leave the technical details to specialists. Already in 1939 caves dug in Palestine and Lebanon had yielded interesting sequences of flake and blade cultures which suggested that an orderly evolution from flakes to blades, and from Middle to Upper Paleolithic, had taken place there, with or without reference to Europe.

From these caves had also come skeletons that seemed related to both modern European and Neanderthal men. When I began this work, the Middle East seemed like a good place to dig in. I will not flatter myself by saying that I thought this problem through when I began the work; yet the problem was clearly there. And after the intervening seventeen years it still resists solution.

The troublesome Neanderthal problem points up the tangled relationship between race and culture, a subject which has grown so complicated and has been so overemphasized that some of the top professional archæologists have repeatedly warned me not to confuse race with culture but to deal with each in a separate compartment. They rightly state that all we know of an ancient people's way of life may be limited to what we can deduce from a collection of broken animal bones and flint.

I cannot, however, accept this warning. From the history of general technology we know that a basic invention is made very few times, if indeed more than once, and that after a new process has been discovered it spreads from place to place and people to people. An invention like that of manufacturing prepared flake cores is spread by teaching. Older hunters teach younger ones how to chip these special cores, and men of one band will pass this knowledge on to their neighbors.

Before the invention of writing, all teaching had to be face-to-face. Before a technique of flint-chipping could be

transferred from one band to another, members of the two
bands had to meet. Once they had gone to this amount of
trouble, they certainly did more things with each other
than chip flint. In every surviving Stone Age society, people who visit one another exchange women. As there is no
reason to believe that this practice is a modern invention,
we may assume that during the Pleistocene, flint lessons
were accompanied by race-mixture. As the breeding populations, to use a biological term, of that time must have
been small, a little mixing would go a long way. The hybrid offspring would without doubt possess some of the
traits of both parental stocks, and through the usual
processes of selection and genetic drift a new race would
be formed.

The classic example of this process in ancient times
may be seen in the skeletons of the people dug up in the
Mount Carmel caves in Palestine. They made their tools
on both flakes and blades. Deep in the deposit at Tabun
Cave, below the level of flakes of a style of manufacture usually associated with Neanderthal man, Miss Garrod found a thin layer of soil in which blades predominated. A little higher up, a fine blend of flakes and blades
had been made, and the skeletons associated with this
industry showed both modern European and Neanderthal features. Whoever the blade-makers were, they did
not just teach a group of Neanderthals how to make
blades and then skip away. They intermarried with the
Neanderthals, and their hybrid children learned both
techniques. So there is more to this race-and-culture business than meets the eye. It cannot be dismissed with a
simple warning not to confuse people with their handiwork, for both are elements in a single picture.

Now that my days of digging caves in the Middle
East seem to be over, I can voice one regret: I have never
found what I was really looking for, and now I never

hope to find it, except in my dreams. That is one complete or nearly complete honest-to-God skull of an Ice Age fossil man. If someone else finds one in a cave in the Hazer Jerif valley, in the other Kara Kamar, or in one of the smaller caves near the Heifer's Outwash, I shall be very happy.

In the course of this work I have been the guest of many governments, and I must have given some of them a lot of trouble. I insisted on seeking caves in remote places. Irate landlords complained that we were ruining the winter shelters of their flocks and destroying their chances of reaping an annual spring harvest of manure. We strained the facilities of country inns, violated local food taboos, and in one place ate up all the surplus sheep. I had an indecent-sounding name (in Persian), my needs for permits fanned interdepartmental rivalries in government offices, and certain officials who were friendly to me got in wrong with their superiors because of my presence. Like the debutante with bad breath, I undoubtedly offended in other ways of which I am still unaware.

I am grateful that, despite all the trouble that I unintentionally caused, my American companions and I were allowed to work day after day in pits and trenches with members of the lowest stratum of Middle Eastern society, the usually unskilled and frequently illiterate tenant villagers, nearly always as poor as mosque mice. It is they who support on their backs the members of the more-or-less Westernized upper crust whom other Americans commonly see. The ideas about the Middle East which many of our fellow countrymen obtain in bars and restaurants and at cocktail parties are different from what we learned in Trench A, level #16.

Now and then I read that a mob has burned the American flag in front of one of our consulates, or that a certain prime minister has made inflammatory statements about us to the press. When I read these things I cannot help thinking how useful it would be if the prime minister or those who incited the mobs were to travel in our country as we did in theirs. At such times I also like to think of my happy days spent in the bottoms of caves with the Absalems, One-Eyed Qasem, Parviz and his men, Khair Mohammed, Saleh the foreman, and even poor epileptic Saleh the British soldier. These workmen and foremen, whose forebears dug trenches for Darius, Harun er-Rashid, and Tamerlane, taught me something that no news reports can influence. The base of the social pyramid in the Middle East consists of a vast and inarticulate body of these decent men, whose tradition of fair play and mutual self-sacrifice will live on long after the present crises have been forgotten.

INDEX

A NOTE ON THE TYPE

THE TEXT of this book is set in Caledonia, *a Linotype face designed by W. A. Dwiggins. It belongs to the family of printing types called "modern face" by printers—a term used to mark the change in style of type-letters that occurred about 1800.* Caledonia *borders on the general design of Scotch Modern, but is more freely drawn than that letter.*

The book was composed, printed, and bound by Kingsport Press, Inc., Kingsport, Tennessee. The paper was manufactured by S. D. Warren Company, Boston, Massachusetts. The typography and binding design are based on originals by W. A. Dwiggins.